Commodity futures and options

Commodity futures and options

A step-by-step guide to successful trading

George Kleinman

 Prentice Hall

FINANCIAL TIMES

An imprint of **Pearson Education**

London • New York • Toronto • Sydney • Tokyo • Singapore
Hong Kong • Cape Town • Madrid • Paris • Amsterdam • Munich • Milan

PEARSON EDUCATION LIMITED

Head Office:
Edinburgh Gate
Harlow CM20 2JE
Tel: +44 (0)1279 623623
Fax: +44 (0)1279 431059

London Office:
128 Long Acre
London WC2E 9AN
Tel: +44 (0)20 7447 2000
Fax: +44 (0)20 7447 2170
Website: www.business-minds.com

First published in Great Britain in 1997
under the title *Mastering Commodity
Futures and Options*
This edition published 2001

© George Kleinman 2001

The rights of George Kleinman to be identified as author
of this work has been asserted by him in accordance
with the Copyright, Designs and Patents Act 1988.

ISBN 0 273 65033 5

British Library Cataloguing in Publication Data
A CIP catalogue record for this book can be obtained from the British Library

10 9 8 7 6

Typeset by Pantek Arts Ltd, Maidstone, Kent.
Printed and bound in Great Britain by Bookcraft, Midsomer Norton

The Publishers' policy is to use paper manufactured from sustainable forests.

About the author

George Kleinman is President of Commodity Resource Corp., a futures and options advisory, brokerage and trading firm located in the beautiful Lake Tahoe region of Nevada. George has been trading for over twenty years on behalf of individuals and commercial commodity users, both large and small.

He entered the business in 1977 as a futures broker with the commodity division of Merrill Lynch. While at Merrill, George was a member of the 'Golden Circle'; top ten commodity brokers internationally. In 1983 he founded CRC and has been highlighted in national publications for trading performance. George has been an Exchange Member for over fifteen years and is currently a member of the New York Mercantile Exchange, COMEX Division, and the Minneapolis Grain Exchange (former board member). He is a member of the National Futures Association and Executive Editor of *Trends in Futures* published by *Futures* magazine. The first edition of *Mastering Commodity Futures and Options* was published by Financial Times/Pitman Publishing in 1998. This revised and expanded version includes new chapters on trading psychology, day trading electronic trading and encompasses his twenty years of trading dos and don'ts. George, a graduate of the Ohio State University with an MBA from Hofstra University in New York, is an avid skier, racquetball player and student of the markets.

Readers who would like to receive a free information packet from George Kleinman with current trading ideas are welcome to request it by phone, fax, or e-mail:

Commodity Resource Corp.
PO Box 8700
Incline Village, Nevada 89452-8700 USA
Phone: 1-800-233-4445
Fax: 1-775-833-1400
e-mail: Geo@commodity.com
www.commodity.com

It is literally true millions come easier to a trader after he knows how to trade, than hundreds did in the days of his ignorance.

Jesse Livermore (1923)

This book is for Sherri

Contents

Preface

Why trade commodities?

In recent years, I've seen more market moves of significance take place in the commodity markets than anywhere else: *moves which can literally make the difference of a lifetime* (for the better or the worse).

More fortunes are made and lost more quickly in these markets than anywhere else. This is due to the leverage the commodity markets possess. Yet, with all the potential these markets have, few really make out well. Do you wonder why that is?

Why this book?

I've been trading full time for over twenty years now. As head of a trading firm working with individuals and corporations alike, I've seen thousands of trades. I've seen fortunes won and lost. After a while you do learn a few things and it's my goal to share some of what I've learned with you. Hopefully, I can save you some of my grief and jump-start you on the road to success. Of course, I'm still learning, and still have a lot to learn, no doubt. Every day is a new challenge, and different from the last. Yet some of the same mistakes I've made are being made day in and day out by those who are on the losing side. I think you can be saved from making some of these same mistakes. This will be discussed in the pages to come.

Without trying to be all things to all people, I've written this book for both the novice and the seasoned trader. It is meant to be a primer and reference source for those of you who have not yet taken the plunge into the shark-infested commodity waters, but are seriously considering this. It is also designed to help those of you who are currently trading and want to do better. We'll start slowly, then build up to the grander concept of a master trading plan. Along the way I think I have some good stories to share with you.

What will it take to succeed? You'll need patience, guts, discipline and a vision. I cannot infuse these qualities into you. I can only tell you what to look for and what to watch out for. It will be up to you to act.

For now, think of this as a game

Financial markets come in many colours, shapes, sizes and flavours. For now, think of commodity futures and options as a *game*: the highest stakes money game in the world. This is where fortunes are made and lost on a daily basis. Sure, there's a loftier purpose. Governments allow most of the traditional financial markets to operate for the purpose of capital formation. Futures markets are allowed to operate as a vehicle of risk transference for commodity producers and users. However, this book is not a scholarly treatise. It is not about investing for your retirement. It's a guide. A guide to winning the game.

A game with consequences

If you choose to play the game, be forewarned it can dramatically affect your lifestyle. For the better or for the worse. You see, commodity futures are a *zero sum* game. For every dollar won by one player, that same dollar is lost by another. Accurate statistics are not available, but it is generally agreed that the great majority of players lose the game. If that's the case, since this is zero sum, then the great minority are winning what this majority is losing. This is one of the reason why the stakes are so high. Fortunes are made in commodity futures and in many cases starting from a very small stake. Luck may play a part in the short run, but in the end those players who play better will triumph. This book is designed to help you play the game better.

For every buyer of a gold or copper contract, bond futures, cattle or Swiss francs, there is someone, unseen but out there, on the other side of the transaction. The buyer is known as *the long*. The seller as *the short*. At any point in time, except for the split second a new trade is initiated, someone is winning and someone is losing. The game can be painful at times. Price movements themselves affect future price movements and it's all a function of who is being hurt and who is being helped. Shorts and longs act differently based on their emotions, and their emotions are affected by price. Your job, as a trader, will be to identify what happens next. People who are right will tend to do certain things on balance. People who are wrong will tend to act differently. Then there are subsets in each group who will not act like the majority. One thing is certain. Markets are made up of people, and people tend generally to act the way they did in the past. With certain stimuli, they will act opposite as to how they generally acted. If you as a trader can predict what the pattern will be, the rewards will be substantial. We will discuss in this book various methods designed to discern and predict these patterns. No method is foolproof, so the best we can attempt to do is put the odds in our favour. If we can do this, and you then approach this in a disciplined manner, success is assured. Sounds simple? If it was so simple most people wouldn't lose and the nature of the markets is to punish the majority. *This book is designed to place you in the minority, because it is the minority who will reap the rewards!*

Why trade commodities now?

I entered this crazy business during the commodities boom of the late 1970s. The Hunt brothers were attempting to corner the silver market, the Carter administration couldn't get a grip on inflation, the currency markets were in turmoil, the Russians were invading Afghanistan, the world was running out of food due to a series of weather disasters, and the Iranians were holding American citizens hostage. Hard assets were in vogue. Paper assets were just that. During the decade of the 1970s, the CRB Index (basket of commodities) appreciated well over 100 per cent. The Dow Jones Index (basket of 'blue chip' US stocks) literally went nowhere for over ten years.

Now we are beginning a new millennium and paper assets are again in vogue. Many have had a spectacular run over the past twenty years, and some commodities have gone nowhere. Yet the pendulum looks as if it is starting to swing back the other way. Commodities, as an asset class, are starting to wake up due to selective global shortages and increasing demand. Here's an interesting (and frightening) fact: the world is adding to its population at the rate of a Mexico every year – over 80 million people. The Chinese population alone is 1.2 billion people. This is more than all the combined populations of North America, South America, Europe and Africa. Chinese grain demand will grow 30–50 per cent over the next five years! In the early twenty-first century their projected copper demand will be 400,000 tons *over and above* their internal production. And this is just China. I think you'll be hearing more and more about commodities in the years to come. Those who can acquire the skills necessary to master this arcane area (skills quite different than traditional stocks and bond investing) will prosper to a degree the traditional investor can only dream about!

George Kleinman

Acknowledgments

Over the years there have been many friends and associates who have contributed to my futures education and trading success. There are a number of floor traders whom I would like to thank for their contributions to my trading career and to this book. First, William G. Salatich Jr, commonly known as Sal, from the Chicago Merc., shared some of his wonderful trading stories, one of which gets the ball rolling in Chapter 1. I also give Sal credit for the *Voice from the Tomb*, a valuable tool which isn't widely known about today. Joe Orlick from the corn pit has provided me with valuable tips and support. The boys at All American Copper in New York, Joseph Santagata and James Gallo, have been friends and associates for over ten years now and do an outstanding job. Thanks Joey for saving my butt a few years back! Kevin McCormack, a trader at the COMEX has been an invaluable associate for just as long. Thanks also to Rand Financial of Chicago, and its President Jeff Quinto, a superior clearing firm and a great partner for our Commodity.com online trading system. Then there is the gentleman cited in Chapter 14 entitled 'Jesse's Secret' who would wish to remain anonymous. You know who you are.

Moore Research of Eugene, Oregon and CQG of Littleton, Colorado (a highly recommended service) provided the charts used in the book. Thanks also to the folks at the Futures magazine group, particularly Ginger Szala, Gerald Becker and Gary Kamen. It is with their permission that I am able to include Chapter 11, 'Day Trader's Secrets'.

There have been clients over the years from whom I have learned more than they've ever learned from me. Three stand out. Since my client list is confidential, I'll just give heart-felt thanks to Bruce, Ivan and Wayne for being cool, calm and solid during the good and bad times as well. John Baird, I'm sure you must be trading in heaven with Jesse Livermore; both of you taught me a lot.

Thanks also to Bill Edlefsen, Fred Carroll, Johnny Morris, Tom Reynolds, and my sons Kevin and Craig.

Finally, without my people at Commodity Resource, particularly Sherri Meadow, Graham Leonard, Ryan Bibbey, Gerry Eick and Justice Litle, this business would be simply impossible. Thanks for putting up with me – I know how difficult I can be! The most credit of all must go to my wife Sherri, to whom I have dedicated this book (my last).

The late afternoon sun offers a few more minutes of warmth as it travels lazily over the canyon and reflects off Lake Tahoe in magnificent hues of oranges and reds. It hints of another magnificent day coming tomorrow.

George Kleinman
Incline Village, Nevada

Do you have what it takes?

A floor broker friend of mine told me the following story. He swears it's true.

In the 1960s, there was a corn speculator who traded in 'the pit' at the Chicago Board of Trade. He was known for 'plunging' (taking big positions). Early one summer, he put on a large *short* corn position for his own account (this is a position which will make money if prices *fall*, but is costly if prices *rise*).

Soon after, the weather began to heat up in the Midwestern United States where the corn is grown. The corn crop needed rain and prices started to rise. Day after day, the sun shone, not a cloud in the sky, and the corn was starting to burn up. The market continued to rally against this guy. He knew if this continued, he would go broke.

Late one trading session, the big trader started a rumour around the corn pit. His rumour was that it was going to start to rain the next morning at 10:30.

The next morning the sun shone, not a cloud in the sky, and the market opened higher. Then, almost miraculously, at just about 10:30, rain started pouring down the windows that look onto the grain trading floor. (The old grain room, located on the fourth floor of the Board of Trade Building, had tall windows which you could see from La Salle Street.) Inside, in the corn pit, a selling panic developed as the traders scrambled to sell out their corn futures. The market went *down the limit!* The speculator covered his entire short position on this break and was saved from bankruptcy.

How did he know it would rain at 10:30 *that* morning? It seems he was owed a favour from his Irish drinking buddy, the chief of the Chicago Fire Department. The chief brought out the hook and ladders and decided it was a very good day to wash those tall windows which looked out on La Salle Street!

So, you're thinking of trading, but you don't know the chief?

In fact, you're thinking of trading cocoa. You've just finished reading a private newsletter, hot off the presses, a first-hand report of how the *witch's tail disease* is devastating the cocoa crop in the Ivory Coast. You have no way of knowing for sure how true this is. You do like chocolate, but you had no idea it all started with a bean called the cocoa bean. (You thought it came out of a can.) Hey, you don't even know quite where the Ivory Coast is. Yet, you're still thinking of trading this bean against the likes of Hershey and Nestlé and whoever else really does know what's going on. Why would you do something like this? Why? To make money, why else?

You do know one thing – the cocoa market is moving. It's moving up and it's moving fast. While you aren't exactly losing money by doing nothing, it's starting to feel that way.

Do you have the guts to act? Do you have the money? Is now the time?

You assume the shorts (those betting on lower cocoa prices) are beginning to experience financial pain. The longs (those betting on higher cocoa prices) are experiencing the opposite emotions – elation, happiness, the satisfaction that comes from being right. The accounts of the longs are growing – money from nothing. The shorts are watching their money disappear.

Let's stop this commentary for a moment, because it's now time for your first lesson: *trading is a human game*. As a result, emotions affect price as much, perhaps more, than the news. You will learn that price movements themselves are a fundamental and in turn affect future price movements. It's all a function of who is being hurt and who is benefitting. It's a function of which side of the market is being 'sponsored' by the 'strong hands'. Shorts and longs will act differently based on price movements which will affect their emotions as much as their pocketbooks.

Your job, as a trader, is to identify what happens next. To do that, I will want you to start thinking about how others feel, because feelings affect actions. People who are generally right tend to do certain things (on balance). People who are generally wrong will tend to act differently. The majority will act a certain way, but be warned, the majority are usually wrong at major turning points (although they can be right in the beginning).

So, are the majority now long or short cocoa? The shorts are in pain, the longs are not, but then again this can change just as fast as the market's tone changes.

Here's lesson number two: on balance, when talking about futures trading, the majority will *not* win. Since the profitable minority will act in a completely different manner, we must learn what makes *them* tick and how to act like *them*.

One thing is certain: markets are made by people, and people generally tend to act the way they did in the past. With certain stimuli, they could act opposite as to how they generally act, but we will be playing the odds here. We need to identify what kind of move the market is in now. Is it a 'normal' move, in which the market will act in a 'normal' way, or is it extraordinary? (At times the market will act in an extraordinary manner, and this can be the very best time to play.) If you, as a trader, are able to predict accurately what the next pattern will be, your rewards will be substantial.

In this book I will present various methods designed to identify profitable market patterns. No method is foolproof, so the best we can do is attempt to put the odds in your favour. My goal is to teach you to approach commodity futures and options trading like a business. This is not a casino. In a casino, risk is artificially manufactured for risk's sake, and the odds are engineered in favour of the 'house'. In the commodity futures and options markets we are dealing with natural risks associated with the production and consumption of the materials that make life possible and worthwhile – food, metals, financials and energy products. We cannot bend these risks to our will, but we do have tools to manage them. Unlike a casino, I believe we can move the odds to our side of the table. To do this, we must be disciplined.

> ✱ If you, as a trader, are able to predict accurately what the next pattern will be, your rewards will be substantial.

You will need patience and you will need guts. I cannot force these qualities in to you, but I can describe to you how the successful trader acts. It is then up to you to act the right way. Plus, to profit in the commodity futures and options, you will need a *systematic* approach; a well thought out *strategy*. I will present to you some good ideas, but it's up to you to actually implement them systematically. After all, a strategy is just a consistent approach to trading.

Do you have what it takes?

OK, so you've decided to risk some of your hard-earned money, go for the big bucks, and trade commodities. This is a *zero sum game*, meaning for every dollar made by someone, it is lost by someone else. Some of the money will go to your commodity broker in the form of commissions, and a very small amount will go to the exchanges for their fee. Then if you are lucky or skilful enough to win, you will owe the tax man some of your profits. When you lose on any particular trade, most of your loss will be transferred electronically to somebody else's account (and you still pay that commission). You will never see this person on the other side of your trade (it could be a corporation), but he (she, or it) is out there somewhere.

You will be pitted against some of the best financial minds in the world: professionals on the exchange floor, exchange members off the floor, Commodity Trading Advisors (CTAs) and Commodity Pool Operators (CPOs), hedge fund managers, commercial firms that use and other commercial firms which produce commodities. Then there are those other individuals with more experience than you have. Can you hope to compete against the likes of these?

I am going to tell you, emphatically, yes! But I didn't say it would be easy, did I? You will need to develop a sensible trading plan and a feel for the markets. This book will help you with these. You must develop certain human qualities as well – qualities nobody can give to you, but you; qualities which are an integral part of every successful trader.

Over fifty years ago, the legendary speculator, W.D. Gann, discussed the four qualities essential for trading success: patience, knowledge, guts, health and rest. His observations are just as valid today, and trust me, you *must* have these (or if you don't, develop them) if you ever hope to compete and win.

Patience

Patience is the number one essential quality for trading success. A good trader will possess the patience to wait for the right opportunity. He or she will not be over-anxious, because over-anxiousness consumes capital, and over time will tap you out. When you are fortunate enough to catch a good trade, when it starts to move your way, you will need the patience to hold it. Perhaps the primary failing of the amateur is to close out a profitable position too soon. In other words, patience is required for both opening and closing a position. Hope and fear will need to be eliminated. If in a profitable position, instead of *fearing* the profit will turn into a loss, *hope* it becomes more profitable. You have a cushion to work with in this case. When in a losing position, instead of *hoping* it will turn around, *fear* it will get worse. If you see no definitive change in trend, then use your essential quality of patience and just wait.

> ✳ Patience is the number one essential quality for trading success.

Knowledge

There is no 'on-the-job training programme' here. The stakes are too high, and the competition too intense. You will need a well thought out and thoroughly researched trading plan before you begin, and you will need to do your homework.

Your plan will always have a mechanism to cut the losses on the bad trades, and to aggressively maximize profits on the good ones. You must be organized and remain focused at all times. If the plan is a good one, you will need the consistency to stick with it during down periods.

My personal goal is to make money daily, or alternatively not lose too much. It is a constant trial to maintain the vigilance necessary so as not to let good judgement lapse. If you are a novice, it makes sense to 'paper trade' before you trade for real. If you are currently trading, you should keep a log book. Log your triumphs and your failures. You will want to avoid making 'the same mistake' again, but I must warn you, all traders do make this 'same mistake'. So, at the very least, learn not to make it so often. By keeping a record of what you did right and what you did wrong, you will be able to identify areas of weakness and areas of strength. If you are not totally prepared on any given day, don't trade. You can't 'wing it' in this business, because the competition will eat you up.

Over time, you will develop what I call a 'trader's sense'. You will know when a trade doesn't feel right, and when this happens the prudent thing to do is step aside. You cannot ignore the danger signals, and when it's time to act, you must do so without hesitation.

So to recap, you must have a game plan and stick to it, but the paradox here is you need to be flexible as well. There are times when it will be best to do nothing and you will need to fight the urge to play for every pot. Plus, as I said before, keep focused. There have been times I've been distracted by 'day trades' and missed the big moves because I missed the big picture. By the time I finally saw the light, it was too late.

The legendary trader of the 1920s, Jesse Livermore, once shared one of his secrets. He attempts to buy as close to the 'danger point' as he can, *then* he places his stop loss. In this way his risk per trade is low. This makes sense, but then how do you know where that 'danger point' is? In 'normal' markets you need to take 'normal' profits, and on those rare occasions where you have the chance to make a windfall, you must go for it. But how to tell when a market is 'normal' as opposed to extraordinary? It takes experience, it takes *knowledge*, and this is an essential quality for success. Knowledge takes study and study is hard work. *This book is a good first step.*

Guts

Call it nerve, courage, bravado, or heart; I call it guts, and this quality is as essential as patience and knowledge. Some people have too much guts, and this isn't good because they are too hopeful and tend to overtrade. Some lack the guts to act (either to enter a position when the time is right, or to cut a loss when it isn't) and this is a catastrophic fault which must be overcome. You need guts to pyramid positions, which is not easy, but this is where the big money is made.

I am going to teach you to learn to trade without hope, without fear, and hopefully with just the right degree of guts. I am going to instruct you to enter positions on what I believe is the proper basis, and then urge you to remember at all times you could be wrong. So you will need a defensive plan to cut the loss when you are. I've been a student in the 'School of Hard Knocks' too many times, but I've never lost my guts. At times I know I've had too much and have overtraded, but then there are some people I know who have an inability to pull the trigger and this is just as deadly.

Looking back only brings regrets, so you need to face the future with optimism, knowledge, patience and guts.

Health and rest

This is the fourth essential quality for trading success. If you don't feel right, you won't trade right, and this is the time to be on the sidelines. If you stick with something too long your judgement will become warped. Traders who are continually in the market without a rest get too caught up in the day-to-day fluctuations and eventually get tapped out. At least twice a year it makes sense to close out all your trades, get entirely out of the market and go on a vacation. When you return recharged, your trading will improve.

> *If you don't have patience, guts, knowledge and good health, all the rules in the world are just so many words.*

These are the four essential human qualities *required* for success. You will need them. Very soon we will delve into specifics which I believe will help you travel this rocky road to trading success. Some of the most important lessons I've learned over the past twenty years are in the pages to come and they should help you make money. However, if you don't have patience, guts, knowledge and good health, all the rules in the world are just so many words.

So, with that said, let's get into the meat of the matter. I'm not trying to be all things to all people, but I do believe this book will appeal to the novice and veteran trader alike. Even in the primer section, which is next, I've included some true stories that I think the veteran might enjoy.

So we begin at the beginning. If you are new to this game, you will need to know how the game is played, what the rules are and how the money works. I will try to be as complete as possible, and if I do this right, at times it might actually appear simple. If it was that simple, however, most people wouldn't lose, and the nature of the futures markets is to punish the majority. So let's begin our journey to join the *minority*, because it is the minority who will reap the rewards!

Basic training: a futures primer

It's not all that hard to pick up the phone and instruct your commodity broker to buy or to sell. These days it is even easier to log onto the internet, push a few buttons and send your order to either an open outcry pit or an electronic marketplace. It's really not all that difficult to learn the math either, or to learn how the money works. The hard part comes later. Yet, some of you who have purchased this book (at least I hope that's what you did) want to start at the beginning and learn the basics. After all, if you haven't been exposed to futures or options before, you have to start somewhere. So we'll start here – it's as good a place as any.

Commodities are not only essential to life, they are absolutely necessary for quality of life. Every person in the world eats. Billions of dollars of agricultural products are traded daily on the world's commodity exchanges: everything from soybeans, to rice, to corn and wheat, to beef, pork, cocoa, coffee, sugar and orange juice. This is how commodity exchanges began. In the middle of the nineteenth century in the USA, businessmen started to organize market forums to make the buying and selling of agricultural commodities easier. Farmers and grain merchants met in central marketplaces to set quality and quantity standards and establish rules of business. Over 1600 exchanges sprang up, mostly at major railheads, inland water ports and seaports.

Around the early twentieth century, communications and transportation became more efficient. This allowed for the building of centralized warehouses in major urban centres such as Chicago. Business became more national and less regional and many of the smaller exchanges disappeared. Today business is global. There remain about two dozen major exchanges, with 80 per cent of the world's business conducted on about a dozen of them. Just about every major commodity vital to life, commerce and trade is represented. Billions of dollars worth of energy products, from heating oil to gasoline to natural gas and electricity, are traded every business day. Metals, both industrial (copper, aluminium, zinc, lead, palladium, nickel and tin), precious (gold) and some of which are both (platinum and silver). Wood products, textiles – how could we live without these. Yet, few of us are aware of how the prices for these vital components of life are set. Plus, today, the world's futures exchanges trade financial products essential to the economic function of the world as well as physical commodities. From currencies, to interest rate futures, to stock market indices, more money changes hands on the world's commodity exchanges every day than on all the world's stock markets combined.

Governments allow commodity exchanges to exist so that producers and users of commodities can *hedge* their price risks. Yet without the speculator, the system would not work. Anyone can be a speculator and, contrary to popular belief, I do not believe the odds are stacked against the individual. In this book, I will share with you some methods designed to help you make money trading commodities. In fact, you the individual have one distinct advantage, and that's flexibility. You can move quickly, like a cat, something a giant corporation cannot do. There are times when many of the big commercials who hedge on the exchange literally hand you your profits on a silver platter, since they are there for a different reason. So, let's start by looking at how the futures contract works and the various participants in the marketplace, what they are each attempting to accomplish, and how they interact with each other.

> ✳ More money changes hands on the world's commodity exchanges every day than on all the world's stock markets combined.

Futures markets are in their most basic form, markets in which commodities, or financial products to be delivered or purchased at some time in the future, are bought and sold.

The futures contract

The basic unit of exchange in the futures markets is the futures contract. Each contract is for a set quantity of some commodity or financial asset, and can only be traded in multiples of that amount. A futures contract is a legally binding agreement providing for the delivery of various commodities or financial entities at a specific date in the future. Before I was in the business, I used to have a vision of the parties involved sitting down at a table and actually signing contracts. It's nothing like that. When you buy or sell a futures contract, you are not actually signing a written piece of paper drawn up by a lawyer; you are entering into a contractual obligation which can be met in one of two ways. The first is by making or taking delivery of the actual commodity. This is the exception, not the rule however, as less than 2 per cent of all futures contracts are met by actual delivery. The other way to meet your obligation, the method you most likely will use, is by *offset*. Very simply, offset is making the opposite, or offsetting sale or purchase of the same number of contracts bought or sold sometime prior to the expiration date of the contract. This can be easily done because futures contracts are standardized. Every contract on a particular exchange for a specific commodity is identical. The specifications are different for each commodity, but the contract in each market is the same. In other words, every soybean contract traded on the Chicago Board of Trade is for 5000 bushels. Every gold contract traded on the New York Mercantile is for 100 troy ounces. Each contract listed on an exchange calls for a specific grade and quality. For example, the silver contract is for 5000 troy ounces of 99.99 per cent pure silver in ingot form. The rules state the seller cannot deliver 99.95 per cent pure. Therefore, the buyers and sellers know exactly what they are trading. Every contract is completely interchangeable. *The only negotiable feature of a futures contract is price.*

> ✳ *Every contract is completely interchangeable. The only negotiable feature of a future contract is price.*

The *size of the contract* determines its value. To determine how much you will make or lose on a particular price movement of a specific commodity, you will need to know the following:

- the contract size
- how the price is quoted
- the minimum price fluctuation
- the value of the minimum price fluctuation.

The *contract size* is standardized. The minimum unit tradable is one contract. For example, an NY coffee contract is for 37,500 pounds, a Chicago corn contract is for 5000 bushels, a British pound contract calls for delivery of 62,500 pounds sterling. The contract size determines the value of a move in price.

You will need to know *how prices are quoted*. For example, grains are quoted in dollars and cents per bushel. $2.50/bushel for corn, $5.50 per bushel for wheat, etc. Copper is quoted in cents per pound in New York, and dollars per metric ton in London. Cattle and hogs are quoted in cents per pound, while gold is quoted in dollars and cents per troy ounce. Currencies are quoted in cents per unit of currency. As you start to trade you will quickly become familiar with how this works. Your commodity broker can fill you in on how prices are quoted on any particular market you decide to trade.

The *minimum price fluctuation* (also known as a 'tick') is a function of how prices are quoted and is set by the exchange.

For example, prices of corn are quoted in dollars and cents per bushel, but the minimum price fluctuation corn can move is $\frac{1}{4}$¢/bushel. So if the price of corn is $3.00/bushel, the next price 'tick' can either be 3.00\frac{1}{4}$ (if up) or 2.99\frac{3}{4}$ if down. Prices can trade more than a tick at a time, so in a fast market the price can jump from $3.00 to 3.00\frac{1}{2}$, but it cannot jump from 3.00\frac{1}{2}$ to 3.00\frac{5}{8}$, since the minimum price fluctuation for corn is a quarter penny. Thus, the next minimum price tick for corn from 3.00\frac{1}{2}$ up would be 3.00\frac{3}{4}$, or down would be 3.00\frac{1}{4}$. The minimum price fluctuation for a gold contract is 10¢/ounce, so if gold is trading for 425 dollars and 50 cents per ounce ($425.50), the minimum it

can move in price would be 425 dollars and 60 cents if up, or 425 dollars and 40 cents if down. Once again, in a fast market, or if the bids and offers are wide, it might jump from 425 dollars and 50 cents to 426 dollars and 00 cents, but in liquid and quiet markets many times the market will move from one minimum fluctuation to the next.

The *value of a minimum fluctuation* is the dollars and cents equivalent of the minimum price fluctuation multiplied by the contract size of the commodity.

eg For example, the size of a copper contract traded on the New York Mercantile Exchange is 25,000 pounds. The minimum price fluctuation of a copper contract is $\frac{5}{100}$th of a cent per pound (or $\frac{1}{20}$ th of a cent). By multiplying the minimum price fluctuation by the size of the contract, you obtain the value of the minimum price fluctuation. In this case it is $12.50 ($\frac{1}{20}$¢/pound times 25,000 pounds).

In the case of the grains and soybeans a minimum price fluctuation is $\frac{1}{4}$¢, a contract is for 5000 bushels, so the value of a minimum fluctuation is also $12.50 ($\frac{1}{4}$¢/bushel times 5000 bushels).

Except for grains, minimum fluctuations are generally referred to as *points*.

eg For example, in sugar prices are quoted in cents and hundreds of a cent per pound. The minimum fluctuation is $\frac{1}{100}$th of a cent, or one 'point'. If the price is quoted at 15$\frac{1}{2}$ cents per pound, your broker would say it is trading at 1550, and if it moves up by a quarter of a cent per pound, this would be a move of 25 points, to 1575.

In some cases, the value of a minimum move may be more than a point. In our copper example, the minimum move is $\frac{1}{20}$¢/pound. A penny move is 100 points (for example if copper prices rise from $1.00/pound to $1.02/pound, we say the market moved up 200 points), but since the minimum fluctuation is for $\frac{1}{20}$¢, a minimum move is 5 points or $12.50/contract. A one cent move is worth $250 or 100 points.

Always make sure you understand what the value of a move is for the commodity you are trading. Your source for this information is your commodity broker. So, if you are trading soybeans, you should know a 1 penny move is worth $50 per contract either up or down, and if you bought three contracts and the market closed up 10¢ that day, you made $1500 or $500/contract. If the market closed down 10¢, you lost the same amount. It may seem confusing at first, but trust me, you quickly understand the value of a minimum fluctuation and the value of a point the first time you write that cheque for your first margin call. Which reminds me of an amusing true story told to me by my favourite copper broker.

> ✳ Always make sure you understand what the value of a move is for the commodity you are trading. Your source for this information is your commodity broker.

On the floor of the COMEX in New York, where copper is traded, the pit brokers always talk in terms of points, rather than dollar values. You will hear a trader saying, 'I made 300 points today,' or 'I lost 150 points on that trade.' It seems a number of years ago there was a big commission house broker (a floor broker who made his living filling buy and sell orders from customers who called in from off the floor), who was pressured by his wife to hire the brother-in-law. The brother-in-law wasn't all that bright, but the broker felt he couldn't do that much damage if he put him on the phones as a clerk. The clerks just take the buy and sell orders over the phone and run them into the pit to be filled.

Well, everything went reasonably well for a few weeks and then the first inevitable error occurred. Apparently, the brother-in-law took an order to buy 5 contracts, and he wrote 'sell' on the order ticket. By the time the error was discovered, it resulted in a loss of 370 points (or $925) which the broker had to make good. After the market closed, the broker took the brother-in-law aside and carefully spoke to him:

'Look, mistakes happen, and fortunately this error was for only 370 points. It could have been much worse, but you have to be more careful. We cannot afford to have any more errors like this one.' To which the brother-in-law replied: 'What are you getting so hot under the collar for? Sure I made a mistake, but it's only points.'

To this day, whenever anyone makes an error in the copper pit, the guys on the floor say, 'Hey, what's your problem, it's only points!'

Many contracts, not all, have associated *daily price limits*, which measure the maximum amount that the market can move above or below the previous day's close in a single trading session. Each exchange determines if a particular commodity will have a daily trading limit, and for how much. The theory behind the 'limit-move rule' is to allow markets to 'cool down' during particularly dramatic, volatile or violent price moves. For example, the rules for the soybean contract state that the market can move 50¢/bushel up or down from the previous close (if it did not close 'limit' the previous day). Limit moves result in expanded limits. So if the market closes at $8.10/bushel on Tuesday, on Wednesday it can trade as high as $8.60 or as low as $7.60. Contrary to popular belief, the market can trade at the limit price, it just cannot trade beyond it.

> ✳ The theory behind the 'limit-move rule' is to allow markets to 'cool down' during particularly dramatic, volatile or violent price moves.

At times of dramatic news or price movements, a market can move to the limit and 'lock'. A 'lock limit move' means there is an overabundance of buyers (for 'lock limit up') versus sellers at the limit-up price, or an overabundance of sellers (for 'lock limit down') at the limit-down price.

For example, suppose in a drought market the weather services were forecasting rain one July weekend, causing the market to trade down on a Friday. However, the rain never materializes and on Monday morning the forecast is back to drought with record high temperatures for the week. It is not inconceivable the market could open 'up the limit' as shorts scramble to buy back contracts previously sold, and buyers are willing to 'pay up' for what appears to be a dwindling future supply of soybeans. Let's say the market closed on Friday at $7.50. It could open at $8.00 on Monday. Now it could trade there, it could even trade lower that day, but suppose 20 million bushels are wanted to buy at the limit-up price of $8.00, with only 10 million bushels to sell. The first 10 million would trade at $8.00, with the second 10 million in the 'pool' wanting and waiting to buy. If no additional sell orders surface, the market would remain limit up that day, with unsatisfied buying demand at the $8.00 level. Now there is nothing to say the market has to open higher on Tuesday (it could unexpectedly rain Monday evening), but all other factors remaining equal, this unsatisfied buying interest would most likely 'gap the market' higher on Tuesday morning.

In fact, some markets have what are called *variable limits*. This is where the limits are raised if a market closes limit up or limit down in a trading session. Soybeans are one of the markets with variable limits. If one or more contract months close at the 50¢ limit on a particular day, the limit is raised to 60¢ the next day. Now, in our hypothetical example, on Tuesday the new limit is 60¢, so the market can move as high as $8.60 or as low as $7.40. The market could open lower or, if the buying interest is still there, it could open 10 or 20 cents higher or, conceivable in the most dramatic markets, up the limit again. Limit moves are rare, but they do occur during shocks to a market. Pork bellies, for example, are notorious for moving multiple limit days after an unexpectedly bullish or bearish 'Hogs and Pigs Report'.

Here's a true story of how gutsy some of the floor traders at the Board can be at times. Bill, who works our soybean orders for us, told me about a day last summer when the soybean market was down the limit. It wasn't just down the limit, it was 'locked down the limit', with 5 million bushels wanted to sell down the limit, and no buyers in sight. It was very quiet. Then, out of nowhere, one large 'local' wanders into the pit and utters 'Take 'em.' 'How many?' they ask. 'All of 'em!' The other brokers in the pit literally fell over themselves selling the entire 5 million to this guy. What could he be thinking? But then, as soon as the 5 million were bought and the quote machines around the world, those that were tuned into soybeans showed this, the telephones around the pit started to ring. Off the floor traders around the world assumed with such a big buyer at limit down something was up and started to buy as well. The market immediately started to rally. When it moved 5¢/bushel off the limit-down price, the large local stepped back in and sold his 5 million bushels. A quick $250,000 profit and it only took 20 seconds!

Trading hours are also set by the exchange for each market. Swiss francs open at 7:20 am Chicago time on the Chicago Merc., and close at 2 pm sharp. If your order to sell reaches the Swiss pit at 2:01 you are out of luck, at least for that trading session. You either have to wait for the next day, or you have the option to trade on the GLOBEX, which is the computerized after-hours electronic market available for the Swiss. Most major markets have after-hours trading but some don't. If you miss the live cattle close at 1 pm Chicago time, you just have to wait until the next trading day. If you miss coffee, you can trade it in London, but there is an eight-hour period where coffee futures are not traded anywhere in the world.

So to review thus far, before you trade in any market, at minimum you will need to know the exchange the market is traded on, the trading hours, the contract size and delivery months traded. You will need to know how prices are quoted so you can put in the right priced order, the minimum fluctuation, the dollar value of the minimum fluctuation as well as the daily trading limits (if any). You will also need to know the types of orders accepted at that particular marketplace. You will want to know what the margin requirement is for the market you are trading, and what commission your broker will be charging you. We'll discuss these points shortly. Speaking of shorts, this is an important concept we'll get into next.

It's as easy to sell short as to buy long

Experienced traders, skip this section. This will become second nature to the rest of you once you start to trade, but experience has shown novices at times have trouble with the concept of *selling short*.

Everyone knows if you buy something at one price, and sell it at a higher price, you make money. If you sell at a lower price than what you paid for it you lose money. When you trade futures, you can buy or sell in whatever order you like. You can buy then sell, or sell then buy. Whichever way you do it, the idea is that the selling price should be higher than the buying price. 'How can you sell what you don't own?' I've heard that one before. Well, here's how. A buyer of a futures contract is obligated to take delivery of a particular commodity, or (and this is what happens most of the time) sell back the contract prior to the delivery date. The process of selling back, which can be done anytime during normal market hours (assuming the market is not 'locked limit down' in those markets with limits, a rare occurrence), in effect wipes your slate clean.

People seem to have no trouble understanding that if you buy 200 shares of Intel stock, you can sell back 200 shares of Intel stock at the stock exchange. If you bought at one price, and sold at a higher price, you make money and vice versa. It is also easy to understand that if you buy soybeans at $8.00/bushel and sell them at $8.20/bushel, you make a profit of 20¢/bushel, which is worth $1000 for a soybean contract (a penny move = a profit or loss of $50). If you bought a contract of 'beans' at $8.00 and sold back at $7.80, you lost 20¢, or $1000/contract. If you bought 10 contracts of July soybeans, you could cancel your obligation to take delivery by selling back 10 contracts of July soybeans. You would then be out of the market and the difference between where you bought and sold would determine your profit or loss on the trade.

In trading futures, since we are trading for future delivery, it is just as easy to sell first and then buy back later. Selling first is referred to as *shorting* or *selling short*. To offset your obligation to deliver, all you need to do is to buy back your contract(s) prior to the expiration of the contract. This process of buying back is known as *covering*. You 'covered your short position' to wipe your slate clean. Now, the purpose of shorting is to profit from a fall in prices. If you believe the price of a particular commodity is going down, due to an oversupply or poor demand, you will want to go short. The objective is to cover at a lower price than you sold.

> ✱ In trading futures, since we are trading for future delivery, it is just as easy to sell first and then buy back later. Selling first is referred to as shorting or selling short.

eg In our soybean example, if you believed prices at $8.00 were too high, and were heading for a fall, you could go short at $8.00. If prices fell to $7.80 you may wish to cover your position and take the 20¢ profit. A short sale at $8.00, covered at $7.80 is a profit of 20¢ or $1000/contract. Of course, if prices rose and you had to cover at $8.20, you would have a loss on the short sale of 20¢/contract, or $1000. 'Sell high, buy back low' can be just as profitable as 'buy low, sell high'.

Kevin 'Mac' who leases my COMEX seat from me, told me a humorous (and true) story. Kevin trades in the copper pit, as does Al, a large commission house broker. Al was large in more ways than one way, and his weight seemed to roller coaster depending on which diet he was on at the time. Diet or not, he was a big guy and this was an advantage which would help him get noticed in the pit. Al was also a colourful guy who liked to play the horses but at heart he was a shy man. Yet, you wouldn't know it when you saw him in the pit because he moved frenetically and possessed a gruff voice. He 'filled paper' for a living, meaning he would execute customer orders in the pit.

Now, this happened in the copper market of 1987–88, a particularly wild time. The day of the stock market crash the market spiked down 10¢/pound, a huge one-day move, to under 80¢/pound (interestingly, just a few months later it was over $1.40). The market was wild and noisy that day, and Al was summoned to the phone to take a large buy order from a New York client. Al was on one of his diets and that day forget his belt. He rushes into the pit, raises his arms to bid for the copper, and his pants fall to his ankles. It was a wild day, but still for a few seconds no one could believe their eyes, and everyone stops trading to stare at Al's boxer shorts. Al turned as red as the hearts on his boxers (he got them for Valentine's Day). Then the silence is broken by Kevin (as he tells it, he didn't stop to think, it just came out) as Kevin yells, '*Look at Al, he's covering his shorts!*'

Now that's a story which is only funny to a commodity trader.

Margin and leverage

One of the big attractions, and what makes futures exciting, is *leverage*. Leverage is the ability to buy or sell $100,000 of a commodity with a $5000 security deposit, so that small price changes can result in huge profits or losses. Leverage gives you the ability to either make a killing or get killed. You need to understand how this important concept works before you trade, and a thorough understanding of the powers and pitfalls of leverage is imperative to sound money management principals, which we'll discuss later.

Each contract that is bought or sold on a futures exchange must be backed by a good faith deposit termed *margin*. This is not like buying on margin in the stock market. When a stock market investor buys on margin, he is in effect borrowing half of the purchase price of the stock from his broker. He is charged interest on the balance, and stock exchange rules prohibit borrowing more than 50 per cent. This provides a degree of leverage, but nothing like commodities.

To see how powerful leverage can be, let's contrast a futures purchase with a stock purchase for cash. If a stock investor buys 200 shares of a stock trading at $10, his purchase cost is $2000. If the stock moves up by 10 per cent to $11/share, he has made $200 on his $2000 investment, or 10 per cent.

Margin in commodity trading is like a good faith deposit. It is just a small percentage of the value of the underlying commodity represented by the contract, generally in the neighbourhood of 2–10 per cent. Margin deposits are set by the exchange and can change with price movements and market volatility. Since we are trading for future delivery, and not borrowing anything, *no* interest is charged on the balance. This is not a partial payment, not a down payment and actually not even considered a cost. If you make money on the trade, upon liquidation you will receive your total margin deposit back, plus your profits. Commissions will be deducted, and they are a cost. Margin is money deposited in your brokerage account which serves to guarantee the performance of your side of the contract. It is a form of 'earnest money' which is deposited by both the longs and the shorts and serves to ensure the integrity of every futures transaction. Margin in effect ensures that you will be paid if you win and the other side will be paid if you don't.

> **✷ Margin in effect ensures that you will be paid if you win and the other side will be paid if you don't.**

When you enter a position, you have deposited, or will deposit the margin in your account, but your brokerage house is required to post the margin with a central exchange arm called the *clearinghouse*. The clearinghouse is a non-profit entity which in effect is in charge of debiting the accounts of the losers and redistributing this money to the accounts of the winners daily.

Now back to our leverage example. The margin requirement for a 5000-ounce silver contract has been running about $2000 in recent years. At $6/ounce, a contract is worth $30,000 ($6 times 5000 ounces). If the price of silver rises by 10 per cent to $6.60, the same contract is worth $33,000. Suppose the same investor puts up his $2000 and instead buys a silver contract. If the price of silver rises by 10 per cent, or 60¢, he has made $3000 on his contract. This is 150 per cent on margin, not 10 per cent. Powerful, but a two-edged sword. If prices fall by 10 per cent, his $2000 is now worth a *negative* $1000. And when you trade futures you are responsible for the total value of a move of any position you hold. In most cases, if a market moves against you, you will have time to liquidate before the account shows a deficit. However, this is not always the case. If you don't use adequate risk control measures, or if a market moves very quickly against you, your account could go into a deficit situation, and *you are obligated to pay the difference.*

There are two types of margin: *initial margin* and *maintenance margin*. Initial margin is the amount which must be in the account before you place a trade. If you do not have enough initial margin in your account, you will incur a *margin call*. Some brokerage firms require the initial margin be in the account before a trade takes place. Others will issue credit for good customers, but generally require the margin call be met within one to three business days. The firm can require same day deposit by bank wire transfer at any time, and may do this in volatile, risky type markets. Maintenance margin is the amount which must be maintained in your account as long as the position is active. If the equity balance in your account should fall under the maintenance margin level, due to adverse market movements, you will be issued a *margin call* as well.

Once the margin call is issued you are required to meet the call, or liquidate the position. If you fail to meet a margin call in a timely manner the broker has the right (and will use it) to automatically liquidate the position for you. This would be done to protect the broker from additional adverse movements in the market, since he is responsible for meeting your margin call, even if you're a deadbeat and don't. If you fail to meet a margin call, and the position is ultimately liquidated at a loss which leaves a deficit in the account, while you are legally responsible the broker is immediately responsible for the deficit. In other words, initial margin may not be the extent of your liability. You are responsible for all losses resulting from your trading activities: if the market moves against you five, six, seven days, and you do not get out; if the market moves limit against you and eats up your margin, you are still responsible for any and all losses. There are ways to manage the risk which we will discuss, but at this point be aware whenever you trade futures your risk is not limited to the initial margin or your account balance. It can go further than that. Options work differently. They will be discussed in depth in subsequent chapters.

> ✱ If you fail to meet a margin call in a timely manner the broker has the right (and will use it) to automatically liquidate the position for you.

Let's look at a typical example. Assume silver is trading at $6.00 an ounce, and the initial margin requirement is $2000. A silver contract has a size of 5000 ounces, so at $6 an ounce the total value of the contract is $30,000, but all that is required to purchase or sell a contract is $2000 (in this example about 6 per cent). A rule of thumb for maintenance margin is that it will be at the 75 per cent level of initial. So if the initial is $2000, maintenance might be $1500. If you have an account of $20,000 with no other positions on, you *could* buy 10 contracts without a margin call (however, this is not recommended since you would be 'overtrading', too highly leveraged and a relatively minor price movement would move you into margin call territory).

For illustrative purposes only, however, let's assume your account balance was at $20,000 and you bought 10 silver contracts. Your maintainence level is at $15,000. If the market starts to move your way immediately, you're OK. Since a silver contract is for 5000 ounces, a 1¢ move = a profit or loss per contract of $50. In this example, the 10 contracts will give you a profit or loss of $500 per penny move. Suppose you buy the 10 contracts at $6.00, and the market closes that same day at $6.05. Your account balance would be $22,500 on the close of business that day. You have an *unrealized* profit of $2500. It is unrealized because the position is still open and not closed out yet. The increase in equity value of $2500 is the result of the 5¢ move in your favour: 5¢ times $50/contract times 10 contracts.

Suppose the next day, the price fell 10¢ to close at $5.95. Your account value would decrease by $5000 to $17,500. You would *not* have a margin call, since your value is still above the maintenance level. If on the next day prices rose 5¢ to $6.00, your equity value would move back to $20,000.

Basically, futures trading is the process of generating a credit or debit daily against your initial position until you close it out. If you make money on any particular day, the unrealized credit balance is immediately credited to your account and debited from the people on the other side of the transaction. You will never know who they are, or see them. It is all anonymous, but they are out there somewhere. If the market closes against your position on any particular day the loss will be immediately debited from your account.

> * Basically, futures trading is the process of generating a credit or debit daily against your initial position until you close it out.

Now, let's get back to our example. The fourth day, the market drops 25¢ to close at $5.75. Your account is debited $12,500 (25¢ times $50/contract times 10 contracts). Your equity balance is now down to $7500, which is below the maintenance margin level, so it's margin call time. You will get a call from your broker, who will tell you about your $12,500 margin call. You see, once your equity level falls under the maintenance margin level you are required to bring your balance up to the initial margin level. You have two choices. You can either liquidate the position in whole or in part, enough to move your equity back above the initial margin level, or you can meet the call. In this case you could sell out 7 contracts, realize your loss on the 7, hold on to 3, get your initial margin down to $6000 and hope the market recovers. If you feel strongly about the position, you can opt to meet the call. Let's say you send in a cheque, or if required wire transfer the $12,500 to your account. Your account balance will now show $20,000, so you are 'off call'.

You have $32,500 into the account at this point, but if you closed out the position at the current price of $5.75 you would have a balance of $20,000 minus transaction costs. If your thinking was right, and the silver market recovers to $6.00, your account balance would grow back to $32,500. You have the right to request the $12,500 (the amount over the initial margin) be sent back to you. If the market fell again however, you could certainly be issued another margin call. It is important to leave a cash cushion in the account so you have the ability to ride out normal market fluctuations without receiving a margin call. My general rule of thumb is *never to margin yourself higher than 50 per cent*. In other words, if your account value is $20,000 I would not put on positions which, at most, would require more than $10,000 in initial margin.

Each market has its own margin requirement. It is based on the volatility of the particular market, and the volatility of the markets as a whole. Greater volatility equal greater risk and higher requirements. The S&P 500 index and the NASDAQ are two of the most volatile of all contracts. It is not uncommon to have a daily range of $5000 per contract in value, or more. The margin requirement for the S&P can be in a normal period from $12,000 per contract on up. I have seen the NASDAQ with $20,000 range days and $30,000 margin for just one contract. On the other hand, corn is traditionally less volatile, and in a normal market might have a price range of $250 per contract. The initial margin might be $400 in a quiet market, and could move up to $750 in a volatile environment for corn prices.

Another point on margins: there is a minimum margin requirement set by the exchange, but individual brokerage houses have the right to charge higher than 'exchange minimum'. This is protect them from overtraders who can tend to plunge (trade in excess of prudent speculation, even in excess of the ability to pay) which would require the broker to make good on his commitment to the clearinghouse. The whole point of this margining system is that all positions are 'marked to the market' by the clearinghouse daily, revalued to the current market price and as such profits and losses are paid daily.

One last point about margins. The exchange allows initial margins to be posted in either cash or (in the USA) US government obligations of less than ten years to maturity. If an investor wishes to post 'T-Bills' for margin he can do so, and many commodity brokers will pass the interest back to the customer. So, in effect, the initial margin earns interest. Other brokers will pay interest on free credit balances and even unrealized profits (before a position is liquidated). Ask your commodity broker if he does this, since it means a few extra bucks in your pocket if he does.

Delivery months

Every futures contract has standardized months which are authorized by the exchange for trading. For example, wheat is traded for delivery in March, May, July, September and December. If you buy a March contract, you need to sell a March contract to offset your position and meet your contractual obligation. If you buy a March wheat contract, and you sell a May wheat contract, you have offset nothing. You are still 'long' March and now 'short' May.

Some commodities are traded in every month, but by convention there are some contract months which are more actively traded than others. For example, gold trades in every month of the year, but the active months are February, April, June, August, October and December. On the London Metal Exchange (where aluminium, copper, zinc, nickel, lead and tin are traded) they have a different system known as 'prompt dates'. The active contract on any particular day is the 3-month. If you buy or sell a new 3-month on, say 10 May, you are in the 10 August contract (assuming 10 August does not fall on a weekend or holiday). Then, to offset your position, you need to sell the 10 August. You can do that prior to 10 August, but your buy or sell price is based on an interpolation of the cash (or spot contract) to 3-month differential on the day you liquidate. The margining procedure is different for the LME as well, so if you are thinking of trading in these markets talk to your commodity broker about how it works.

Which month should you trade? This is a general rule of thumb only, but unless you have a specific reason for trading a specific month (for example, you want to be short December corn, because this is the first 'new crop' month and you think there's a big crop coming, so despite tight supplies in the near market, you think this month will fall faster), trade the active month. The active month is the one with the highest open interest. Your broker can tell you which month this is for any particular commodity at any point in time. The reason for this is the active months have the most players and therefore the most liquidity. You can get in and out with a smaller degree of *slippage*. Slippage in effect means having your order filled at a different price than that which existed as the last trade.

> ✳ *Unless you have a specific reason for trading a specific month trade the active month.*

For example, you want to buy gold, the last quoted price is 401.10, but the best bid is 401.10, and the best offer 401.30. It is a fast moving market, and you want in. You buy at the market, and even though the last trade is 401.10, your price fill comes back at 401.30. This 20 points represent $20, and probably went into the pocket of a floor broker. It is legal, and as long as there were no lower offers in the pit, it is the price you pay for the 'liquidity' the floor brokers provide.

More about this later, but for minimum slippage it is best to trade in high volume, active markets. I've also found that a good commodity broker, who uses the better floor brokers (there are good and bad floor brokers) will tend to, on balance, get you better fills thus reducing the costs associated with slippage.

It also doesn't make sense in most cases (there are exceptions to this rule as well) to trade in a *delivery month*. So avoid entering positions that are close to delivery, since you'll need to 'roll over' into the next contract sooner. The rules are different for each market, but in many cases a contract enters actual delivery the last day of the month prior to the delivery month. For example, for March wheat the *first notice day*, or first possible day the shorts can make a delivery, is the last trading day in February. What happens if you fail to sell out, and are still in the contract on first notice day? Well, there is a possibility you will get actual delivery of the wheat. I say possibility, since the shorts are not required to make delivery the first day or the next. A short is only required to make delivery if he has not covered his contract prior to the *last trading day*. The last trading day for March wheat is in the third week of March. So the delivery period lasts for about three weeks. A long can receive delivery, at the discretion of the shorts, any one of the days in the delivery period. If the cash price is above the futures on first notice day, the shorts may not find it lucrative to deliver, and wait. If the cash price is under the futures, odds increase for deliveries.

Now, just because deliveries are made on any particular day does not mean you will get delivery on any particular day. Early in the delivery period, the number of open contracts generally exceeds the deliverable supply. If open interest in the March wheat is say 100 million bushels, and the deliverable supply in the elevators licensed for delivery is 20 million bushels, the odds of delivery are great only if you have a contract purchased months ago, rather than days ago. This is because deliveries are assigned to the 'oldest date' first. The oldest long is first in line for delivery. However, as the delivery period progresses, the odds of receiving a delivery increase as the number of outstanding contracts is liquidated down, and your date becomes fresher.

So what happens if you do get delivery? Contrary to popular belief, you will not get a load of wheat dumped on your doorstep (or worse yet a load of hogs). You will receive a warehouse receipt which states you now own 5000 bushels of wheat in, say, a Toledo elevator. Since you are now in a cash contract (the delivery offsets your futures) you are required to post the full value of the contract. So your leverage is gone. If your margin deposit was $700 for the futures, you now need to pony up an additional $19,300 if you received delivery at $4/bushel. If you don't have the money in your account, since your broker will have to post this amount, he will charge you interest on the balance. There are other fees involved as well, including an additional commission, insurance and storage costs. You can pass your delivery receipt on to someone else. Since only the shorts can make delivery (and you are *long* a warehouse receipt), you will need to sell a contract short and then instruct your broker to make your delivery on your short contract. This is the way you can sell your warehouse receipt.

> ✳ *So what happens if you do get delivery? Contrary to popular belief, you will not get a load of wheat dumped on your doorstep.*

The point here is, in most cases, there is no good reason to be trading in a delivery month unless you have a good reason. A good reason might be a belief there is not enough of the commodity available to deliver, which could cause a 'short squeeze', a panic situation for the shorts. However, this is a game for very sophisticated traders. Of course, as a short you have no chance of receiving a delivery (since it is at your discretion as to when to make it), but then your chance of being 'squeezed' increases with each day you are in the contract during the delivery period. If you are in there on the last day, and your broker hasn't forced you out, good luck in making the delivery. This is a game for the commercials.

When I was at Merrill Lynch, I remember one of the commodity brokers had a client who refused to liquidate a long sugar position prior to the delivery period. He thought there was no sugar, but there was. The sugar contract is written so that you can receive delivery at any one of a hundred ports around the world. He got his sugar on a barge off Bangkok, Thailand, and it cost him plenty for us to find a cash operator and dispose of this 'distress merchandise' (because the commercials knew he had no use for 112,000 pounds of sugar on a barge) in the cash market.

One last point: most financial futures (stock indices, currencies) and even some of the agricultural (feeder cattle, lean hogs) are 'cash settled'. Any positions still open when the contract expires are closed at the settlement price. The amount paid/received is calculated for everyone (who remained in at expiration) based on this common price.

Brokers and commissions

Margin may not be a true cost (you will get it back at the end of the trade, plus any profits, or minus any losses), but commissions are. Unlike stock transactions, most commodity brokers charge on the *round turn*. This means there is no fee charged on initiation of the trade (whether it be a new short position, or a new purchase, known as a long). The commission will be charged on liquidation (the buying back, or covering, of a short, and/or the sale of a long). This is your broker's fee for his services. Commissions range across the board and by broker. There are two major types of 'commission firms', the discounter and full service.

Commissions, while important, should not be your main consideration when choosing a broker. Low commissions do not mean the best service. My firm is a full service firm. Our commissions are competitive for full service, but are generally a bit higher than discounters. I am not trying to say there isn't a place for discount brokers. Our firm also offers online trading at very reduced rates for the self-directed trader. If you are relatively sophis-

> ✱ Low commissions do not mean the best service.

ticated, know exactly what you want to do in the marketplace, do not require advice or additional services, only need order execution, then you should certainly consider using a discount or online futures broker. However, you need to evaluate what you're receiving. With some firms, not all, discount commissions equal cheaper service. All firms use brokers in the open outcry pits to execute trades. Some use company brokers, but most use independents, or members of the exchange who fill 'paper' or public orders. Not all independents are created equal. Bigger firms, with larger orders, can tend to attract the bigger (and better) floor brokers. This is because the floor brokers are paid a small fee per contract executed (the floor brokers, unlike the off-the-floor brokers, are paid on both the buy and the sell). If a floor broker can be a bit louder, a bit more aggressive, or is known to hold a large 'deck' of orders, he will tend to do a better job than the novice or floor broker with a small deck. The better floor brokers attract the bigger decks.

In our firm, we additionally pay some floor brokers who do an outstanding job an additional or higher fee per contract executed. I'm not sure many discount brokers would do this. We do this, because if a floor broker can be a bit quicker, if he can at time buy the bid, or sell the offer for us, and get us a bit better price fill for our customers, then this means money in our customers' pockets and is more important than a low commission. Bottom line, whichever broker you ultimately choose, you must evaluate how timely and accurate your price fills are. You also will need to see how fast your broker can get back to you with price fills. Additionally, you need to evaluate how much help your broker is providing you with, and how much help you require. A knowledge-able full service broker, who can provide you with profitable recommendations, is worth many times the commissions charged. Just as impor-tant, is your broker helping you to control your risks properly on the bad trades. Is he helping you to avoid the classic mistakes, such as over-trading? These are factors you will need to evaluate. A brokerage relationship is very personal, and who you trade with can mean the difference between profit and loss.

> ✳ *A knowledgeable full service broker, who can provide you with profitable recommendations, is worth many times the commissions charged.*

One last thought about commissions: the fee per contract traded when talk-ing about commodity futures is generally quite low when compared with other types of investments. It can be one-half of a percentage point of the total account value. It is a higher percentage when compared to the margin deposit, but still quite small. The other side of the coin is that futures traders are much more active than more traditional investors, and *total* commission costs for an active trader can run up substantially over time.

One last thought about brokers. There are brokers who do both securities (stock) and commodities business. I'm sure there must be some of these dual types who excel at both, but I've not met one. Many of our clients who previ-ously had troubles in commodities seem to have come to us from brokers, in many cases from a major 'wire house', who was one of these 'Jack of all trades'. On the other side of the spectrum are those who know what they are doing and trade only electronic markets, such as the S&P 'E-mini'. Price fills and quality of order execution are generally uniform for the electronic markets. However, if you need help, remember commodity trading is a full-time business, very intense, and you should go with a specialist.

The players

There are two major types of participants in the futures and options markets: the *hedger* and the *speculator*.

Hedgers account for up to half of all the participants in most of the major futures contracts (although there are a few dominated by hedgers, and others with a very small contingent of hedgers). Hedgers use commodity exchanges to offset the risk of fluctuating prices when they buy or sell physical supplies of a commodity.

For example, a copper mining company may sell copper futures to 'lock in' a sale price today for their future production. In this way, they protect their profit margins and revenue stream should copper prices fall in the future. Should copper prices rise, they will lose on their futures position, but the value of their physical metal will rise. The copper mine, a producer, is just trying to offset, or hedge, his price risk. A hedger can be a buyer or a seller.

A copper tube manufacturer, who buys copper as a raw material in the production of copper tube used for plumbing, might buy copper futures to 'lock in' his cost of copper for future purchase. If the price of copper rises, he will have a profit on his hedge, which can be used to offset the higher price of physical copper he will need to purchase in the marketplace. If the copper prices fall, he will show a loss on the futures side of the transaction, but he will be able to buy the copper cheaper in the marketplace.

In either case, the copper mine, or the tube manufacturer have the ability to hold their contracts into the delivery period. They then have the option to make or take copper delivery through the exchange at an approved warehouse licensed to do business on the exchange. This is as important in theory as practice because it is what allows physical commodity prices and the exchange-traded contracts to come together in price. If the price of the commodity is too high in relation to the futures price, then those people involved in the use of a particular commodity will buy the low priced futures contracts and take delivery. Their buying in effect pushes prices up to 'meet' the physical price. If the price of a futures contract is too low in relation to the actual commodity, then producers of that commodity will sell the contract to make delivery, since the higher priced futures (in relation to the physical) just might be their best sale. Their selling pushes the price of the futures down to the cash price. This whole process is known as *convergence*. This potential process of convergence is what makes the system work. However, in practice only 1 to 2 per cent of all commodity contracts ends in delivery. Odds are that you, as a speculator, will never get involved in a delivery, and there is no need to. In fact, most hedgers also do not use the markets to actually make or take delivery. They are using the futures as a pricing tool, to help stabilize their revenues and their costs.

I have a client, a major manufacturing firm, that publishes a catalogue twice a year with prices which they honour throughout the catalogue date. They use copper and zinc in their manufacturing process. They know what their profit margin is based on today's price of copper and zinc. If they did not hedge, and lock in the six-month price of copper today, and the price went up during the time the catalogue was distributed, their entire profit margin could be wiped out. The other side of the coin, if copper prices fell and their published price remained based on the old higher prices of the raw materials, they could have reaped a windfall profit. However, they are not in the business of speculation, they are in the manufacturing business. They are more than willing to forgo the chance of a windfall to be assured of a profit margin which will allow them to keep the plant running and avoid layoffs.

So a few times a year, we sit down together and determine where to buy copper and zinc futures to lock in a price they can live with for the next six months. Once they know this price, they can publish their catalogue with peace of mind, knowing their profit margin is secure. If the price of copper rises, they will have to pay the higher price in the cash copper market, but their futures contracts will rise in value as well, and the profits from the futures offset the higher price which must be paid in the physical market. If the price of copper falls, they will show a loss on their futures, but this will be offset by the lower price they will enjoy in the cash market when they buy their copper.

In this particular case, the firm has documented an additional cost savings advantage by using futures. In the past, they used to 'lock in' their price by buying six months' worth of copper and zinc and placing this metal in large warehouses. At times there were so many tons of metal that they also had to rent space in warehouses they did not own. Not only did this involve the cost of maintaining these warehouses (you have to pay fork lift operators to move the stuff around), but think of the cost of money to finance thousands of tons of heavy metal. Now that they are assured of a future price, they maintain just two to four weeks' worth of physical metal on location, and have eliminated the need for many of these warehouses. The savings in interest on money alone is in the hundreds of thousands of dollars. This firm has never taken delivery on the futures. Actually, they do not even use the type of copper which is specified in the futures contract (the pure or 'virgin' metal), they use scrap copper. However, since the price of scrap moves in the same direction as the price of the virgin metal, this is a good *cross-hedge* for them which works well in their risk management programme.

Many of the products hedged on a futures exchange are actually cross-hedges. For example, diesel fuel and jet fuel are similar to heating oil, and the three are often priced within a few cents of each other. A major airline might use the heating oil contract to hedge their jet fuel needs, and a trucking company might use the same contract to hedge their diesel fuel needs. It should be mentioned, there is a related tool that can be used effectively by hedgers called an option, which we will discuss in depth later in the book.

✳ *The definition of basis is the difference in cash and futures prices.*

Basis risk

The definition of *basis* is the difference in cash and futures prices. Each and every contract traded has what are called specifications, which make the contracts fungible and standardized.

For example, let's look at the contract specs for heating oil traded on the New York Mercantile Exchange:

Trading unit 42,000 US gallons (1000 barrels).

Trading hours 9:50 am – 3:10 pm New York time.

Trading months 18 consecutive months commencing with the next calendar month.

Price quotation In dollars and cents per gallon (for example, $0.7575 or 75.75¢/gallon).

Minimum price fluctuation $0.0001 (0.01¢) per gallon or $4.20 per contract.

Maximum daily price fluctuation 40¢/gallon for the first two contract months. Back months 4¢ per gallon, rises to 6¢/gallon if the previous day's settlement price in any back month is at the 4¢ gallon limit.

Last trading day Trading terminates at the close of business on the last business day of the month preceding the delivery month.

Grade and quality specifications Industry standards for fungible No. 2 heating oil.

Delivery FOB seller's facility in New York harbour, ex-shore. All duties, entitlements, taxes, fees and other charges paid.

Now this is an example of how a typical contract is written. It is standardized in that all contracts created are exactly the same. Contract specs for all the exchange-traded contracts are available from your commodity broker or the exchange (a listing of the exchanges is in the Appendix). As a speculator, you really are not concerned with the delivery specs since you will not be involved in delivery – you'll be out long before.

What about the hedger? This particular contract calls for delivery of No. 2 heating oil in New York harbour. Not all heating oil is used in the New York area, and prices in other cities will vary due to differences in transportation costs, storage costs, as well as local supply and demand considerations. A wave of Arctic air sweeping through Europe will no doubt raise the price of heating oil globally, but the price will rise faster in Rotterdam than in New York if NY is experiencing a warm winter. These differentials are known as the *basis*. The basis can be stable and predictable at times. For example, if it costs 3¢/gallon to transport heating oil from New York to Boston, the basis in Boston may predictably run at 'plus 3¢/gallon' all other factors remaining equal. However, if Boston is under deep freeze, and New York isn't, the basis can move up to 'plus 4¢'.

For the manufacturing firm I deal with, for example, the price of scrap can at times be at the price of the virgin metal (when there is a scrap shortage), or at times be as much as 4 or 5¢/pound under. The point here is that the hedger has what's called *basis risk*. Basis risk is almost always far less than the price risks involved without a hedge. A hedger who does not hedge is just like a speculator, in that he is assuming the natural risks of the marketplace. Once again, I will point out that most hedgers close out their futures positions long before the futures contract expire, and most long before the delivery period even starts. Then they take or make delivery of the physical commodity they are involved in through normal channels, using their normal suppliers. Yet, knowing that each contract is actually keyed into a specific actual grade of the underlying commodity keeps the value true to life. No matter what the underlying commodity is, each exchange ultimately guarantees the purchase and sale as well as the delivery grades for quality and quantity. This is why quotations from the exchanges for most of the commodities traded are used as pricing standards by companies and individuals around the world.

A hedging example

The primary thrust of this book will be geared towards the speculator and how he or she can use the commodity futures and options markets to make money. However, it is important for all traders to understand how a typical hedge might work to understand why these markets exist in the first place. Remember, the perfect hedge is rare; there is always some basis risk present. However, the concept is the same, no matter if we are discussing a packing plant hedging their live cattle needs or a bank hedging interest rate risk. Hedges come in two basic forms: the *short* and the *long*.

The short hedge

A short hedge is entered into to protect the value of an inventory. Let's look at an example using crude oil. An inventory of 1000 barrels of crude oil constantly changes in value, from wellhead to consumer, even before it is processed into gasoline or heating oil. The value changes as the price of crude changes and this also occurs daily. A short hedge is used by the owner of a commodity to essentially lock in the value of the inventory prior to the transferring of title to a buyer. *A decline in prices generates profits in the futures market on the short hedge.* These profits will be offset by depreciation in the inventory value.

Let's say an oil producer is afraid of a price decline. In August he anticipates he will sell his August production in September. His production is 1000 barrels a day for 25 days. The cash price in August is $20/barrel, and October futures are quoted in August at $20.10/barrel. Here's what the producer might do in the futures market: he sells 25 October futures (each contract is for 1000 barrels, so this represents his August production of 25,000 barrels) at $20.10, which 'locks in' a value of his inventory equivalent to $502,500 ($20.20/barrel times 25,000 barrels). Let's suppose he was correct about the price falling, along comes 15 September and the price of crude has fallen in the cash market by $2/barrel. Since the futures mirror the cash fairly closely, the futures will also fall in price. Let's say the futures on that date were quoted at $18.00/barrel. The cash price on 15 September is now $18, or $2 less than the price at production time – $20. He sells his product in the cash market to the refinery for a total of $450,000 ($18 times 25,000), or $50,000 less than what he could have received in August. However, the futures have also dropped, and he also buys back his October futures contracts on 15 September (this offsets his position: he does not have to make delivery) for $18. Remember he sold for the equivalent of $502,000, he buys back at the equivalent of $450,000, and the difference of $52,000 is his gain in the futures. The futures gain of $52,000 offsets the cash market loss of $50,000, and he had in effect protected the value of his inventory at the August price.

Now what if he was wrong and the cash price rose? Let's say instead of falling to $18, the cash price rose to $21 by 15 September and the October futures rose to $21.10. His 25,000 barrels will realize him $525,000 in the cash market, or $25,000 more than he could have received in August. However, his futures have also risen to a total value of $527,500 ($21.10 times 25,000). When he buys his contracts back he will realize a futures loss of $25,500 ($502,000 minus $527,500). So, the futures loss of $25,500 must be taken into consideration with the extra cash profit of $25,000 – he still comes back to about the August price. The short hedge has protected the value of his inventory at about $20, which is the number he was happy with.

The farmer in Nebraska, who wants to 'lock in' the price of his corn for harvest time in the fall, while it is still in the ground in the summer, would use a short hedge in much the same way.

The long hedge

The long hedge is entered into by a commodity user (buyer) to fix acquisition costs, and in effect assure a certain profit margin.

For example, let's suppose an ethanol producer (ethanol is a corn-based fuel additive) uses 1,000,000 bushels of corn to meet the ethanol requirements for his major customer during the peak summer driving season. It is April, and July corn is quoted at $2.50/bushel on the futures. By July, depending on weather and exports, the price of corn could be much higher or lower. This big customer wishes to enter into a contract with the producer for delivery at today's price in August (for ethanol the producer will manufacture in July). The producer knows he can make a profit at today's ethanol prices *if* the price of corn remains at $2.50. He calculates his gross profit at $2.50 corn to be $50,000. His profit will be greater if corn prices fall, his 'break-even' is at $2.70 corn, and if corn prices rise above this level he would actually wipe out his profit margin and start to see red ink (assuming today's prices for ethanol which could also fluctuate).

To keep his customer happy and loyal, plus to assure his plant will continue to run at capacity, he enters into an agreement to deliver ethanol at today's price to the big customer in August. Rather than take the risk of the marketplace, and run the risk of potentially selling his product at a loss in the summer *should* corn prices rise, he forgoes the gamble of a windfall profit (should corn prices fall) and enters a long hedge in the futures market. He buys 1,000,000 bushels of July corn in the futures on 15 April. This is the day he also enters into his cash contract for delivery of ethanol to his customer next August. The price of July corn on 15 April is $2.50. A drought develops, and in July, when he needs to go into the cash market to purchase the million bushels, the price of corn has risen to $3.00 in both the cash and futures. It has gone up by 50¢/bushel which is an additional cost to him, over and above the April price, of $500,000 (1,000,000 bushels times 50¢/bushel).

However, the futures have also risen by 50¢, and he sells his July futures contracts purchased for $2.50 at the then prevailing price of $3.00. He thus realizes a futures *gain* of $500,000, exactly offsetting the additional cash loss of $500,000. In this way he assured his $50,000 gross profit on the transaction. If he had not hedged, he would have lost $450,000 on the cash contract instead of a profit of $50,000.

Now if the weather had been good, and it looked as if a large crop was forthcoming, prices might have fallen to, say $2.20 by 15 July. His cash corn cost in this case would be $300,000 less. If unhedged, and he had entered into a cash contract for ethanol at the April price, he could have realized a windfall profit of $350,000 versus $50,000, all other factors remaining equal. If hedged, he loses $300,000 on the futures transaction (a fall of 30¢/bushel times 1,000,000 bushels). However, the ethanol producer has made this decision; if he can always enter into profitable contracts with his users, he will remain in business. Sure, if corn prices fall he is out the extra $300,000 profit in this example, and this 300 was probably transferred from his account to some speculator(s) he will never see, but this is OK. He is not in the gambling business, his business is ethanol production. He will gladly forgo the chance of a 'windfall' for the ability to keep the plant running profitably.

This simple example demonstrates that the objectives of hedgers and speculators are not the same. The speculator is always looking to make money on his transactions. The hedger is not always looking necessarily to profit on the futures side of this transactions. His goals are to lock in a price which will assure a profit, or prevent a loss for his business, either the production or consumption of some product. The bread baker who wants to lock in his future wheat purchase price would use a long hedge in much the same way.

The reality

In these examples, I have kept the basis fairly constant. In reality, it can change. If a short hedger (one who sells futures) experiences a *widening* of the basis (where cash prices have fallen to a greater degree than futures, either cash has fallen faster, or risen slower than futures), a basis loss may result. In other words, the short hedger's cash position loss may be greater than the gain realized on the futures side of the transaction. Or, in a rising market, the gain on the cash side of the transaction would not be as large as the loss on the futures side. Conversely, a basis gain would occur with a *widening* basis on a long hedge. The futures would rise in price to a greater degree than the cash. A *narrowing* basis yields additional gains for a short hedger (the cash falls less, or rises more, in relation to the futures) and incremental losses for the long hedger (the cash falls less, or rises more in relation to the futures). Basis gains or losses are a risk to the hedger, but not nearly as big a risk as what is called 'flat price' risk. The price of heating oil may move 20¢/gallon in a couple of months, while the basis might move 1¢ either way. The flat price move was a result of a warmer than normal winter, while the basis change was due to the fact that it was colder in New Haven than New York that particular winter. The hedger has to be concerned about basis. The speculator may look at basis changes to help him determine the strength or weakness of a market, but this is really more of a hedger's concern.

It doesn't matter if you use copper or soybean oil, or need to purchase euros six months hence, any futures market where prices fluctuate creates price risk for the commercial participants. This creates the need for a hedging tool. Remember, hedgers are not trying to make a killing in the market. They wish to offset price risks. On the other hand the *speculator* is trying to make money by buying low and selling high (or vice versa). A speculator is a participant in the marketplace who is neither a producer nor a user of a commodity or financial instrument. By definition he does not have or want the underlying commodity. It could be you or me.

> ✳ *A speculator is a participant in the marketplace who is neither a producer nor a user of a commodity or financial instrument.*

Without speculators, or traders, the system would not work; they add *liquidity*. Speculators often take the other side of the bids and offers in the marketplace put out by hedgers. At times they take the other side of a speculative bid and offer, and at times different hedgers may be on both sides of a transaction. However, a trade cannot be completed unless someone is willing to take the other side and if there were only hedgers and no speculators the system would not operate smoothly. By assuming the risks the hedgers are trying to avoid, the speculator will make money if he is right and lose when wrong.

In our ethanol example above, when the manufacturer made the $500,000 in the futures market, somebody, or bodies, lost that money. Those people could have been speculators betting the crop would be good and prices would fall. On the other hand, if prices did fall, this hedger's loss might have been made by speculators betting on lower prices.

There are various types of traders who fit the speculator category. There are *pit traders*, also called *locals* or *professional traders*, who stand in the pit and trade for their own account. Many of them are *scalpers*, who are just trading for 'ticks' or minor fluctuations. A local may, for example, scalp a small profit by selling 5 May copper contracts to a hedger who is buying at 98.10¢/pound, and then cover (or buy them back) from a speculator who is selling at 98¢/pound. The tenth of a cent represents two price ticks (a tick is a minimum fluctuation), for copper this is 0.05¢/pound or $12.50/tick, or $25 per two ticks, or $125 for a two-tick move on a 5-contract position. In this example, the local made a profit of $125, and he did provide liquidity for both the hedger and the speculator. The hedger wanted to establish a longer term buy hedge, and the speculator wanted to establish a new short position.

The scalper is 'making a market' here. At times, without the scalpers, a market can be thin, with buyers and sellers bidding and offering prices away from each other. So the local who is a scalper is providing an economic service, and this is why he is allowed to exist. I am not trying to say he is a wonderful person, or a bad person, he is out to make a profit for himself (or herself, about 1 per cent of pit traders are women). I am also not trying to insinuate being a local on the floor is a licence to print money. If a local's judgement is off, he can get caught in an adverse market swing and his modest scalp turns into a healthy loss.

I lease my COMEX seat to a local, and since I guarantee his performance I receive duplicate account statements. I see as many losing trades and losing days as winning days, but on balance he is making money and this is why he is still around. He is a scalper (primarily) and trades hundreds of contracts a day, but he may trade 2 or 5 or 10 at a time, and he holds them for very short time periods. He is usually out or 'flat' by the end of the day. At times he will hold a small position overnight, but most days he is out by end of the day, win or lose. The local, as an exchange member, has the advantage of very, very low fees, just a few dollars per transaction. This is why the pit trader can trade so many contracts and trade them for just a few ticks and make money.

For the rest of us, commissions and slippage (the inevitable difference between buying the 'offer' and selling the 'bid') would eat us up if we tried to scalp. There are pit traders who are also 'position' traders, in effect hold a position for more than seconds, however most off-the-floor speculators do not try to scalp. While some speculators may be *day traders* (in and out during the same trading session), more hold a position for a few days, weeks, and in rarer cases for months. When trading futures, holding for months is the exception (although the 'big money' can be made with longer term positions; more about this later).

Speculators can be big commodity mutual fund managers, a lawyer in Toronto, a farmer in Montana (who is not hedging), a software engineer in London, or you! The risks in these markets can be high – so, by definition, are the rewards for the speculator.

The exchange 'open outcry' and the clearinghouse

It is not commonly understood that the exchange does not set the prices of the traded commodities. The prices are determined in an open and continuous auction on the exchange floor by the members who are either acting on behalf of customers (you and me), the companies they work for (if a hedger), or themselves (for their own account). The process of the auction which has been around for over one hundred years (and has already been replaced outside the USA) is called *open outcry*. This is not like the typical auction at Sotheby's where a single auctioneer announces the bids. At the exchange, people are not only competing to buy, but also to sell, and they all can be doing this simultaneously. Every floor trader is his own auctioneer. The democratic feature of open outcry is that only the best bid and offer are allowed to come forward at any point in time. If a trader is willing to pay the highest price offered, he yells it out, and by law all lower bids are silenced. By exchange rules, no one can bid under a higher bid, and no one can offer to sell higher than someone else's lower offer.

> ✳ If a trader is willing to pay the highest price offered, he yells it out, and by law all lower bids are silenced.

While each trader in the pit can see who the other floor trader is, the customers remain anonymous. At times, customers who are entering or exiting a large position act through various floor brokers, so as not to 'tip their hand'. Since this is an anonymous auction, prices quoted on futures exchanges are widely accepted and used as reference prices for the underlying commodity. This is known as *price discovery*, since anyone, anywhere can discover the price. For commodities which are not exchange traded (tungsten, coal and onions, for example) a few large players can set the price, and the bid to offer spread (the difference between where the buyers can buy and the sellers can sell) is generally much wider than the exchange-traded commodities. As a result, middlemen can take a greater percentage out of the middle, making many of these thinly traded cash markets much less efficient. This is one of the benefits of a futures exchange to a free society. By helping to manage risks and broadcast price, a well-run business can bring its goods and services to market more efficiently at the lowest possible price.

How is the price determined?

Conspiracy theorists would tell you it's the big banks or seven families, a clergyman would tell you God. A simpler explanation is supply and demand, or in other words buyers and sellers. If the buyers are more aggressive than the sellers, prices go up. If the sellers are more eager, prices go down. In a free market, prices are determined by what the seller can get from the buyer. Prices are made by what someone is willing to pay for a given product. You might think any given price is too low, or too high, but at any point in time the market sets the price.

How do the participants know they will get paid?

Investors trade futures to make money. Commercial interests use futures to lessen the risks in their businesses. Both groups want to make sure that if they make money on their transactions, they will get paid. This is the job of the exchange – to guarantee each trade. While a trade may be conducted between two parties on the floor, it is ultimately the exchange's responsibility to act as the seller to every buyer and the buyer to every seller. Each exchange is made up of many member firms, some of the largest and best capitalized names in banking, brokerage and private industry. They all individually and collectively guarantee against default by any one party. Each player in the marketplace, whether he be a farmer from Des Moines or an automobile manufacturer in Stuttgart, must deal through a clearing member. Each participant must post a good faith deposit (*margin*). If a doctor in Los Angeles buys 10 gold contracts, he is required to have on account or to quickly send in the margin money required for 10 gold contracts to his broker. His broker is either a clearing member or dealing through one. Whether he sends the money or not, the clearing member is still obligated to post this margin money at the exchange. The seller of the 10 gold contracts, whoever that is (it could be a mine which is hedging, or another speculator who believes prices will fall), is also required to post the margin and so is his clearing firm. The exchange must know that participants have sufficient funds to handle losses they could potentially experience in the markets.

> ✳ *While a trade may be conducted between two parties on the floor, it is ultimately the exchange's responsibility to act as the seller to every buyer and the buyer to every seller.*

The margin is determined and set by the exchange. It is generally stable, but can be changed by the exchange based on market volatility and risk. Margin is generally the amount of money the exchange determines sufficient to cover any one-day price move. It should be noted that the exchange determines the *minimum* margin necessary to hold each contract. However, any one brokerage firm or clearing firm can charge an individual customer a higher margin rate than the minimum if they feel they require additional protection against customer default. As an additional safeguard, the clearing members contribute to a pool of funds, a guarantee fund, that can be used in the event any one member defaults.

There has never been an exchange default, although individual customers of clearing firms, and even clearing firms at time, have gone into default. If an exchange defaulted, it would mean the members collectively defaulted and we would all be trouble since the whole global financial system would be in jeopardy. So, bottom line, I would not be concerned about being paid if you win.

What are they doing on the floor?

You have probably seen photos or films of the exchange trading floors. In the years to come these trading floors may become relics of the past, but for now they remain with us in the world's largest exchanges based in the USA. Traders, many wearing wildly coloured jackets, stand in the trading rings around a bar or pits which are arranged like amphitheatres with steps descending to the centre. They gesture wildly, screaming out buys and sells. Men and women who work for the exchange are silently punching keys on computer terminals or in some cases handheld computers. These people are reporters, listening for completed transactions so that they can broadcast the price to the information vendors who in turn transmit the price, almost simultaneously, to quote machines around the world. You'll also see people running back and forth, dodging telephone cords and each other. Around the 'floor' you'll see huge wallboards that flash a series of never-ending, always changing, numbers.

> ✳ *Traders, many wearing wildly coloured jackets, stand in the trading rings around a bar or pits which are arranged like amphitheatres with steps descending to the centre. They gesture wildly, screaming out buys and sells.*

The shouting, gesturing and jumping around by the pit traders give the floor a chaotic appearance to the uninformed. In reality, it is quite orderly. The running people are carrying customer orders from the clerks, who receive them by telephone from buyers and sellers around the world, to the floor brokers in the pits who will bid or offer the order in the pit to the other floor brokers who also have orders to buy or sell. The 'runners' also are taking *confirms*, or completed trades, back to the phone *clerks*, who then report back to their customers. In some pits, the orders are *flashed* into the pit directly by phone clerks by hand signals, or at times by just plain old-fashioned yelling. In the pits, the floor brokers, who are holding bids (or orders to buy) are crying out how much they are willing to pay, and what quantity they are willing to purchase to other brokers in the ring. Sellers are crying out their offers (orders to sell) with price and quantity. When a buyer and seller meet, they cry out 'Sold' or 'Done' or 'Take it'. These are the words the reporter is listening to hear, and when they are heard they report the price (not the quantity) which is then transmitted around the world electronically.

Each floor broker wears a badge with a number of letters to identify him to the other brokers. When a trade is completed (or *executed*) each selling broker must record each transaction on a card which shows the commodity, quantity, delivery month, price and badge number or name of the buyer on the other side of the transaction. The pit card must be time stamped immediately and submit-ted to an exchange employee after completed transactions. In some of the more active pits, thousands of contracts are bought and sold each and every minute. The card is then sent to the data entry room where operators key the data into the exchange's central computer system. Since both sides of the transaction are submitted in the same manner (the buyer submits a card, and the seller a card with the opposite side of the same transaction), there is a dual audit trail.

What's the difference between a floor broker and the broker you'll use to place your orders?

A floor broker is buying and selling futures on the floor either solely for himself or filling orders for his customers who are the brokerage houses. He cannot take customer orders from the public, but he can fill them. The exchange has strict rules for floor brokers who trade for their own account as well as filling cus-tomer orders. The basic rule is that they can never trade for themselves *ahead* of customer orders. A broker off the floor is licensed by the federal government to execute trades for the public. Your broker will call the floor to have your trades executed on your behalf. The same rule applies to the broker who places your orders for you. He or she cannot trade for their own account ahead of a customer order. The customer always comes first.

Most of the trading is done during the official hours the trading floor is open. However all the major exchanges, for most of their major contracts, also have in place after-hours electronic trading systems which are active after the trading floor is closed. These are computer terminals where transactions can take place electronically, and the contracts created are the same as during normal trading hours, so they can be sold or bought, in other words offset, the next day or whenever, on the exchange floor.

How do the floor brokers do it?

The more energetic the better: when you see the pictures of the traders in the pit, here's what you're looking at:

- Palms in: 'I'm a buyer.'
- Palms out: 'I'm a seller.'
- Hands away from body, arms outstretched, fingers moving: 'Here's my price' (prices 1 – 5 quoted with vertically extended fingers; 6 – 9 fingers horizontal, zero a closed fist).
- Hands held near head: 'This is how many I want.'

Of course, they're yelling too. Do mistakes ever happen? Well, these are human beings, right?

Sal tells the story of a novice floor broker in the deferred cattle futures (the months that are thinly traded), who wrote the book on how *not* to open a market. The day after a bearish Cattle on Feed Report, the broker had orders for 30 contracts to sell, and only 5 to buy. He bid 20 lower for the 5, and offered 30. A local trader sold the 5 immediately, and seeing the other markets were sharply lower screamed an offer to sell 50 contracts 100 lower. The novice panicked and offered his 30 contracts limit down. The local bought his five back (limit down) for a tidy profit. The novice had to answer as to why the opening range was 130 points, and he made both sides of it!

Quote recently heard from a feeder cattle broker on a very volatile, wide-ranging, whipsawing type day: 'I've 10 left, I'll pay half on ten, sell ten at a quarter (the lower price), anybody want 'em?'

Finally, Sal tells the story of the best order he ever got as a floor broker. He was working for the now defunct Mitchell-Hutchins. 'I was told to go into the bellies, don't bid for the front contract, but just start buying the rest. I was also told to report back to the desk every 15 minutes and report how I was doing. I was told to keep my ears open for any large offers to sell that came into the pit, and if I heard them I was supposed to buy 'em, and after they were gone, bid higher. My final instructions were, by the end of the day, "Have the bellies limit up!"'

Quote from a pork belly trader: 'If God told me bellies would be limit up tomorrow, I would still go home long only five contracts.'

'Open outcry' versus electronic

Virtually my entire career in this industry was involved with the traditional open outcry auction style trading methods, and this is evident from much of what I have written in this book as well as many of the stories from traders' lore. However, as Bob Dylan once said, 'The times they are a changin''. While just a few years ago all futures trading took place in open outcry pits, today the volume for purely electronic markets has probably outpaced the traditional. While the large US exchanges are still primarily open outcry, virtually the rest of the world's exchanges are purely electronic. There are no trading pits, rather computer terminals matching up trades. The advantages of the electronic markets are the low cost of execution and clearing and a perception of a more level playing field (since it is first come, first served with an electronic timestamp). Some industry experts predict all futures trading will eventually go electronic. They just may be right, but this is probably still a number of years away in the USA. While electronic execution of trades may make for better speed and efficiency, the new technology will not help with your trading decisions. This is where this book is designed to help you.

> * While the large US exchanges are still primarily open outcry, virtually the rest of the world's exchanges are purely electronic.

The regulators and regulations

The first level of regulation is the exchange. Recall, the exchange does not take positions in the market. Instead, it has the responsibility to ensure that the market is fair and orderly. It does this by setting and enforcing rules regarding margin deposits, trading procedures, delivery procedures and membership qualifications. Members who violate the rules can be fined and/or expelled. A sophisticated, intricate system of safeguards virtually guarantees against counterparty credit risk and default. An individual member may default, but the party on the other side of the transaction has always been paid. This statement cannot be made of over-the-counter, or non-exchange markets.

Each exchange is composed of non-clearing members and clearing members. All members need to meet business integrity and financial solvency standards, and all members can trade on the exchange, but the standards are higher for clearing members. Each clearing member (there are over sixty on the NYMEX alone) must show a minimum working capital of $2million plus must own two seats. They must also deposit 10 per cent of the firm's capital (up to $2million) into the guarantee fund, which is $160million for the NYMEX alone. Yet, even if one clearing member goes under and the guarantee fund cannot cover it (has never happened), every clearing member has agreed to cover a loss on a pro-rated basis. The clearing members represent some of the largest firms in the world, from Merrill Lynch to Citibank to Exxon. As a result, the financial strength of the exchange is based on the combined financial capability of all its clearing members.

The clearinghouse ensures that all trades are matched and recorded and all margin is collected and maintained. It also is in charge of ensuring deliveries take place in a orderly and fair manner. The compliance department of the exchange sets capital-based position limits on each clearing member. In addition, the exchange places position limits on customers. The limits are always lower in the spot or delivery month. For example, the maximum number of contracts any customer or entity can hold in crude oil is 10,000 in all months, with 5000 in any one month, and 1000 in the spot month. There is an exemption from position limits for 'bona fide' hedge transactions.

Looking over the exchange regulators, are the governmental regulators. In the USA, the Commodity Futures Trading Commission (CFTC) regulates the futures and options markets. Customers maintaining large positions are required to be reported to the exchange and the CFTC by the customer's futures commission merchant. The reporting level in crude oil, for example, is 300 contracts. Additionally, in the USA, the National Futures Association, a self-regulatory body, oversees its members which comprise the brokerage community. Finally, the world's major exchanges have an agreement, for example, in the UK with the Securities Investment Board (SIB), to share financial information on common members.

> ✳ *Looking over the exchange regulators, are the governmental regulators.*

How to place an order

OK. Let's do a bit of time travelling. You've finished the book, you've done your homework, you've opened an account with a commodity broker, and you're ready to place your first trade. What's the procedure? Very simply, you need to instruct your broker (either by telephone or by internet order entry) which commodity you want to trade, the quantity (in terms of numbers of contracts), the month and whether you want to go long or short. You then need to tell your broker how you want your order executed.

Market order

This is an order to buy or sell at the prevailing price. By definition, when a commodity is bought or sold 'at the market' the floor broker has an order to fill immediately at 'the next best price', but in reality it is the 'next price'. I've seen advice in trading manuals which effectively states 'you should never use a market order'. The reasoning has to do with the bid/offer spread. In an auction market, traders make bids and offers. The bid is the price put out for immediate acceptance. The offer (sometimes known as the 'asked price') is the price at which the seller is 'offering' for immediate sale. In most cases, unless the floor broker is able or willing to pass along the 'edge' to the customer, you will buy at the offer and sell at the bid. You potentially lose this difference. It may be small, but you can lose it by placing a market order.

I totally disagree with the advice 'never to use market orders'. For one thing floor brokers are out there who *are* able to buy the bid or sell the offer and pass this along to us, the customers. If I consistently don't like the price fills received by a certain floor broker in a certain market, I go out and find myself a new one. There are many around. In the markets I trade actively, I personally know the brokers on the floor who are filling our orders. I find this personal bond makes for better fills. However, this aside, there's a more important reason to use market orders in many cases, even if you have to give up the bid/offer spread. For one thing, if you use a limit order at a specific price, there is no guarantee you will be filled. The market may have to move away from the direction you think it is moving to get filled. Most important, with a market order you know you will be filled. This is important in a fast moving market, because these are the ones you most want to be in. By definition, you will be filled on every bad trade at a limit price (since it has to move against your bias first) but you could miss some good trades. If a market is moving like this – 50, 55, 60, 65, 60, 70, 80 to close at 120 – and you placed a market order at the 60 level first time you see 60, you might get 60 or 65 or even 70, but you know you are in a trade which is at least starting out right. If you limited your price to 55, you might never get on a good move. Who knows, the next day it could open at 150?

Limit order

When you place this type of order you know what you will get, worst case (you could get better), but there are strings attached. With a limit order, the floor broker is prevented from paying more than the limit on a buy order, or less than the limit on a sell order. Unless the market is willing to meet your terms, you will not get in. The drawback of a limit order is there is no guarantee you will get in. You could miss some markets. You are not even assured you will get in if your limit is hit. In the above example, if you placed a limit order to buy at '50 or better' and the market touches 50, this may be your trade, or it may be someone else's. You can only be reasonably assured you are in if the market trades *lower* than 50. There is nothing more frustrating than to place an order to buy at 50, see the market trade there once, call the floor to see if you are filled, only to receive an 'unable' just as the market's crossing 75. That's not to say there isn't a place for limit orders. I like to use them in quiet, back and forth type markets so as not to give up the slippage seen with a market order. I also use them to take profits on a good position. I try to let the market reach out to my limit price. After all, if the market doesn't reach my limit, I can always go back to a market order.

> **✱ With a limit order, the floor broker is prevented from paying more than the limit on a buy order, or less than the limit on a sell order.**

Stop orders

Stop orders or 'stops' are used in two ways. The most common is to cut a loss on a trade which is not working (also known as a 'stop loss order'). A stop is an order which becomes a market order to buy or sell at the prevailing price only if and *after* the market touches the stop price. A 'sell stop' is placed under the market; a 'buy stop' above the market.

For example, you buy July sugar at 11¢ (1100). You buy it because your analysis suggests the market is going to go higher. However, you do not want to risk more than approximately 50 points. So you give your broker a sell stop, to 'sell July sugar at 1050 stop'. As long as the market moves higher, fine and good, your stop will not be elected. However, if the market trades down to 1050, your stop loss automatically becomes a market order to sell. Depending on the speed and direction of the market and the skill and luck of the floor broker who has your order, you will be out at the next 'best' price. It most likely will be 1050, or slightly below say 1049. In a fast market, it could be lower, say 1048, or it even could be higher, say 1051, if the market upticks after the stop is hit.

A stop can also be used to 'lock in a profit' as well as 'cutting a loss'. In our sugar example, let's say the market starts to move in your favour, up to 1150. You might decide to cancel your 1050 stop and move it up to 1104, thus assuring a worst case break-even, or small loss after commissions. The market continues to move up, reaching 1210. You move your stop up to 1150, thus assuring a profit on the trade, even if it trades back down. This is termed a *trailing stop*, which occurs when you move your stop with the market.

A buy stop is placed above the market to liquidate a losing short position. You go short sugar at 1201, and place your buy stop *above* the market at 1253 to limit your loss. You can always cancel and move your buy stop lower, should, for example, the market move in your favour.

Stops can also be used to initiate positions. They are used by momentum traders who want to enter a market moving in a certain direction.

For example, a trader believes if gold can trade above the 'psychologically significant' $400 mark, it will move higher. She places a buy stop at 401. If the market remains under 401, she never enters the market, and potentially avoids a 'do nothing' or, worse, a losing trade. If the market reaches the 401 level, she will be in at the next prevailing price. The hope is the market keeps moving, to 402, 403 and on up. Once in, the trader can place a sell stop, at say 396 to limit losses should this turn out to be a 'false signal'. Of course, the risk is the market could run up to 401 and back down again. In this case, it would have been better to limit the price at a lower level, or not use the stop to initiate the trade at all.

Yet, if used correctly these can be good orders to enter with. A sell stop would be used under the market to initiate a new short position if not in the market.

There is, additionally, a variation of a stop order called a *stop limit*. With a stop limit order, if the stop price is touched a trade must be executed at the exact price (or better) or held until the stated price is reached again. The risk with the stop limit is the same as with a straight limit: that is if the market fails to return to the stop limit level the order is not executed, so I normally do not recommend their use. They can, in a fast moving market, defeat the purpose of the stop (to stop your loss).

> ✳ *The risk with the stop limit is the same as with a straight limit: that is if the market fails to return to the stop limit level the order is not executed, so I normally do not recommend their use.*

Market if touched orders

Also called MITs, they are the mirror image of stops. An MIT is placed above the market to initiate a short position.

For example, you are long platinum 405, and you want to take profits at 410. You could place a limit order to sell at 410, but you cannot be assured you will be filled if the price touches 410. It would have to trade above 410 to have a reasonable assurance you are out. An MIT at 410, becomes a market order if 410 is touched, which will assure you are out at the next prevailing price. MITs tend to be filled better on average than stops because you are moving with the prevailing trend. In a market which moves 40950, 410, 41050, 411, an MIT at 410 would be filled at either 410, or perhaps 41050. If the next 'tick' after 410 was 409, you certainly could be filled at 409 (since the MIT became a market order) but it is more likely a buy stop at 410 be filled at 41050 in this example. An MIT could also be used to initiate a new short position *above* the market. An MIT to buy is placed *under* the market to exit a short position, or enter a new long. If the market is trading at 100, you might place an MIT to buy at 99 but you would place a stop to sell at 99. See the difference?

These are the major types of orders you will use. There are other exotic orders which I have not found useful in practice, with the possible exception of the OCO. OCO stands for *one cancels the other*. It is used on both sides of the market either to take profits or to cut losses; one cancels the other.

For example, you buy silver at 700, you want to take profits at 750, and cut the loss if the market trades down to 675. You could place an order with your broker to sell at 750 or 675 stop, one cancels the other. In this way, you are assured if one side is hit the other side will be cancelled. This is significant in volatile markets. If you placed two separate orders, and the market first runs up to 750, takes out your position at a profit, then trades down to 675, you could be sold into a new short position you didn't want.

That concludes our discussion of the basics. If this is your first exposure to commodity trading you now know just enough to be dangerous. If you're a novice, hopefully this has shed a bit more light on the game. If you've traded awhile, nothing new yet, but hopefully there is a lot of new stuff for you in subsequent chapters.

Let's conclude this chapter with a true story which happened to a commodity broker friend of mine. Remember, it's a common and good practice to place your stop loss order at the same time you place your trade. A good broker will remind you of this. There is a belief that the floor traders will 'run the stops', and I'll talk more about this later in the book. However, I've found the proper and judicious use of stops is essential to successful trading. The best markets will never reach your stop. I cannot count the times a stop has saved me from a bad trade turning into disaster. In any case, my commodity broker friend Tim tells the story of Elmer, a farmer client of his from rural Minnesota.

> ✴ I've found the proper and judicious use of stops is essential to successful trading. The best markets will never reach your stop.

Tim suspected Elmer was growing a bit feeble, but then again Elmer had been trading for many years, and he had always been the eccentric type. Tim recounts the day that Elmer called him up prior to the market open.

Elmer to Tim: 'Tim, a miracle happened to me this morning.'

Tim to Elmer: 'What's that Elmer?'

Elmer to Tim: 'Tim, I was shaving this morning, and just as I looked in the mirror, the Holy Spirit came to me and said, "Elmer, today you should buy 50 March wheat market at the open".'

The way Tim tells it, he didn't hesitate, he didn't cross-examine, without stopping to pass Go, he immediately asked Elmer, 'Elmer, did he tell you where to place your stop?'

Advanced futures

A broker took on a customer he was told to be very careful with. The money was thought to be 'mustache money' (Mafia). They opened the account with $50,000 and initiated a long platinum position. The market went down, and they bought more. The market went down more. Margin call time. The broker was becoming a bit nervous with the position but when he called them the reply was, 'Sure we'll send you more money, no problem.' When the call went that easy, he felt much more relaxed. The market kept going lower, they kept adding to the position, the margin calls continued, and the Mob continued to send money. The broker was talking with the mustache man one day and confided that he was not sure platinum was going to rebound any time soon. The response was simple, 'Let's get this straight. You can have all the money you want, just remember we don't take losers!'

Zero sum game

There's an old saying, 'To make a small fortune in commodities, start with a big one.'

You may be getting the impression that the odds are stacked against you. I don't feel that way at all. It is true that most people lose trading commodities, but not because the odds are stacked against them. Every buyer of every losing trade could have been a seller and made money on that same trade, and every seller of every losing trade could have been a buyer and made money on that trade. There is the profitable minority that is doing this. Not on every trade, but on balance. So what's the key? Is it how you analyze the market? We will discuss various methods shortly, but the real determinants of success or failure are emotion and psychology. All winning traders understand this. Trading emotionally, or on 'gut feelings', will ring your

> ***** There's an old saying, 'To make a small fortune in commodities, start with a big one.'

death knell. You will need to understand mass psychology which is what makes markets move in trends. You will also need to understand when the real trends are turning, and the majority is wrong. Sound money management is crucial.

Money management

If emotions will kill you in the markets, then the opposite must be to be unemotional.

> Years ago, a friend of mine whom I respect as a very successful trader, cashed in on what I knew was a major score in wheat. I saw him in the Members' Dining Room and said something to the effect, 'You must be feeling damn good, having cashed in right at the top.' He was a calm sort of fellow, and I still remember what he said. 'George, when the markets treat me well, I don't dance in the streets, and when they don't, I don't beat myself up. Always remember this: slow and steady wins the race.'

Years later, I think I know what he means by this. You need to concentrate on trading correctly, and not the money. If you trade right, the money will come. If you trade wrong, you're doomed.

A loser hopes too much. He has an inability to get out of a losing trade early enough because he keeps hoping the market will turn back his way. Sometimes it does, but far too often his broker is the one forcing him out. Invariably, once he's forced out, the market does come back his way, but it's too late. Why do so many people sell at the bottom, or buy at the top? It's because they're acting emotionally instead of intellectually. There is one way to avoid this – *do not get attached to any position*. This should not be an ego thing. There is always another market tomorrow and another next week.

I've seen thousands of trades from hundreds of brokerage clients over the years. I've seen what those who make money do, and I've seen what the losers do. Invariably, the losers make the same mistake. They make money initially, and they may even have more winners than losers, but there always seem to be those few large losses which wipe out whatever good went before.

A few years ago the Chicago Mercantile Exchange had an ad campaign in which they tried to teach the public how to trade (an impossible undertaking). There was one full-page magazine ad which pronounced, 'Do not risk thy whole wad.' How profound. Yet, this is the mistake too many novice traders make. They bet too much on one trade, or one market. This is the first tenet of good money management. *You must know in advance how much you are risking on a trade, and unless it is a small percentage of your risk capital, don't take it*. I could start to get into theoretical probability theory here, but common sense is better. Some of the most important advice I can give you early in the book is to plan for slow and steady gains with minimal drawdowns. The way to do this is cut the losses quickly on the bad trades. How much should this be? Definitely not more than 10 per cent of your total trading capital, and ideally 2–5 per cent per trade. If you start to trade and risk 5 per cent on each trade, you will need to be wrong 20 times in a row to be totally wiped out. It would have to be a very poor trading system to do this (and I think we'll be able to give you some ideas that will help you develop a good trading system which also fits your person-ality). If you win on only half your trades, but your net profit is 10 per cent on each winning trade, and your net loss is 5 per cent on each losing trade, on your first 20 trades

> ✳ *Plan for slow and steady gains with minimal drawdowns. The way to do this is cut the losses quickly on the bad trades.*

you are up 50 per cent. Not bad, and you were only right half the time. On the other hand, if you are risking 25 per cent of your capital on each trade, four losing trades in a row and you're done for. If you trade long enough, there will come a time when you have four losing trades in a row, this is inevitable. To avoid major drawdowns, I have a couple of other tips:

- First of all diversify. Don't put all your eggs in one basket, and don't put all your chips on one roll of the dice. This lessens the opportunity for any one trade to be your last.

- Then stick with the trades that are working, and cull the ones that aren't. If you don't have the discipline to get out of the bad trades when you need to, make it your own personal rule to place a stop loss order physically in the market the moment you enter any trade.

- Tell your broker, if you haven't given him that stop, he is supposed to twist your arm to get it. Believe me, your stops will not be hit on the best trades.

- Finally, once you have a reasonable paper profit on a trade, move your stop, and never let it turn into a loss.

Contrary opinion theory

Sometimes it pays to be contrary, at least according to the contrarians. Since this chapter is about not doing what the losers, the majority, are doing, this is a good time to introduce the contrary opinion theory. The concept is simple: if all the bulls have already bought, there is nobody left to buy. The market will fall of its own weight. If a piece of bullish news fails to move the market up, this is the clue. When all the bulls run for the exits, there will be no cushion of new buyers to soften the decline and it will be particularly severe. The reverse is true if 'all the bears' have already sold.

The father of contrary opinion is recognized to be Humphrey Neill who published *The Art of Contrary Thinking* in 1954. His book is still available. Basically, he proposed compiling a 'bullish consensus' which gives a percentage estimate of how many newsletter writers, analysts and traders are bullish or bearish a particular commodity. You can try to do this yourself, or subscribe to a commercial service. For example, Consensus Inc. of Kansas City, MO publishes a weekly newspaper with their 'Consensus Index of Bullish Market Opinion'. The consensus is expressed as a percent of a market, with 0 per cent indicating there are no bulls in a market and 100 per cent no bears. The lower the reading, the more 'oversold' or bullish (closer to a bottom) the market is.

Contrary opinion is not a hard and fast trading system. The way to use it is to watch closely for signs of a turn in the marketplace when the index is high (over 80 per cent) or low (under 20 per cent). I am always on alert when a market is very bullish or very bearish. Everyone knows about it, the story is on the front page of the commodity section of the *Wall Street Journal*, the *Financial Times*, the evening news or the cover of a major news magazine. In the summer of 1993 when the floods hit the Midwest and thousands of acres of good crop land were under water, it seemed everyone was bullish soybeans (including myself), with consensus ratings over   90 per cent. *Newsweek* had a cover story on the floods. The cover had a picture of a farmer up to his neck in water. Looking back, we now know that issue came out on the very day the contract high for that year was reached in the grains.

> ✳ *I am always on alert when a market is very bullish or very bearish.*

Spreads, straddles and switches

These are actually three terms you will hear for the same animal. I'll use the most common, spread, but you can substitute the other two if you'd like. Spreads are a more sophisticated way of trading which fits well into the game plan of many traders. I know some traders who only trade spreads because they feel this is the best way to limit some of the risks inherent in futures and options. In fact, this is the main purpose of spreading: to reduce risk.

When you enter a spread, the objective is not necessarily to make money on a rise or fall in the market, rather a change in the relationship between different prices. When you put on a spread, you buy one contract while *simultaneously* selling another. You are long and short in two related commodities, or two different months of the same commodity, at the same time. The relative changes between the two are what will determine your profit or loss.

There are two major categories of spreads: intramarket and intermarket. As we discuss each, the concepts should start to sink in.

Intramarket spreads

These consist of buying one month in a particular commodity and simultaneously selling a different month in the same commodity. Examples would be buying July corn and selling December corn, buying March crude oil and selling May crude oil, buying May cotton and selling October cotton. Since you are trading two different months in the same commodity, one long and the other short, their prices will tend to move in the same direction.

So how can you possibly make money here? Well, they move in the same direction, but they don't have to, and even when the two months move in the same direction they tend to move at different *speeds*. Many times when you gain on one side of a spread, you will lose on the other. What you're looking for is a bigger gain on the winning side than loss on the losing side.

Let's look at an example. Assume you put on a spread between March COMEX copper and July COMEX copper in December of the previous year. You are buying the March and selling the July. When you buy the near month and sell the distant it is called a *bull spread*. A *bear spread* (short March and long July) is the mirror image. In a bull spread, you are predicting the near month will either rise faster than the distant, or fall slower. Either outcome will be profitable. Spreads can tend to be more reliable and more predictable than outright positions, which is why many traders like them. There are no 'sure things', but they can tend to put the odds in your favour. Look at this particular example. The March copper, most years, tends to gain on the July due to seasonal considerations. March is historically a high demand time of the year for copper due to inventory rebuilding prior to the peak building season. Suppose March is trading at 102 and July is trading at 101 when you 'put on' the spread in December. You have put on this bull spread, long the March short the July, with the March trading at a 100 points (1¢ per pound) *premium* to the July. (If the March was at 100 and the July at 102, you would say you were long the March and short the July 'with the March 200 points *discount* to the July'.) So a few months goes by, and in February copper has risen in price, and both months have gone up – but at different speeds. The March is trading at 115 and the July at 110. The spread has now *widened* from 100 points premium the March to 500 points premium the March, and you feel it is time to take your profits. You would give your broker an order to do the reverse transaction, that is sell the March and buy the July. This will offset both sides of the spread and wipe your slate clean.

Let's look at the result. The March has risen from 102 to 115, so you have a 13¢ or 1300 point profit on this side of the spread. The July, the short side, has risen from 101 to 110, so you have a 9¢ or 900 point loss on this side of the spread. The difference between what you gained and what you lost, 1300 minus 900, is your profit – in this case 400 points. Note, you don't need to calculate both sides to determine your profit; this works out neatly to be the spread differences: 500 minus 100 = 400. Since a point in NY copper is worth $2.50 per contract, this is a gross profit (we're not taking commissions into consideration here) of $1000 per spread.

But you may ask, why trade the spread when you could have made more by just buying the March outright? In this case, March rallied from 102 to 115, a 1300 point move; this is $3250 versus $1000. It all has to do with the risks. Spreads generally move slower. Yes, you can lose in a spread as well, but at times you can gain even if the market didn't move the way you planned. What if the economy weakened and March copper fell 1300 points. If you were long you would have lost $3250 per contract. The spread could certainly fall 400 points, but it is also possible traders would turn bearish the whole market, both months could go down the same amount, thus resulting in no loss. You are more interested in the difference between the months than the outright 'flat price' movements.

The ability to profit in both an up or down situation is one of the advantages of spread trading. Also, the margin requirements for spreads are generally much smaller than outright positions, since the exchange recognizes in most cases spreads will be less risky. If you are long May corn and short September corn, and the President declares a grain embargo, odds are both months will be down sharply. You are somewhat insulated from dramatic news and price shocks in spreads. Lastly, spreads can move slower, giving you more time to react, and many traders feel they are more predictable.

Intermarket spreads

These consist of buying one commodity, and simultaneously selling a related commodity. Examples would be buying silver and selling gold, buying hogs and selling pork bellies, buying Minneapolis wheat and selling Chicago wheat. In these examples, the two markets are related, they generally move in the same direction because the same market forces affect both, but they will move at different *speeds*.

For example, you might decide to buy July corn and sell July wheat. They are both grains, both can be used for animal feed and both are export commodities. They will tend to move in the same direction, but if the fundamentals are strongly opposed, they could move in opposite directions. It is March and you believe the supplies of corn are tight, but wheat supplies will grow bigger closer to the harvest in the early summer. July corn is at $3.10 and July wheat at $4.50, so you buy the corn and sell the wheat with corn at a 140 discount to the wheat. (You always read the order with the long or the buy side first.) Intermarket spreads cannot be classified as 'bull' or 'bear' like an intramarket.

Suppose a few months go by and both corn and wheat fall in price, corn to $2.80 and wheat, under harvest selling pressure, to $3.60. You decide it is time to *unwind* the spread. You buy the July wheat and sell the July corn. This offsets both sides of the spread and wipes your slate clean. The long side, the corn side, shows a loss of 30¢, the short side a profit of 90¢. Your gross profit is the difference of 60¢, and since in grains a penny move is worth $50, this is a profit of $3000. Note, you put the spread on at a 140 discount, took it off at an 80 discount; the difference between 140 and 80 is 60. In this case you wanted the spread to *narrow*, you wanted the lower priced corn to gain on the higher priced wheat, and it did. If the corn fell by 40¢ and the wheat by 20¢, you would have lost 20 on the spread. If there were some weather problems with the new crop wheat, and the spread widened to 190, since wheat went up 40 cents and corn fell 10, you would have lost 50.

Special spreads

There are certain spreads which are actively and commonly traded. In some of the markets there are spread brokers who only trade spreads and will make a market both ways in the common spreads. The exchanges will give the trader a break on the margin rate for trading these spreads. For example, while it may cost $700 to margin a wheat contract, because Kansas City and Minneapolis recognize inter-market spreads between their two respective wheat markets, a long Minneapolis wheat, short Kansas wheat spread might only require $500 total (or $250 a 'side', not $1400).

Grains

The new crop/old crop spreads are popular among traders who try to determine how the relationship will change between one crop which has already been harvested, and another which is either in the ground or yet to be planted. These would include (as common examples, there are many others):

- Long May or July corn/short December corn
- Long May or July soybeans/short November soybeans
- Long May or July soybean meal or oil/short December soybean meal or oil
- Long May or July oats/short December oats
- Long March or May wheat/short July or December wheat

Popular intermarket grain spreads include:

- Long or short wheat versus corn
- Long or short corn versus oats
- Long or short soybeans versus corn

The soybean crush is used by the soybean processors to lock in profit margins. This involves the purchase of soybeans (the raw material) and the sale of the products, soybean meal and soybean oil. The 'reverse crush' involves the purchase of the products and sale of beans.

Cotton

The old crop/new crop July cotton versus December is quite popular and can be volatile.

Meats

The hog versus cattle, cattle versus feeder cattle, and hogs versus pork belly spreads are the most popular. Some traders like to trade the 'cattle crush' which involves a purchase of corn and feeder cattle (the two 'raw ingredients') versus the sale of live cattle (the 'finished product').

Energy

By far the most popular energy spread is the purchase or sale of heating oil versus the unleaded gasoline as traders try to take advantage of the seasonal tendencies of these two products to move away or towards each other. The 'crack spread' is the simultaneous purchase and sale of the crude oil contract and the products, gasoline and heating oil.

Metals

The gold/silver ratio spread: this is calculated by dividing the price of gold by the price of silver. It represents the number of ounces of silver required to equal the price of one ounce of gold. In 1980, when gold was $850 and silver $50 the ratio was 17, however in 1996 with gold at $350 and silver at $5 it was 70. I'm not sure there is an average or a 'correct number' here, but recently the ratio has traded between 30 and 70, with the average for the past century at 32.5. The purchase of platinum versus the sale of gold is another popular metal spread, with a margin break for buying one selling the other.

Interest rates

The TED spread is an interesting one because it is a *limited risk* spread, so I'll elaborate a bit on this one.

The TED spread involves buying 90-day US Treasury Bill contracts and simultaneously selling 90-day Eurodollar contracts. Treasury Bills ('T-Bills') are short-term obligations of the US government. The rates of interest paid on these will fluctuate. However, T-Bills are generally believed to be one of the safest investments in the world, since you are assured of getting your principal back plus interest upon maturity.

Eurodollars are similar to T-Bills in that they are also short-term paper, and they are denominated in US dollars. However, there is one major difference. They are not government obligations; rather those of major banks outside the USA and therefore outside US banking regulations. Because they are not backed by the full faith of the US government, they have more risk than T-Bills. Greater risk = greater return. Therefore, Euros always will have a higher *yield* than T-Bills. For example, if T-Bills were yielding say 5 per cent, Euros might be yielding $5\frac{1}{2}$ per cent. If the yields were the same, investors would buy T-Bills. (Why get the same return for greater risk?)

This is why TED is a *limited* risk spread. Euro yields will never go below T-Bills, but there is no limit to how far they can go above. In its history the 'narrowest' it has ever been is about 40–50 points or 0.4 per cent–0.5 per cent over T-Bills. Historically, when it's anywhere below 60, it's time to do the TED since the risk appears small. There are two main factors which will move the TED: interest rates and stability in the financial system. When investors become concerned about the financial markets in general, there is the traditional 'flight to quality' as they sell Euros (and other investments such as stocks) and buy T-Bills. For example, when the Continental Illinois bank had problems in the 1980s, the spread widened out to over 300 basis points. When the stock market crashed in 1987, the TED rallied out to 175. TED also tends to increase if inflation heats up.

Other popular interest rate spreads are the MOB (Municipal Bonds versus Treasury Bonds), and the NOB (Treasury Notes versus Treasury Bonds).

Other limited risk spreads would include *carrying charge* spreads. Carrying charges are the cost to hold a commodity from one month to the next, and would include storage costs and interest. For example, if it costs 3¢ a month to hold wheat, and the July/September wheat spread was trading at 8¢ premium, the September, the risk on this one is low. Unless interest rates would rise dramatically, the likelihood September would rise much more above the July is low. However, should a bull market develop in wheat due to tight nearby supplies, there is no limit to how far July could rise above September. These are spreads to watch for. Limited risk carrying charge spreads can *only* be found in storable commodities. There is no limit to how spreads can change for perishable commodities such as live cattle.

It is important to know, *if you ask,* that many commodity brokers offer a commission discount if you trade a spread as a spread (meaning you enter both sides simultaneously and exit both sides simultaneously). Yes, you can 'leg off' a spread, meaning you can liquidate one side and leave the other intact, but it generally is not a good idea. You put on the spread because it is a lower risk transaction.

> ✳ You can 'leg off' a spread, meaning you can liquidate one side and leave the other intact, but it generally is not a good idea.

Novice traders, when a spread isn't working to form, have been known to take off a profitable leg of a spread, leaving the unprofitable on, hoping it will come back and profits can be realized on both sides. For some reason, this usually doesn't work. (It would be better in most cases to take off the unprofitable side, since this is the side that isn't working.) But no matter which side you take off, you are immediately incurring the risk of an outright transaction. It is rather like splitting sixes in blackjack because you don't like a 12 against a dealer's ace showing. You're asking for trouble, most cases. By the way, if you leg off a spread, you immediately lose your margin advantage; your account will be charged full margin for the outright position.

Normal or inverted?

When analyzing a market, the spreads can give you a clue as to how bullish or bearish a market is. Typically, markets are termed 'normal' or 'carrying charge'. In London they would say the market is in *contango* (no, Alice, contango is not a dance). This occurs when the distant months sell at a higher price, or premium, to the near months. An example of a 'normal' copper market is as follows:

March copper	99.05
May copper	101.15
July copper	102.95
September copper	105.25
December copper	107.10

Since it costs money to store copper from one month to the next (storage costs, insurance, and the cost of money or interest), this is reflected in the configuration of futures prices.

However, at times, markets take on an opposite configuration where the near month is trading at a premium to the distants, as illustrated:

March copper	103.50
May copper	101.25
July copper	100.05
September copper	98.15
December copper	95.95

This is called an *inverted* market. In London they would call this a *backward* market, or say the market is in *backwardation*. What can cause a market to invert? Generally, a perceived or real near-term shortage. This can be caused by weather (cold weather will tend to push the nearby natural gas over the back, or even nearby cattle over the distant since cattle do not gain weight well in cold weather and could conceivably be 'pushed back' or not ready for market in a timely manner). It could be caused by a mining strike, or a government programme, or excellent near-term export demand; actually, any number of things. The important point here, is that the spreads can give you a significant clue as to the strength or weakness in a market.

> ✳ *The important point here, is that the spreads can give you a significant clue as to the strength or weakness in a market.*

Here's the general rule of thumb: *when the bull spreads are working (the near months are gaining on the back months), this a bullish sign and the market should be played from the long side. When the bear spreads are working (the near months are losing on the back months), this is a bearish sign and the market should be played from the short side.*

As with every other rule, there are exceptions. November beans could be gaining on July beans in June because the new crop, which will harvested in the fall, is burning up due to drought and there are adequate near-term supplies, but as a rule this works. I am always sceptical if I am short a market and the bull spreads are working. Something is definitely wrong.

Another trading tip: *Watch for spread to cross 'even money'.*

For example, **March sugar is trading at 1090, and October at 1110, a normal market. Over time, you notice the spread is starting to narrow, and then one day crosses zero – March has moved up to 1130, and October is trading at 1128. I've noticed when spreads 'cross zero', this is many times a significant indicator of a change in the supply/demand balance of the commodity being studied. Go with the flow. If the market crosses zero to the upside, play the bull spreads, or play the market from the long side. If the market crosses zero to the downside, play the bear spreads, or play the market from the short side.**

I'll end this discussion of spreads with a caveat. Since the margins are much lower on spreads, there is a natural tendency to overtrade, that is to put on too many. Just because spreads are limited risk does not mean there isn't risk, and on rare occasions can have greater risk.

A number of years ago, a friend of mine had on the long July/short December cotton spread. Some change in government policy was announced one afternoon, after the market's close (I forget the specifics), but I do remember the next day the market opened limit down in the July and limit up in the December. He was wacked to the max on both sides.

The 'Voice from the Tomb'

There are at least two old-time grain traders I know who swear by this, and you might just want to check it out.

The story goes like this: there was a millionaire grain trader who died and left nothing to his three children. After their mother died, he raised them by himself and dedicated his life to his children. But the children were lazy and thought they would inherit all the money. He thought his children wasteful, and believed they took him for granted. When he died all the money went to charity. All he left them in his will were the following dates of when to buy and when to sell. The will said that if they strictly followed his advice they would have the fortune they always thought was going to drop in their laps:

Wheat
Sell March wheat on 10 January
Buy May and July wheat on 22 February
Sell July wheat on 10 May
Buy December wheat on 1 July
Sell December wheat on 10 September
Buy March wheat on 28 November

Corn
Buy July corn on 1 March
Sell July corn on 20 May
Buy December corn on 25 June
Sell December and March corn on 10 August

This is the advice of 'The Voice from the Tomb'.

Here's a true story from the the Chicago Mercantile Exchange. One day before a major government Cattle Report, a large trader in the cattle pit bought 100 contracts at steady money on the day to initiate a new long position. Several smaller traders in the pit also bought, figuring this guy knew something and they would 'coattail' him. Then the first wave of selling hit the pit. The market moved 50 points lower on the day. Instead of panicking, the large local bought more. So did the 'coattailers'. Then the second wave of selling hit the pit. At 100 points lower, the big guy bought more. So did the 'coattailers' (but at this point their coattails were feeling a bit tight). Then the third wave of selling hit the pit. The market went just about limit down (it can only move 150 points, or 1.5¢ per pound under the previous day's close and then if there are more sellers than buyers it can 'lock limit down' and traders can conceivably be locked into a position until the next day). But the big guy bought even more. This time, however, the 'coattailers' ran for exits, they just couldn't take it anymore. Just as they sold out they heard the big guy say, 'Now we've got 'em right where we want 'em.' Only one 'coattailer' had the guts to hang on. As it turned out, that third wave was the last wave of selling, and the market ended up closing higher on the day!

Perhaps this is where the following expression comes from: 'I bought the first break, I bought the second break, I *was* the third break.'

A diabolical story

The same floor broker who told me the story of the corn speculator and the fire chief told me this one. He says he *knows* this is true.

My floor broker friend trades at the Chicago Merc. A number of years ago, he hired one of the main characters of this story as his clerk, which is how he got to hear it. The clerk left my friend to work in the S&P pit, and this lasted for about a year. Then this fellow had an opportunity to join a college buddy of his in San Diego to become a commodity broker. He quickly packed, left Chicago and moved to the West Coast.

The San Diego office he joined produced some business but nothing spectacular. Customers would come, many would lose and leave, and new ones would come to take their place. One afternoon, staring from their office window (which looked out over the Pacific) our two buddies spawned an idea. They discussed how the customers would lose money. In fact 80 per cent of the trades would ultimately be liquidated as losers. With this thought in mind, our two heroes placed an ad in the paper to hire rookie commodity 'trainees'.

After interviewing a number of applicants, they hired ten 'average Joes'. They told the newly hired gentlemen they would perform the normal duties of a commodity broker, servicing customer accounts and the like, but in addition they were each going to be given a rare opportunity. The ten would each be given a $50,000 account with the firm, 'no strings attached', to 'manage' a portfolio of commodity trades. *If* they could show profitable performance they would share in the profits and receive a bonus.

They could each trade the $50,000 accounts however they saw fit, but there was just one procedure they had to follow. Unlike other trades for customers of the firm, if they were going to place a trade in their 'managed' accounts, the order had to go through one of the two principals, either the owner or the guy from Chicago. You have to ask yourself why these two would trust ten novices, ten raw rookies, with $500,000 of their money. Well, you see this was all a diabolical scheme the two hatched that one afternoon.

What would happen is one rookie broker would call to buy 10 cattle, another would want to sell 100 soybeans, another buy 2 copper or short 5 silver. The two guys behind the scheme would call the various trading floors and *sell* 10 cattle, *buy* 100 soybeans, *sell* 2 copper, and *buy* 5 silver. In other words they would do exactly the *opposite* of what their 'traders' wanted them to do. You see, the money in the 'traders'' account was fictitious. The firm's money was in reality *the other way*, with opposite positions. The next day, fictitious position sheets would be distributed to the 'traders' showing them what the rookies believed to be true.

Eighty per cent of the novices who trade lose money. Inevitably, the fellow who 'bought' the cattle couldn't stand the market moving against him, so he would call one of the two to liquidate his 'losing' position. This was their signal to call the floor, buy back their shorts and actually make money! The next day, the cattle 'trader' would show a losing trade on his sheet, his $50,000 would be something less, but in reality the two were cashing in. This pattern continued with the guy in the beans, the guy in the copper, etc.

In the very first week, one 'trader' lost his whole $50,000. He was immediately summoned to the bosses' office. Thinking he was about to be fired, before anything was said, he started to cry. He said he had been married for a year, just had twins, and really needed this job. He would do better, he would learn from his mistakes, please give him another chance. Imagine his surprise when he was given another chance. The boys couldn't wait to 'recapitalize' his account with another $50,000. They also couldn't wait for him to leave the office so they could laugh their asses off. By this fellow 'losing' $50,000, they actually made $50,000 in the real markets. This was better than printing money.

The scheme proceeded much the same way for a while. One 'trader' would blow out, then another. The two bosses were finding it increasingly difficult, however, to supply the traders with the fictitious statements along with every transaction. They just couldn't keep up with the paperwork and started falling behind. Nevertheless, they continued on with the plan until the silver trade.

This was all happening during the early 1980s, the same time the Hunt brothers tried to corner the silver market. Silver ran up to about $50 an ounce, and one of the 'traders' calls to sell short 5 silver. Of course, the firm actually buys 5 silver. The silver market moves erratically sideways for a few days, then starts to fall.

In the meantime, the 'trader' who sold the silver goes back to Kansas to visit his mom. While he's visiting, a tornado hits the town. A tree falls on the house, the roof collapses, and he ends up in a hospital bed unconscious. He remains in a coma for two weeks.

Meanwhile, our masterminds back in San Diego are wondering where the hell he is, and when he's going to take his 'profit' so they could take their loss. In New York, they raise the margins, declare silver is for liquidation only, and the market start its famous collapse. The masterminds go belly up. The guy in the coma awakens, demands a newspaper, and screams in ecstasy when he sees how far silver has broken. He immediately calls San Diego, anticipating praise and dreaming of his big bonus. Instead he hears two words: *'You're fired!'*

An options primer

Options have been touted as 'the best of both worlds'. '*Unlimited* profit potential, with *totally limited* risk', the radio ads shout. Sounds wonderful, does it not? Why would anyone trade anything else?

The reality is, as in every other financial instrument, there are major advantages to trading options, but there is certainly no free lunch. There are probably more ways to lose money when trading options than with any other financial instrument. You give something up for the limited risk feature, but it may just be worth it to you to give this something up. Then again it may not. I know traders who trade *only* options and wouldn't think of touching futures. Many do quite well. I know others who tell me options have never worked for them; they despise the added costs. Like anything else in the speculative world, options require good judgement, a sound game plan, and a bit of luck wouldn't hurt either.

This chapter is designed as an 'Options 101' course for beginners and those who want to brush up. We will discuss the basics: what an option is, how they work, the various ways to play and the jargon. In the following chapter we will attempt to delve into some of the more advanced strategies for the more serious student.

Options

Definition: An option gives the buyer the right, but *no* obligation, to buy or sell a stated quantity of a commodity at a specified price on or before a specific date in the future.

Options are often compared to insurance. When you buy insurance, let's say house insurance, you pay a premium for certain rights. These rights are yours, but there are limits to the payoff according to the policy. This analogy works to some extent for a hedger (to be discussed later), but there are major differences when speculating. For one, the option buyer theoretically has no limit to his profit potential. Insurance policies have a stated limit. Insurance is not transferable between parties, and is usually specific to a person or property. Options are standardized and can be sold in the marketplace, in most cases. Actually, while we plan to spend some time here discussing options, how they operate and the jargon of the trade, they are actually quite simple. There are just two types, and the features are fairly straightforward. They offer the speculator and the hedger alike ammo which should be considered for any arsenal.

The cost of an option is also called the *premium*. The premium is a one-time cost and the maximum exposure the buyer has. No matter how far prices of the underlying asset rise or fall, the option buyer knows what his maximum exposure and therefore maximum risk will be. Yet, the profit potential is not fixed.

✱ Like anything else in the speculative world, options require good judgement, a sound game plan, and a bit of luck wouldn't hurt either.

Just as in futures, the profits are only limited by how far the market moves in the stated time period. Options are now available for just about every futures market, from orange juice (an old adage says 'never sell call options during freeze season'), to pork bellies, to gold, copper, heating oil, Eurodollars – you name it. The more liquid and active futures markets, you guessed it, generally have the most liquid option markets. There are exceptions to every rule, however. In a strange quirk of fate the white wheat options traded on the Minneapolis Grain Exchange have a larger volume than the underlying futures contract. Don't ask me why.

Just like futures, options trade in designated contract months. Check the expiration dates, since in many cases the options expire in the month *preceding* the futures to which they correspond. March grain options expire the third Friday of February, for example. For cash settled futures contracts, such as the S&P 500 and feeder cattle, the options and futures expire the same day. You may have heard the term 'triple witching hour' which refers to the simultaneous expiration of futures, stocks options and futures options the third Friday of March, June, September and December. All this activity is supposed to cause wild and crazy fluctuations, but in many cases this has been a non-event in my experience. In many of the active markets, there are options traded every month of the year. For currencies, as an example, the January, February and March options are based on the March contract. There are also weekly and bi-weekly options during each month for currencies. Consult the exchange tables or your broker for the specifics on option months and expiration dates by market. Most of the rules for options are set by the exchange.

An option for what?

Options can be converted into the underlying futures contract at the discretion of the buyer; this is the right to exercise. This is why the size of every option is the same as the contract it represents. By *exercising* an option, the buyer receives either a long or short position at the option's strike price. An owner of a *call* option who exercises his option receives a *long* futures position. An exercise of a *put* receives a *short* futures.

The primary advantage

For options the primary advantage is definitely the limited risk feature. Unlike futures, the most you can ever lose as an option *buyer* (we'll discuss option selling shortly) is what you pay for it. You could lose less by selling out prior to expiration, and, yes, you can even make significant bucks trading options, but you have a defined and maximum risk and you know to the penny the worst case scenario at the outset. No possibility of margin calls, and for many no sleepless nights since you know the worst case scenario. This statement cannot be made for futures.

> ✳ The most you can ever lose as an option buyer is what you pay for it.

The primary disadvantage

The primary disadvantage of options is the premium. It must be paid upfront, and the cost must be recovered in part or in whole via a favourable movement in price or you lose. You can even be right when buying options, but if the market doesn't move far enough you still lose.

Look at it this way: if you buy a wheat option good for the current market price for say $1000, and the market goes nowhere, it stays at the same price for the life of the option, you are out $1000. The market moved nowhere, and the seller of the option keeps your $1000. He only needs a stationary market, a move in his direction, or a move which will not cover the premium in full, to profit. If you bought a futures contract, and held it for the same time period, you are out nothing other than commission costs. In this case the 'limited risk' option was definitely more costly than the 'higher risk' futures contract.

Of course, in this simplistic example we do not know what transpired in the interim period. The market could have sold off wildly, resulted in a margin call or a stop loss being hit in the futures, and then recovered. The futures trader could have been knocked out, perhaps more than once, while the option trader (not subject to margin calls) could just sit it out. You see, there are no easy answers here, and we've only scratched the surface.

Types of options

The two types of options are puts and calls.

Call options are bought by bullish traders. A call option gives the buyer the right, but no obligation, to *purchase* the underlying asset at an agreed upon price (known as the *strike price*) within a specified time.

Put options are the mirror image of the calls. A put option gives the buyer the right, but no obligation, to *sell* the underlying asset at an agreed upon price (the strike price) within a specified time. They are bought by bearish traders who anticipate a weaker market.

What is the underlying asset? It is, for exchange-traded options, the corresponding futures contract. Call buyers have the right to exercise into a long futures position and put buyers into a short at the *corresponding strike price*.

A word about strike prices. Remember I said most of the rules are set by the exchange where the options are traded. This applies to the strike prices at which options trade. They are listed at set intervals. For example, wheat options trade every 10¢/bushel: $3.50, 360, 370, etc. Beans, a bigger contract, trade at 25¢ intervals: $6.75, 700, 725, etc.

I should note, in this and the following chapter I will always refer to exchange-traded options. This is because these are the options available to the general public. For your information, certain brokers and institutions also offer *OTC*, or *over-the-counter* options which are dealt directly off the exchange. OTC options are completely flexible with the exact details, such as date and quantity, freely negotiable between the buyer and seller. These are very common in the currency markets, but generally only available to big players in lots of $1million minimum.

Exchange-traded options (the ones you most likely will be involved in) are standardized. The exchange sets the strike prices, size, specifications, expiration date and style (American or European). Most importantly, the exchange eliminates the counterparty risk. If an exchange member goes belly-up the clearing house (consisting of all clearing members) guarantees performance. If the bank on the other end of your OTC option has one rogue trader too many, there is no guarantee you will be able to collect, even if you are profitable. While the risk of a large money centre bank or multinational brokerage firm not performing is slim, it is nevertheless a risk. I have personally witnessed a number of rock solid, old-line firms go out of business over the past decade or so, and believe me it can happen. One last advantage of exchange-traded options – quotations. It may seem like a minor point, since you are able to get a quote from the counterparty for your OTC option. However, with the OTCs it comes directly from the other party (and whose interest do you think is foremost in this case?). Quotes on exchange-traded options are publicly disseminated by a third party, the exchange, based on actual trades in an auction-like environment.

✳ *I have personally witnessed a number of rock solid, old-line firms go out of business over the past decade or so, and believe me it can happen.*

Styles

There are two *styles* of options: *American* and *European*. The basic difference is in the rules of exercise. An American-style option can be exercised by the buyer at any time before it expires. The European can be exercised only on the expiry date. All other factors being equal, the European will generally be slightly cheaper than the American since they can only be exercised on the one date and therefore involve less uncertainty for the seller. The vast majority of exchange-traded options are American style, and the vast majority of OTC are European.

How are option prices quoted?

In terms of futures, ticks.

For example, a 101 Euro call might be quoted at 99 bid/102 offered. The settlement price is 101. These are ticks, and since a tick for the Euro contract (on the IMM) represents $12.50, at 101 the option is worth $1262.50. A 390 wheat call at 22¢ goes for $1100 (it is a 5000 bushel contract so each penny is worth $50).

One major exception, major because it is probably the most liquid of all futures options, is the US Treasury Bond options. The futures have a minimum tick equal to $31.25. The options have a minimum tick equal to half the futures tick, or $15.62.

Buy 'em and sell 'em

Option buyers, whether it be puts or calls, pay a premium. Who gets it? The option seller receives the premium. Option sellers (also called option writers) are in many cases professional traders on the floor of the exchange. This is because the public generally prefers buying options. However, anyone can be an option seller. You could be an option seller. Why would you want to be an option seller? Well, it does put the odds in your favour. You receive the premium, it is credited to your account, and becomes a cushion against an adverse market move.

Call options are sold by bearish traders. Call options are also sold by traders who expect a market to go nowhere over the specified time period. Call options are also sold, at times, by bullish traders who wish to receive protection, cover a long position, or to gain additional income for a long position. More about this later.

Put options are sold by bullish traders. If the market moves up and remains above the strike price within the specified period, the put seller will keep the premium with no penalty. Put options may also be sold by traders who feel the market is not going anywhere. They are sometimes sold by bearish traders who are looking for protection to cover a short position, or to gain incremental income for a short position.

The primary advantage of selling options is that the seller receives the premium income paid by the buyer immediately. All he needs to make money is for either a quiet or stable market or a move away from the buyer. Or the market must move in favour of the buyer less than the premium received. In other words, there is a wider range of price movement in which the option seller will profit. The odds are in the seller's favour, and this is why professionals like to sell them.

The drawback of selling options is the unlimited risk. This is the mirror image of buying options. Since the market can theoretically move an unlimited amount away from the strike price, the risk cannot be predetermined. It is sort of like Las Vegas. Think of the option seller as the house. We all know the house has the advantage, but this doesn't mean any individual on any particular evening couldn't make a major hit on the house.

How options work

Let's look at a typical example. You are bullish gold and want to play this market using options. It is January, and the price of gold is $400 per ounce. You're a bull, remember, so there are two basic strategies you can employ. You can buy a call option, or sell a put option. But there are other decisions to be made. It's like the kid who goes in to buy his first pack of cigarettes. The clerk asks which brand? He says Marlboro. Standard or Menthol? Standard. 100s or shorts? Shorts. Box or soft pack? Box. Lights or Regulars? With his head turning, the kid runs out of the store rationalizing they aren't good for you anyway and this just isn't worth it.

Well, options come in a variety of flavours as well. The simplest way to participate in the options market is to buy a call (if you think the price will rise) or buy a put (for the bears). Let's suppose it's December and the price of gold is $399 an ounce. You can buy an April 400 call for say $6/ounce or $600 for one option. This option gives you the right but not the obligation to receive an April futures contract at a price of $400 at any time, your discretion, prior to the expiration date (which in this case is mid-March). You can pay less for an April 420 call, or more for an April 380 call. You can pay more for a June 400 call, or less for a February 400 call. You can pay much less for an April 500 call, or a lot more for a February 340 call. The permutations are endless.

Of course, you can sell any of these as well. I'm often asked by clients who have a market opinion 'which is the best option for me to buy?' How do you determine this? Well, it depends not only on your outlook, but your outlook for your outlook. There are still a number of issues and factors we need to discuss, the first of which is time.

Time

You have to decide how much time you want to pay for. A basic rule of thumb is, and this should be no surprise, the more time you want the option to have before it expires, the higher the premium. You can go far out, receive a lot more time for your position to work, but this is not generally a good idea. Recall, there is no free lunch. Long dated options cost more, at times quite a bit more. You are tying up more money for a longer period of time. This money can be used for alternative transactions. Plus, the farther out you go, the less liquid the options become. You are generally dealing with a market professional who will quote a wide bid to offer spread. If you want to liquidate the option in the options market (as opposed to exercising the option) you will have to deal with this spread once again. These are additional hidden costs. The cheapest options are the closest options. The problem with a short dated option is, and I think this is obvious too, you have a much shorter time for the market to move your way. Unlike futures, it not only has to move your way, but do it quick. This works at times, but the market doesn't always know *your* option's expiration date. I should point out, there are no simple formulas which will tell you how much is a fair price to pay for time at any particular point. A 6-month option may or may not be twice as much as a 3-month option. You are dealing with the spreads of the underlying commodity which of course can change, and many times the near month will move faster than the back month and this will be reflected in the option's cost.

> ✳ A basic rule of thumb is, the more time you want the option to have before it expires, the higher the premium.

Time decay

All else being equal, the time value of an option decreases very slightly each day (providing there is still a reasonable amount of time left until expiration). The rate of this decrease becomes more rapid as the option gets closer to expiration. This is termed the normal time decay which works to the detriment of the buyer and the benefit of the seller. As an option gets close to expiration, time value becomes less and less. The main thing that matters at this juncture is the relationship between the strike and the underlying commodity. This is because at expiration the option can only be worth something, or nothing – that's it. Also remember, you might buy a call because you thought a particular commodity would increase in price, but you could show a loss even if you are right and it does. The reason for this is that the extent of the rise was insufficient to compensate for the time it took to occur.

In, at and out of the money

If you look at an options price table you will first of all see the two major categories (puts and calls). Then you will see listings for different months out into the future. Under each month you will see a variety of different strike prices,

prices at which the options can be *exercised*. Oh, I forgot to mention this feature: a very important feature, actually, of options, and one that makes options on futures more complicated than futures.

Let's look at our gold example. You are bullish gold and decided to purchase the April 400 dollar call when April gold was trading at $399. April gold futures subsequently rise to $425/ounce. At this point the option has *intrinsic value*. That is because the price of the underlying asset (in this case April gold futures) is above the strike price. At $425/ounce, the 400 call has $25 of intrinsic value. This is now an *in the money* call option. It is in the money by $25. Since a gold option is for 100 ounces, and every $1 is worth $100 per option, the value of this option will be at least $2500 ($25 x $100/ounce). Another way to look at this is the right to buy at 400, when the current price is 425, must be worth *at least* 25 since it is already profitable by this amount. It could be worth more, of course, if there was still *time value*. Time value is that portion of the premium price other than intrinsic value. It is dependent on time, but there are other factors as well which determine an option's value.

By definition, a call option is in the money when the market price of the futures is *above* the strike price of the option. A cocoa 1400 call is in the money when the futures are trading at 1458. A call option is out of the money when the futures price is below the strike. The same call is out of the money when the futures are at 1361. Since puts are always the mirror image of the calls, a put option is in the money when the market price of the futures is below the strike price of the option. A 1400 cocoa put is in the money at 1361 futures, but out of the money at 1458. Out of the money options have time value only.

How are option prices determined?

Like futures, options are traded in an auction-like environment in a pit on the floor of the exchange. They are traded by open outcry just like the futures. In most cases, the option pit is adjacent, sometimes right in the middle of the futures pit for the same commodity. The futures traders are looking at whatever technical or fundamental factors they use to determine the value of the particular commodity they are trading. The option traders are looking at the futures. It goes without saying that an option's premium price is determined by the underlying asset. If we dissect this a bit deeper, we see that any particular option's premium has two basic parts. In fact, we just mentioned them: time value and intrinsic value.

Options that are *out of the money* have only time value. These options have no value other than potential value.

For example, the April $400 gold call was trading for $6 per ounce in December and would have cost the buyer $600. The price of April gold at that time was $399, so the option could not have been exercised at a profit. Nobody in his right mind would exercise an option to receive April futures at $400 when they could go into the marketplace and buy it $1/ounce cheaper. So why would anyone in his right mind pay $600 for this right? You guessed it: this option has potential. To buy futures, the risk is potentially greater than $600. Yes, you could buy April futures at $399 and place a $6 stop. This would essentially provide the same risk without having to fork over the $600, but there are some major differences. For one thing, when you buy an option for $600 you know that your maximum risk is guaranteed. If you purchase futures, with a $600 stop loss the stop could be filled at, at times better, more times a bit worse than your stop loss point. It is entirely possible April gold could close one afternoon at $394.10, not elect your $394 stop, and open the next day at $390. The overseas market fell due to sales by the Belgium Central Bank, London gold fell $4.10/ounce and New York (where you bought your contract) opened in line with London due to arbitrage selling. So now your projected risk of $600 per contract has turned into a $900 loss which is 50 per cent more than projected. This can happen. It cannot happen with options, which gets back to the main advantage.

There is another possibility and that is the market could trade in a range. It could fall $6 or more, stop you out of your futures and then eventually trade back up to profitable levels. This underscores another main advantage of options purchases, and that's *staying power*. The other side of the coin has to do with the cost. If you are right in your analysis and willing to take the risk of the futures, you are guaranteed to make more than in the options. If the price of gold rises to $425, and you bought your contract at $399, you have the ability to cash in with a $2600 profit per contract ($26 times $100/ounce) minus fees. You have the right to sell your option, and/or exercise it as well, but your profit has to be less than the $2600. Remember, you paid $600 for time. $600 for the potential to make a score. Some time has passed and some time value will have disappeared. You will not get back the $600, only a portion of it.

Let's review a few concepts and hopefully confuse you a bit less. Calls that have a strike price above the market (for example, a $400 gold call with the market at $399) and puts that have a strike price below the market (a $390 put with the market at $399) will have premium made up of time value only. In the money options ($400 call with the market price at $425, or $440 put with the market at $425) have both – that is time and intrinsic value. The more an option is in the money, the more valuable it becomes, so by definition it becomes more expensive. Another way of looking at this is a simple formula:

Time value = premium minus intrinsic value

Also, time value increases for options with greater time to expiration. I hope this is an obvious one to you (if not we have real problems with communication). It makes perfect sense, since the more time an option has to expiration, the more potential the buyer of the option has for something to happen which could increase the value of the option. The seller is taking additional risk (there's more time for something to get screwed up from his standpoint) and demands additional compensation for the additional risk.

OK. We know in the money options have intrinsic value as well as time value. Out of the money options have time value only. You'll hear the term *at the money* as well, which refers technically to an option whose strike price is equivalent to the underlying futures price. In practice, at the moneys are those options whose strike prices are close to the price of the futures.

In our example, with April gold at $399 the 400s are at the money. The 410s are definitely out of the money and the 390s are certainly in the money. The 360s are *deep in the money*, and what would you call the 500s? You could call them *deep out of the money* – I would call them a long shot. Long shots are generally cheap. You can buy quite a few out of the money options for relatively little money. This means if something extraordinary occurs you stand to make a killing. A good analogy would be the Megabucks slot machines we have here in Nevada. The state's casinos link up for the Megabucks jackpot where $3 can win $10 million or more. People do win these, but how many do you know? Of course, the jack does pop out of the box every once in awhile.

I had a client once with way out of the money wheat calls (worth about a penny if I remember right) and only three days to go. It looked hopeless and I felt he should have salvaged the penny so he could at least cover commissions. Then something happened called Chernobyl. We had never traded a nuclear accident before, and the rumours started to fly. The whole Soviet wheat crop was wiped out. This was the first rumour. Wheat went limit up the next day, and the day after. The options came back from the dead and my client eventually cashed them out on expiration day for 39¢/bushel each. In other words, they were selling for $50 each just days before and blossomed to $1950 on expiration day. It was good thing he had to sell that day (and did not exercise) because after the facts became known, and the extent of the radiation damage was deemed not as severe as first feared, wheat prices came all the way back down.

You do hear other stories of rags to riches, as cheap options come to life (I had Euro puts, almost worthless, then the day of the Soviet coup they blossomed to 50 points or $625. When Yeltsin stood on the tank and the coup failed, the next day they were worthless again. Sometimes you need to be nimble. The point is, deep out of the money options can hit at times, but they are long shots and generally a loser's game. I prefer both buying and selling at the moneys in most normal situations. With deep in the money

✱ *Sometimes you need to be nimble.*

options you tie up capital which can be used for diversification. Deep out of the moneys generally expire worthless. Given the choice I also prefer to pay more for time. More about this later.

To recap, we have now discussed how an option's value is determined: time and the relationship of the strike price to the underlying futures price. Oh, I almost forgot, there is another component and it is *volatility*.

Volatility

Very simply, as the volatility of a market increases, so do option premiums. This is a very important determinant in pricing options. Sleepy markets supposedly have lower potential price movements and option buyers bid less. I should point out, however, some of my best option purchases have been 'cheap' buys. When everyone is buying, the smart money is selling. The reason premiums increase with higher volatility is very simply that option sellers demand higher premiums to offset the higher risks which options entail in a more volatile environment.

Many of the option pricing models place a great deal of emphasis on *historic volatility*. In determining 'fair value' you are asked to input this number (for example, if the market is moving at a rate equal to 20 per cent of the price annualized, this is your historic volatility). I have personally found this to be an academic exercise of limited value. It is only a prediction, and the past is not necessarily a good predictor of the future. In fact, my experience has shown the opposite.

Quiet markets lead to more volatile markets and vice versa. When volatility is high, option prices are excessive and, while it takes guts, this is the time to be selling. On the other hand, an old timer once told me 'never sell a quiet market'. It works more times than not.

Let me sum this up another way. In general, the premiums will reflect recent market conditions. In explosive markets they are larger than quiet markets. The risk equals the reward. However, there are those situations when the majority does not see a change coming. Premiums could be tiny just before a major move comes, options are their cheapest when they are the best buys. Conversely, at the pinnacle of expectation, premiums are at their highest, and good sales just before a change in trend or the start of a sideways move. This is where the opportunities arise.

One last point about volatility: on a percentage basis volatility affects at and out of the money options to a greater extent than in the money options. Here's the reason. In the moneys have both intrinsic and extrinsic (anything other then intrinsic, mostly time) value. Intrinsic value is not directly affected by changes in volatility. So a change of, for example, 10 per cent in volatility may change the option's value by 2 per cent, while it will change an at the money's value by 10 per cent. Out of the moneys are affected most by changes in volatility since they can only become profitable when the market moves to them. A change of 10 per cent in volatility could result in the option price moving by, for example, 50 per cent or more. This percentage move is also easier to accomplish for out of the moneys since they are cheaper.

Interest rates

I should mention there is another factor which theoretically determines option premiums, and that is the cost of money or interest rates. I am not going to dwell on interest rates here, or discuss the various models for option pricing since I have found these variables to be more theoretical than practical. In most cases, the professionals on the floor will exploit minor degrees in option mispricing and this is not what we are playing for here. We are in this for more major moves which can be exploited, or as a hedger options as a tool for price protection.

How do changes in price of the underlying commodity change the option's premium?

Here's the basic rule of thumb, all other things being equal:

- *At the money* options move at a 50 per cent rate of change. For example, if the S&P moves 200 points, an at the money will increase or decrease by about 100 points.
- *In the money* options move at a 50–100 per cent rate of change, depending on how deep in the money they are.
- *Out of the money* options move at 0–50 per cent rate of change.

Again these are rules of thumb. I have seen days when in a quiet market both puts and calls lose premium regardless of the move of the market. Then again, in times of wild fluctuations, both puts and calls can gain premium. However, in normal markets these rules work fairly well. An at the money will move at half the speed of the futures. The next strike price up may move 60 per cent of the futures, if a call and an up day or a put and a down day, the next 70 per cent and so on.

Delta

If you trade options, you will hear the term *delta*. This is what we are referring to here. Delta values range from 0 (for very deep out of the money options) to 1 (for options so deeply in the money they move just like the underlying futures). At the money options have a delta value of 0.5. Calls have a *positive delta*, while puts have a *negative delta*. So if a 100 copper call trading for 210 points (or 2.1¢) has a delta of 0.6, a 1¢ (or 100 point) move in the copper price will result in a move of 60 points in the value of the call to 270.

Delta hedging

You will also hear the term *delta hedging*. Many professionals on the floor who specialize in selling options to the public strive to manipulate their position always to be neutral delta hedged. In this way, they look to maximize the benefits of time decay.

This is best appreciated by means of a simple example. You bought 10 March 600 silver calls for 23¢. They are in the money and have a delta of + 0.7. You are bullish silver longer term, but do not like the way the charts look temporarily and instead of selling out the position, wish to hedge it. You would sell short 7 March futures to hedge your 10 calls. For normal moves in price over relatively short periods of time, the 7 futures will offset the change in value of the 10 options.

You still have the risk of loss of time value, but that's essentially it. If volatility increases you could possibly gain a bit. On balance, however, to be delta neutral is a no win/no lose position which should be used for short-term protection only.

Gamma

Gamma is an interesting concept in theory, but I have found it of limited use in practice. There is really no need for the average trader to monitor gamma, but since you might hear the term we'll define it here: gamma is the extent to which the delta itself is changing in relation to the underlying price move. For those who wish to constantly achieve delta neutrality, it is something to keep an eye on, but a more detailed explanation is beyond the scope of our discussion here.

> ✳ Gamma is the extent to which the delta itself is changing in relation to the underlying price move.

Should you exercise profitable options?

When you exercise an option you receive the underlying asset. In the case of a put option you receive a short futures contract (the seller or option writer receives the other side of the transaction, the long position).

For example, let's say it is March, you felt soybean prices were overvalued and purchased May $7.00 put options when the May futures were $7.02 for 10¢/bushel. The futures fall to $6.85. The puts will reflect the increased intrinsic value in this case. They will trade for at least 15¢, which is the difference between the strike price and intrinsic value, or amount the option is 'in the money'. The put buyer could exercise his option, receive a short futures at $7.00 and if desired could cover the short futures at $6.85 in the futures market to realize the 15¢. An automatic profit of 5¢/bushel, or $250 per contract, which is the difference between the purchase price of the option and the futures profit.

This example does not include commissions, and this is one of the basic reasons more options are not exercised. Instead of paying the commission to receive the futures, and an additional commission when you offset the futures, it is much simpler and easier to sell the option back *in the options market*. Most option transactions take place entirely in the options market. Once you are in the futures, which is what happens when you exercise, you assume the additional risks of futures as well. You can still lose more than your initial investment if not careful, and you also are required to post margins required for futures. In fact, option buyers never have to get involved in the futures at all. Option premiums will reflect the change in value of the underlying futures.

> ✴ *The most profitable, least costly and easiest way to liquidate an option is just to sell the option back into the options market rather than exercising it.*

However, there is another good reason not to exercise options in normal markets. You will be giving up, in most cases, some additional money, which represents any time value remaining.

Let's look at our soybean put option example above. The put value will always include any cash value, or intrinsic value which is determined by the underlying futures. When the market is trading at $6.85, the $7.00 put is 15¢ in the money and will have 15¢ in intrinsic value. Yet, depending on how much time is left until expiration, this put will also have some time value associated. It may be trading for 20¢ or more if a lot of time is left, or perhaps 16¢ if just a few days are left. This is an *in the money* put in this example. The $6.75 will also have a quoted value. With months left it could be 10¢ or more, with days left only a penny or two. This is an *out of the money* option which has no intrinsic value. Its total price consists of time value, or potential to become profitable based on time, market outlook and volatility.

In conclusion, the most profitable, least costly and easiest way to liquidate an option is just to sell the option back into the options market rather than exercising it.

Should you *ever* exercise an option?

There is only one instance when I would consider exercising a long put or call. On the last day there generally is no time value left. Options are priced according to their cash value. This can also happen, at times, to deep in the money options prior to expiration. You would think you could always sell an option for at least its cash or intrinsic value, but this is not always the case. At the very end you are dealing with a local or professional trader, most likely a member of the exchange. The public is not interested in selling in the money options on the last day. The locals will require a sweetener to take the other side of your transaction if you are looking to sell an option like this, and you may need to give up a small piece of the premium you earned to liquidate in the options market at an illiquid time.

So, looking at our soybean put example, let's say the market was at 660 and you try to sell your 700 put for 40¢ with very little time remaining. You may not get the order filled. You may need to price it at 39¢, which would guarantee the local a modest 1¢ ($50/contract) profit. He will just offset the transaction in the futures market which guarantees a profit. Now you could do this as well. You could buy the futures at 660, exercise the 700 put, be assigned a short futures at 700 which will offset with your long from 660 and result in a 40¢ futures profit. Your net profit would be the 40¢ in this example, minus your original option cost minus commissions.

This is something to consider if it makes more sense than letting the local take the sweetener. Or, if you still feel the market is going to move in the direction of your option, consider exercising a profitable option on the last day. No need even to consider this prior to the last day, but on the day of expiration this is something to think about. Remember, you are subject to the margining requirements of futures. In many cases, however, for a deep in the money option you will have this covered – at least temporarily. A greater concern is that you are now in the futures; something option buyers have been trying to avoid. The risk is no longer limited, and an unfavourable move in the underlying futures can now wipe out your profit. Use a stop to prevent losing what you made.

If selling options puts the odds in my favour, why not do it?

More options are sold by professional traders than the public. They like getting the head-start option selling (also called option *writing*) entails. Yet, anyone can take the other side of an option purchase. The field's wide open. It is something to consider, but think about the following points.

The primary advantage of buying options is the option writer's disadvantage

When you sell an option, you agree to provide the option buyer with either a long position (when writing a call) or a short (when writing a put). You receive the premium, but since the market can theoretically move an unlimited amount away from the strike price, the associated risk is also unlimited. The greater the premium received, the lower the risk to the option writer. The lower the volatility (not always an easy thing to predict), the lower the risk to the option writer. As a general rule of thumb, the less time until expiration, the lower the risk to the option writer.

The option writer is also subject to the risk of exercise. This is a right specifically granted to the option buyer, which the seller has no control over. When a call option is exercised by the buyer, he is credited with a long futures position at the strike price; the seller the short side of the transaction (at the strike price). If a put is exercised the buyer is credited with the short and the seller the long. An option will only be exercised by the buyer when it is profitable for him to do so. No reason to if it is not, since this is the reason he or she is in options. The buyer would just walk away from an unprofitable option, either let it expire worthless or sell it back to the option market if there is time value left. By definition, if an option is exercised against the seller it will be unprofitable to the seller. The only time it would not be is if the seller sold the option in the aftermarket after it was already unprofitable to a previous seller. The risk of exercise, and the unlimited potential risk, are the risks all option sellers must, by contract, accept.

> ✳ As a general rule of thumb, the less time until expiration, the lower the risk to the option writer.

So why take these risks? The option seller has a head start. He receives the premium. This will insulate his risk to some extent, and he can make money in more situations than the buyer. The buyer needs a move in his favour. If he holds the option until expiration, the buyer needs not only a favourable move, but a move which will exceed the premium he paid, to realize a profit. The seller can make money if there is a move favourable to his position (up when selling puts, and down when selling calls). He also makes money in a quiet or stationary market – something the option buyer cannot do. Third, he can profit even if the market moves against him, as long as it moves to a lesser degree than the premium received.

You will no doubt hear the warnings against 'naked' option writing. So, how risky is it to sell options? Well, it is risky, certainly more so than buying, but actually less so than futures. This is because you receive a premium, and in the case of writing out of the money options, you have the additional cushion of the gap between the market and the strike price. Furthermore, there are defensive strategies the option writer can employ to protect him or herself. The writer can always buy back his short position, just as a short futures trader can buy back his. A stop loss can be used in the option market, just as in futures. Some options are not all that liquid; and you need to take this into account, but many of them trade very actively and are as liquid, in some cases more so than many futures markets. Finally, the option writer can buy (in the case of selling a call) or sell (for a put) a futures against his option if he gets into trouble. This strategy is used by professionals in many cases to become more neutral, a strategy we will discuss later.

Let's say you are bullish corn, you are looking for an up move, but not necessarily a major move. You can buy futures, buy calls, or sell puts. It is late September and December corn is trading at $3.00/bushel. You can buy the futures at $3.00, have unlimited upside, and theoretically unlimited risk. You can buy the December 300 calls for 10¢/bushel, or sell the December 300 puts for 10¢. You project the market will make a move to the $3.10 level, so decide to sell the puts. Yet, any close anywhere above $3.00 at expiration and you keep the entire premium, in this case 10¢ or $500 per option (minus the inevitable commission of course). So if the market does close at $3.10 you keep the premium (since the 300 put expires worthless and is abandoned by the buyer). This is a profit, the same as the futures buyer who bought at $3.00 and sold at $3.10. However, the put seller realizes the same profit at $3.00 at expiration, while the option buyer only breaks even. You can even be wrong, and not lose. At expiration, if the market drops to $2.90, while the futures buyer is sitting with a 10¢ loss, the seller can still get out of his obligation in the options market at about 10¢ or no worse than a break-even. Wrong, and no loss. The beauty of selling options is that you can also be wrong and still profit. In this example, if the market fell to $2.95 by expiration, the option can be covered at 5¢ for a 5¢ profit. Wrong, and a profit; an impossibility with futures or any other investment I can think of.

The odds are really in the option seller's favour, since the majority of options do expire worthless and are not exercised. However, the payoffs are not as potentially high. Here's the rub. The most the option seller will ever receive is the premium, never a penny more. The risks are greater. For some traders, the risks are just too high for the potential gain. This is the tradeoff: sellers have odds in their favour, buyers have greater potential. This is not to say sellers are stuck with the position. Just as in futures, the risks can be managed. Just like a short seller in the futures, the short option seller can get out by covering his position in the option market. Stop loss orders are accepted in options to cover shorts and should be used. Should you write options? The answer is there is nothing wrong with it for those who understand the risks and how to manage them. There are some traders, those who just cannot find it in themselves to cut the losses (one of the most important lessons I am trying to teach in this book), who should probably only buy options and nothing else. You know who you are.

> ✱ *This is the tradeoff: sellers have odds in their favour, buyers have greater potential.*

Options – a prime hedging tool

Hedging is the offsetting of risks from other positions. While I personally prefer futures to options as a speculator, I also believe hedgers should strongly consider options. They truly can offer the best of both worlds.

A cattle feeder should know what his break-even cost is, as an example. He knows what he paid for the calf, he knows his feed costs (he hedged his corn, of course), he knows his vet costs and labour, he has an allowance for death loss, and he can to the penny calculate his cost of money to finance the whole operation. So he would know, for example, his break-even is 70¢/pound for the finished product (a market-ready animal 120 days hence). What he doesn't know is what his ultimate selling price will be on that date. After all, we are dealing with the unknown to some extent here. The futures 120 days out could be trading at 73¢ and by selling the futures today, he can guarantee himself a 3¢ profit. This isn't bad, except cattle feeding is a risky business. There are some periods of windfall profits, where 10¢/pound or more can be had. There are other periods where 120 days of work and risk result in a net loss. If a 3¢ profit could always be locked in, a lot of the risk and uncertainty would be taken out of the equation, but in the real world it is not always possible to lock in a profit. So, bottom line, you need the windfall profits at times to offset the marginal profits and losing periods that also occur. Futures hedges lock out the windfall profits. If you sell futures at 73, and the price at finish is 80, you have a futures loss of 7 which offsets the windfall cash gain of 10. The net result gets you back to your 3¢ profit.

Today, most cattle feeders just accept the risk of the marketplace. They feed cattle and hope a decent price is there for them in four or five months to reward them for their efforts. Sometimes it is, but there are also many *former* cattle feeders out there. On the other hand, the big, profitable, corporate cattle feeders use options. This should tell you something.

Here's how it might work: the feeder in this case could buy a 120-day live cattle put at say, a 73 strike price for 2¢/pound. He is in effect 'locking in' a 71¢ selling price (73 minus 2). If the price falls to, for example, 66 at expiration, when his cattle are ready, he will take a 4¢ bath in the cash market. His break-even is 70, so a sale at 66 is a 4¢ loss. However, to offset this loss, his option will be worth 7¢, for a net profit of 5¢ before commissions (recall he paid 2). Add the 5 back to the 66 and in effect he gets back to his 71¢ worst case break-even. So he is giving up 2¢ of potential profit for the ability to avoid catastrophic loss. The real beauty of the options, unlike futures, unlike forward contracting in the cash market, is that his upside is totally unlimited. If prices rise to 80 he reaps a 10¢ profit in the cash market. This will be reduced by the cost of the option, in this case 2¢ down to 8¢, but his upside is unlimited.

The bottom line is the farmer has a tool in which he can guarantee himself a price floor, a worst case scenario, while not constructing a ceiling (which is what he is doing with futures hedges). There are precious few opportunities for the farmer to reap windfall profits, and he needs them to offset the mediocre or worse than mediocre years. Options are a tool which if used properly achieve this goal. A powerful tool!

This concept works just as well in financial futures.

A US company receives an order for equipment not yet built from Germany. They will be receiving Euros on delivery in six months. The Euro is trading today at 95¢ to the dollar. The profit margin is good, but could be wiped out by exchange rate fluctuations. There could also be a windfall gain if the currency moves up in relation to the dollar within the time period. The company is not in the business of currency speculation, however. Their business is building equipment. The common practice is to hedge in the currency forward using the Interbank market (the electronic market between banks for foreign exchange trading). This may be prudent, and certainly makes more sense to a manufacturing business than floating in the wind. Options can be just as prudent and they offer something else, a sweetener – the possibility of *improving* on a position while limiting the risk for a predetermined cost. The company can purchase an option giving it the right to sell Euros at, say 95¢ to the dollar in six months for 250 basis points. A 95 put. A standard contract traded at the IOM (a division of the CME) is for 125,000 Euro. The minimum tick is for $12.50/contract, so a quote of 250 points will cost the company $3125. If the order is for $1,000,000 in equipment (today's exchange rate) they might buy about 8 of these puts. Profit insurance, so to speak. If the Euro rises, the company loses the premiums, but can reap an additional currency profit which is theoretically unlimited. If the Euro falls, the company sells the put for a profit, and this will offset the cheaper currency. They are willing to pay the $25,000, which will reduce their bottom-line profit to assure a profit.

Finally, let's look at this from the other side. If a company places an order for merchandise or equipment and is required to pay for it on receipt, some time in the future, this firm also has a currency exposure. A rise in the value of the Euro, or yen, or whatever currency will mean higher costs. A fall would cheapen the purchase and add to bottom-line profits. Unless the firm's purchasing people are gamblers, which translates into being a hero or a bum (and bums don't keep their jobs), they will hedge this risk. The traditional method is to forward contract in the Interbank market or buy futures. Both methods 'lock in' a price or cost of the currency. However, buying calls just may be a better way to go: establishes a ceiling price on costs, yet allows for windfall profits if the currency falls by more than the option price in the time period.

Stock index options

How many times have you been right about the direction of the stock market, but *your* stocks went nowhere. Well, you guessed it, there's a simple way to gamble on the stock market without having to be a stock picker. A trader who is bullish can buy S&P 500 (or any of the other) stock index call options. The bear would, of course, buy the puts. Or, when the premiums are high, a sale may be warranted. Much of the volume in the S&P is institutional, where a portfolio manager uses the futures or options for protection. Yet, any individual can use S&P at the money puts for price protection. They allow the buyer to sell the S&P 500 index (500 biggest stocks representing over 80 per cent of the US market) at today's market price. One put protects 250 times the index. In other words, if the index is at 1300, one at the money put will 'protect' a $325,000 stock portfolio (250 × 1300 = 325,000) for a specified period. The option gives the buyer the right, but no obligation, to sell the S&P 500. It will increase in value by at least $250 (minus the purchase price) for every point the S&P falls (a point is a move from say 1300 to 1299). It can be sold prior to expiration. If prices rise by expiration the purchase price and commissions will be lost, but no additional funds would ever be required.

* Well, you guessed it, there's a simple way to gamble on the stock market without having to be a stock picker.

This is a hedge, however, and if you 'lose' on the put, hopefully your stock portfolio rose. If the market falls by the same amount as the premium, you'll get your purchase price back. In other words you're protecting your portfolio from a fall of *greater* than the premium paid. If the market falls by a greater percentage, you will lose on your portfolio but gain on the put option. Why wouldn't a bear just sell his or her stocks? For long-term investors, wary of a market dip, this is cheaper and easier. Selling $325,000 worth of stocks would involve numerous and costly commissions. The commission on one S&P option will generally be less than $100. Plus, you need not forgo dividend income on your stocks, worry about long-term capital gains taxes, and if your stocks outperform the market in general you will have a relationship gain. If the market declines, the investor/hedger can sell his put at a profit, and hold on to the stocks. If the market rises, the stocks will be worth more, and the put has to be considered insurance which just didn't need to be used.

This covers the basics. If you've have enough of options (they're not for everyone), go ahead, skip the next two chapters. They are useful, however, trust me on this. So, if you are intrigued and starting to see some new ways to make money here, let's proceed to some of the more sophisticated techniques.

Advanced option strategies

Entire books have been written about options. Many of them get way too precise, and go over such academics as butterfly spreads and other strategies which may look good theoretically, but in practice are seldom useful. We will be spending three chapters here on options, and no doubt I will leave something out, but I plan to cover the basic strategies and sub-strategies which I feel are worth your consideration.

Buying options to protect futures

This simply involves buying a put when long futures, or a call when short futures. This is sometimes known as creating *synthetic* options, since a put with a long futures is somewhat like a call, and the call with the short futures is somewhat like a put. You can make a case, that if you buy an at the money call option while simultaneously holding a short futures position (synthetic put), or buy a put option while simultaneously holding a long futures position (synthetic call), the overall position will act just like a put or a call (so why bother?). However, I think it is a better strategy. This strategy gives you added flexibility, and I use it quite a bit.

Let's look at an example. Suppose you are fundamentally bullish the hog market, but are concerned that the upcoming Hogs and Pigs Report could move the market substantially (perhaps in your direction, but there are no guarantees). In fact, the Hogs and Pigs Report, released by the USDA quarterly, has a reputation for moving the market locked limit – at times consecutive multiple limit days in a row. Lock limit moves, or abnormal moves in markets without limits, is a risk every futures trader has to accept. If the report was a bearish surprise, you could lose many times your initial margin as you may not be able to get out the first day, or even second. A real

nightmare when you're caught on the wrong side of a three-day locked limit report; it does happen. Of course, the report could confirm your fundamental bias, and if not in and the market starts moving limit in your direction, you may never be able to enter at a reasonable price. You could buy a call, of course, but here's a more flexible approach.

You buy the hogs at 72, and simultaneously purchase a 72 put for a premium of 180 points, or $720. If the report is bullish, you can abandon your put for whatever the market will offer and reap your profit on the futures. A bearish report? You are fully protected, and regardless of how many limit moves the market makes you know your worst case scenario – in this case a $720 maximum risk plus fees. If worst comes to worst, you can exercise the put and you will be assigned a short futures position which will automatically offset your long. You always have the right in this case to sell your 72 purchase, for 72, which is a wash. You are out, at most, the cost of the put.

However, here is where the flexibility comes in. These reports are funny animals. I have seen markets open limit in the direction of the report and close totally opposite by day's end. The markets will trade off the reports, but the reports are not always right, and the smart money will use the news as an opportunity. It is almost always a bullish sign if a market closes opposite the direction a report indicates it should. Let's say in this case they were looking for 3 per cent more hogs and the report indicated there are 9 per cent more. Bearish. You are glad you had the foresight to buy the put. They are talking two, maybe three, limit days down. The market opens limit down, at 70. The put increases in value from 180, to say 310 at the open. The market should stay limit down, and if two days down the put should theoretically trade up to 400 or higher. You place a sell stop *on the put* at 230. Remember, as the market rises, the put loses value. The only way for the stop to be hit is for a rally, at least sometime during the day. If the market stays weak, you leave the put in place. But the market starts to rally, you are stopped out of your put at a modest profit of 50 points, and still have the long futures. However, you have the long futures in an environment where the market is trading. In effect the abnormal situation is more normal, more manageable. You can now place a stop under the futures. If the market keeps rallying (the Hogs and Pigs Reports have been shown to be inaccurate 40 per cent of the time, but nobody knows for sure until six months down the road when the pigs actually materialize or they don't) you have a good position. You had protection if the report proved unmanageable, and in effect if it was a good report, this was a 'mistake' you liked to make since the futures would rise more than the put would deteriorate. You had a lot of flexibility here.

This is only one of the many variations and permutations of using options in conjunction with futures. They give you staying power, while allowing you the choice of lifting one side or another at any time. If your technical or fundamental bias changes, you can always lift one side and use the other. If you reach your profit objective on the futures, you can liquidate and hold the option. It is possible the option could 'return from the dead' and earn you a double profit.

Another variation on this theme involves buying options to protect profits for a position which has already moved your way. You'll see later I'm a big fan of riding a trend for all it's worth. In a big move, a market always seems to go farther than reason alone might warrant. However, at the end of a move a market can get overheated and when you know the top is in, it could be too late.

> ✳ You'll see later I'm a big fan of riding a trend for all it's worth.

When you feel the end is near, but there is no reason fundamentally or technically to liquidate, why not just buy an option to protect profits. It could be money well spent, and if you are too early, once again this is the kind of mistake you like to make since you will make more on the futures than you spend on the option.

Writing options as a hedging strategy

In the previous chapter, we discussed a company which has foreign currency risk and the purchase of options to hedge this risk. A more sophisticated strategy involves the selling of options to generate additional income.

Let me explain. What if a company needs to buy Japanese yen, and is happy with today's rate of exchange? To generate additional income, the manager could sell at the money put options. Say the yen was trading at 80, and the 80 puts for 90 days were priced at 200. By selling the puts, the company's account is credited with the premium, in this case $2500 per option. In effect, the company is saying they are willing to buy yen from the option buyer at 80. If the value of the yen rises, the puts will remain unexercised at expiration time and the company keeps the entire premium. This is a hedge, in that the money can be used to offset the higher yen. If the yen has risen by less than 200 points, the company is money ahead. If it rises by more, the company can buy calls or futures or forward contract at an appropriate spot (if it is unwilling to accept any additional risk in the marketplace). If the yen falls, the company just honours its commitment to purchase yen at the higher price (it will be assigned long futures at 80, a price it was willing to live with), but it will still keep the 200 points which will effectively lower the purchase price to 78.

This strategy works best if the outlook is for a stable, or slightly rising, slightly falling market. By receiving the premium, the traditional costs of hedging are not only reduced, they can be paid for, plus.

Covered option writing

The advantage of *buying options* is that your risk is limited and predetermined, and the profit potential unlimited. This is the attraction. Be aware, however, that most options will expire worthless and the premiums will eventually disappear. Therefore, buying options is generally a losing proposition. This is not to say you cannot make good money in a major bull market, but be advised most of the professionals on the floor I know sell options (generally to the public); they rarely buy options.

The advantage of *selling options* has to do with the fact that you capitalize on the time decay of options. Since the premiums people pay for options will eventually disappear, the option seller will gain this. Writing options is generally a winning strategy. However the big disadvantage is that the risk is unlimited, and the profit potential is limited to the premiums received.

✳ When option premiums are high, the general rule of thumb is that it is better to sell options than buy them.

When option premiums are high, the general rule of thumb is that it is better to sell options than buy them.

The advantage of *futures* is the profit potential is unlimited, but so is the risk if you do not employ risk management techniques (stops). Stops are not foolproof, but they generally work efficiently. The main problem with stops is that in a volatile market you can be stopped out only to have the market eventually go your way. And if you do not have stops you don't know what your risk is.

Covered option writing takes advantage of the high option premiums, but does limit your risk to some extent and allows more room to work in a volatile market. It basically involves selling call options and buying futures, or selling puts and shorting futures. There is still very good profit potential if this is all we do, over time.

For example, last April I bought the November beans at 800 and sold the 800 calls for 45¢. This gave me 45¢ in downside protection. At expiration if the market was anywhere above 755 I still would have some profit on this trade. If the market was anywhere above 800 – at expiration we would keep the 45¢, or over $2250 gross per contract. This is a good profit. The disadvantage of this strategy is that the most we can make on each one is 45¢. So if 'beans in the teens' becomes a reality the covered positions are limited.

Now here is how I overcame this disadvantage. I looked to pyramid the position every 25¢ or so up. So if the market moved to, say, 825 (this number is not written in stone, depends on circumstances) we buy more futures at 825 and sell the 825 calls for 45¢ or more. At this point our lower buys look safer. The 800 covered writes we can ride to theoretically 755, so the market would have to fall 70¢ before we're in big trouble here. If we happened to have the 750s on at this point, they would look real safe, etc. Now if we add every 25¢

up and take in say an average of 40¢ each time, if the market is strong we make 160 for every 100 move up. With a call option, if you pay 40 and the market moves up 100 you make only 60.

So this is actually more profitable than just buying calls in a major bull move, if we pyramid. In down periods, we are better able to ride out the fluctuations than if the futures are not covered. In a sideways market you will make money with this strategy as well, while you would lose just buying calls. Of course, there is also risk if the market goes down with this strategy. With options the risk is limited. With the covered position the risk is less than futures, but you still need to monitor the position and use a risk point on the futures if the market looks too weak.

Option spreads

Futures can be spread in many different ways, but options can be spread in even more. Only with options can one spread two different contracts of the same month. They can be constructed in a variety of ways to fine tune market outlooks. I'll be honest, I generally do not spread options. However, some of these strategies are very popular, and they do fit nicely with some trading styles. So I will touch on the basics here.

> **＊** *Futures can be spread in many different ways, but options can be spread in even more.*

Vertical call spreads

This is where two options of the same month, but *with different strike prices* are spread against each other. The vertical call spread is bullish, and the vertical put spread is bearish.

Let's look at an example. Say you're bullish wheat. It's March, and May wheat is trading at $4.20. You buy the May 420 call, pay 22¢, simultaneously sell the May 450 call take in 7¢. Your cost (not including commissions) is the difference between the two premiums, in this case 15¢ or $750. The difference (always a *debit*) is your maximum risk. If the market at expiration closes below 420 you lose the 22, keep the 7, a max-risk of 15. Your maximum profit is the difference between the strike prices minus the debit. 450 − 420 = 30 − 15 = 15. Above 450 you lose penny for penny what you make on the 420. So your maximum profit is at or above 450 (returning 30 for your 22 investment in the lower priced call, but you keep the 7 for a total of 15).

So why do people do this? In some respects bull spreading calls offers the best of both worlds. The risk, as in buying options, is strictly limited. You lower your overall cost by benefiting from the time decay of selling premium. You are selling premium on the greater out of the money option, which is more likely to expire worthless, than the lower priced option. The main disadvantage is the profit is absolutely limited, which eliminates one of the main advantages of buying options. However, there is still a premium cost, one of the main disadvantages of buying options. You also have double commissions.

Vertical put spreads

These are the mirror image of the call spread. You are mildly bearish the stock market.

It is July, the September S&P is trading at 750. You buy the August 740 put (which keys off the September contract and expires the third Friday in August) for 1800 points, and sell the 710 for 450 points. Your maximum risk is 1800 minus 450, $3375 (1350 points). You lowered your maximum risk by $1125 versus just buying the 740 put. Your maximum profit happens under 710 and is the difference between the strike prices, in this case 30 points or $7,500 minus the debit of $3375 or $4125 minus commissions.

By writing a lower priced put against a higher priced put you take on less risk for a lesser potential profit. For call spreads, by writing a higher priced call against a lower priced call you do the same thing. There are quite a few variations here for all tastes, but in practice if you use too high a priced call, or low a priced put, you do not receive enough premium to lower the cost sufficiently.

Calendar spreads

Also known as *time spreads*, this strategy takes advantage of the tendency of nearby options to decay faster than the distants. It involves the sale of an option in one month, and the simultaneous purchase of an option (usually the same strike price) in a later month.

For example, you might sell a September 1500 cocoa call, and buy a December 1500 cocoa call for a net debit. If the market remains fairly stable, you eventually gain the premium in the nearby to cheapen the ultimate cost of the distant, or there will be a net gain on the entire position after some time passes (you can liquidate both sides at any time).

One of the potential pitfalls in this strategy is that the spread values of the underlying commodity can change, perhaps favourably, but contrary to expectations as well. Many times, the nearby month, which will affect the short side of the spread, will move more dramatically due to higher open interest and greater speculative play. So the risk cannot always be predetermined to an exact level like the vertical spreads. However, on balance I think there is merit in this strategy if monitored and massaged when necessary.

Straddles and strangles

These option spreads involve both puts and calls. The straddle involves buying or selling puts and calls at the same strike price. During the life of a straddle it is almost a certainty that one or both of the options will be in the money at any point in time. The strangle involves different strike prices. It is less likely that both or even one of the strangle legs will be in the money at any point in time. However, it is certainly quite possible. There are two sides to each of these market plays, so let's examine the four possibilities a bit deeper.

Buying a straddle

 It is late September and the December T-Bonds are trading at 10503. You buy the December 105 call and the 105 put. The call is trading for 2 full points and $\frac{1}{32}$. The put is trading for 1 and $\frac{31}{32}$. So your cost is the sum of both premiums, in this case 4 full points or $4000 (plus the inevitable commissions of course). So at expiration, bonds must move over 4 points, above 109 or below 101 for this strategy to be profitable.

The advantage of this strategy is you know the maximum risk to the penny. The disadvantage is you must overcome double premiums to be profitable. Why would anyone do this? There is only one situation this makes any sense at all. You anticipate a *volatile* market but do not have any idea which direction the market will move. Let's suppose there's a big unemployment report coming out which will determine Fed policy. You know this report will move the market, but have no clue as to how it will come out or be received. After the report you can decide if you want to cut the losses on the bad option, and let the good one roll, or if the move is dramatic enough for the good one to cover the premiums of both.

I've found this strategy only works if you are willing to manage it. To overcome the time decay of two options you need to be very right over time. At times, after a move of significance, it could make sense to take a profit on the good side, and hope the other comes back from the dead; or cut the loss on the unprofitable side, and look to maximize the good side. There are no hard and fast rules here. It takes management and smarts. So the report comes out, unemployment is up dramatically. Since this indicates a weakening economy, the thought will be the Fed could lower rates which is *bullish* bond prices. So now we see how the market reacts to the report. It is not the news, but how the market reacts to the news that's important.

❋ There are no hard and fast rules here. It takes management and smarts.

In this case, bond prices move up dramatically. They rally over $2\frac{1}{2}$ full points to close at 10718. The call gains about a point and a quarter. The put loses a point. Due to the delta pricing of options, the first leg of the move will be the least profitable for this strategy. As your profitable option moves deeper into the money, it will act more and more like a futures contract and become increasingly profitable. The out of the money will lose comparatively less, since it will have less to lose. Of course, at any time you have the choice of selling out one leg of the straddle or both. If, at some point, your indicators tell you the move is over you might wish to take profits on the call, and hold onto the put hoping the move reverses to the downside. You could, if you are looking for a major bull to unfold, cut your loss on the put and hold onto the call. In this case, you would realize a loss of about a point, and most likely be out about $1000 or so on the *realized* side of the equation. Now if, at expiration, the market fell back under 105, you would lose your entire call premium and this 'limited risk' trade would cost you over $3500 per straddle.

This is why it is important to protect profits on the good side of the spread. You could place a stop on the call at break-even (for the call) which would limit your risk on the entire position to about the put loss, while leaving your upside open. Once you are out of the put, you need a move (at expiration) to over 108 to show a net profit. Every point move above this level will result in a $1000 profit per point per straddle. The important thing to remember is you need to use sound judgement and good money management when using a strategy like this. At expiration one side of the straddle will expire worthless, so you need to make this up somehow.

Selling a straddle

Somebody was on the other side of the previous example. Most likely, the buyer of the straddle bought from two different sellers, but you could be a seller of the straddle too. This is a strategy which places the odds in your favour, but opens up the risk level as well.

 In the above example, the seller of the December T-Bond 105 straddle receives both premiums. In this case about 4 points. If the market doesn't move, and at the expiration date closes exactly at 105, he gets to keep *both* premiums. The odds of this outcome are small, but as long as the market remains within a range he will make something. In this case, he has 4 points to work with. If the market stays within the relatively wide range of 101 to 109 some profit is possible. The market must move outside of the range for the straddle writer to lose. The problem with this strategy, in many cases, comes in the timing of the move. If the market moves fast (either direction), and volatility increases, the seller could get into trouble. Just as in any limited profit (in this example the profit is limited to an absolute maximum of $4000), unlimited risk strategy this one needs to be managed.

If the unemployment report results in a ho-hum reaction, you may wish to stay with the entire position. If there is a dramatic move, it certainly could make sense to cut the loss on the unprofitable side, but then look to 'lock in' a profit using some form of risk control measure (a stop comes to mind) on the profitable side.

Buying a strangle

The strangle is similar to the straddle but with an important difference. The strangle player uses different strikes, usually at either side of the market price. As a buyer, your risk is limited. Your leverage increases since a major move will result in a greater profit on funds at risk.

Let's go back to our T-Bond example. In the straddle you purchased the 105 call *and* put with the market trading about 105. The strangle buyer might buy the 108 call for one point *and* the 102 put for just under a point. So your cost is about $2000 instead of $4000. Your risk is cut in half. Your outlook is most likely the same as the straddle buyer; that is you are looking for a substantial move in a volatile market, but don't have a clue as to direction. The disadvantage is that the market must move *substantially* for you to show a profit. In the straddle example above, at expiration, the profit zone is outside of 109 or 101. For this strangle, the range has widened to 110 on the upside (108 plus the 2 points in premium paid) and 100 on the downside. However, if bonds soar to 118 at expiration this strategy would result in a gross profit of $8000. The 102 put would expire worthless. The 108 call would be worth $10,000. The cost was $2000, resulting in a gross profit of $8000, or 400 per cent. In our straddle example, the gross profit would be $9000 at 118. The 105 call would be worth $13,000 minus the $4000 cost = $9000. While the gross profit is higher, the leverage is lower. On a $4000 risk, the net profit was 225 per cent. For the same risk, you could have purchased two strangles resulting in a gross profit of $16,000.

Don't forget, I am hypothetically assuming a major move here. They do happen, but don't count on them coming often.

Selling a strangle

This strategy, which would involve taking the other side of the above, is profitable most of the time. This is because most out of the money calls expire worthless, or do not overcome the premiums paid. In this case, you are writing two out of the money calls. This does not necessarily put the odds doubly in your favour. If a major bull or bear move takes place, the strangle seller could find himself in big trouble. So I repeat, you need to manage these option spread strategies, and this becomes of primary importance for the strangle writer. He has a lower potential profit than many other plays. The risks are less, but they are still there and very real.

In conclusion, the strangle buyer pays less than the straddle buyer, but his profit potential is less. The strangle seller has better odds of a profit, but his risks are higher. The strangle and straddle sellers can do very well in quiet, trading range-type markets. The buyer does well during major bull or bear moves, and particularly well in runaway moves. Your market outlook is not as important using these strategies, as the *degree* of the move. Premiums will vary by market conditions. So you need to vary your strategy based on these conditions and your outlook. The one rule which will always hold true is that the rewards are higher with the risks!

Butterfly spreads

In an effort to be complete, since you will hear this term if you trade long enough, I'll tell you what a butterfly spread is and then give a word of advice. A butterfly spread is a combination of both a bull spread and a bear spread. It involves three

> ✱ Your broker may like the butterfly, but I suggest you fly away from them.

strike prices, for example buying a May 290 corn call, selling two May 300 corn calls, and buying a May 310 corn call. They are limited risk, but the profit potential does not generally justify the costs involved. Remember, you have the commission costs (in this most simple case there are four of them). Then you have to overcome the bid to offer spreads on three positions for both the in and the out. Your broker may like the butterfly, but I suggest you fly away from them.

Ratios

Ratios involve buying or selling a greater number of calls or puts on one side of the transaction than the other. They are basically a combination of strategies already discussed, and can be useful in certain situations.

Ratio writes

We talked about covered option selling or covered writes. Simply stated, a ratio write involves selling a greater number of options than the underlying futures position. The most common is the 2:1.

It is 15 September. You buy December cotton at 8055, and simultaneously sell two December 86 calls for a premium of 130 each. So you are taking in 260 points in premium – for cotton a point is worth $5. Therefore, this strategy gives you $1300 in downside protection. There is still downside risk here, but it is less than an outright futures position. The market at expiration must move below 7795 for this strategy to produce a loss (not including commissions). With the futures, any move under 8055 will result in a loss. Profits will also be higher on a 'normal' bull move compared to an outright futures position. If the market on option expiration date closes at 8305, a

single futures position will show a gross profit of 250 points, or $1250. The ratio write shows a much more impressive profit of $2550 since the 86 calls expire worthless and the premium is kept in full. It should be noted that this profit is also greater than naked call writing. In this example, the naked call seller receives the $1300 not the $2550.

The rub? This ratio write has a two-sided risk, which is not seen in either covered or naked writes. If the market falls substantially, the risk on the futures is not limited. If the market rallies substantially, the upside risk is unlimited as well. There's an extra naked call to contend with. A ratio call writer has a neutral to slightly bullish outlook. A ratio put writer (short December cotton and sell two December puts) has a neutral to slightly bearish outlook.

I've stressed this before, and I'll do it again. This is a strategy which can be quite profitable, but must be managed. The ratio writer should know his break-even point, both above and below the market, and manage the position when it appears threatened. The best positions are those which have a wide enough profit range to allow for defensive action should it become necessary.

> ✳ I've stressed this before, and I'll do it again. This is a strategy which can be quite profitable, but must be managed.

Ratio spreads

A 2:1 ratio call spread involves buying one lower priced call and selling two higher priced.

For example, with May beans trading at 689, you might buy a May 700 call for 14¢, and sell two 725 calls for 7¢ each. Under $7.00 there is no real risk other than cost on this one. In fact, if you can establish the spread at a credit initially, there is no downside risk. The maximum profit occurs at the upper strike price at expiration. If the market expires exactly at 725, you keep the 14¢ plus show a gross profit of 11¢ (25 – 14) on the 700. The 25¢ in this case is the maximum profit.

The profit potential is reduced above the upper strike price since the loss is theoretically unlimited for the naked portion of the spread. The greatest risk for ratio call spreads always lies above the market. Ratio put spreads, you guessed it, have their risk below the market.

Ratio spreads and ratio writes are similar in that they both involve uncovered writes and both have predetermined profit ranges. The difference is the downside risk (for ratio call spreads) or upside risk (for puts) is small and in some cases non-existent. Again, you would use this strategy in a neutral, or mildly bullish or bearish environment. There are virtually unlimited permutations of ratios and strike prices which can be used. Just use good judgement.

Reverse ratio spreads

As the name implies, this is a strategy opposite to the more commonly used ones, and therefore you don't hear much about it. Nevertheless, I like it. It involves selling a call or put at one strike price, and buying a greater number of calls at a higher strike price, or buying a greater number of puts at a lower strike price. This is also commonly called a *backspread*. You want to look for backspreads you can establish for a *credit*, and are looking for a relatively substantial move for the best profits.

 Let's look at an example. It is February and May sugar is trading at 1112. You sell an 1100 call for 65 points, and buy two 1200 calls for 23 each. The spread is established at a credit of 19 points (+65 – (23x2)). If May sugar expires under 1100, all the calls will expire worthless and the credit of 19 points is the profit. In fact, this is your maximum downside potential. You don't put on a bull backspread looking for a down move, but if you are totally wrong and the market does fall, you can still earn a slight profit. This strategy has limited risk. The maximum loss comes at expiration at the purchased calls. In this case, at 1200 the 1100 call sold will show a loss of 35 points (100 points of intrinsic value minus the 65 received), and the 1200 calls will expire worthless. Therefore, the total risk on this one is 35 + 46 or 81 points. The risk is never more than this. The real profit potential comes when the market moves above 1200, with no limits on the maximum profit potential. If the market expires at 1300, the short call will show a loss of 135 points, but each of the 1200 calls will show a profit of 76: 76 × 2 – 135 = 17. A relatively small profit, but now the profit potential is unlimited. The short and one long call will offset each other, but the added call will gain with the futures. At 1400 the strategy results in a 117-point profit, 1500, 217 and so forth. The profit range (without fees) is anywhere below 1119, anywhere above 1283, but not in the middle.

Very simply, this is a bullish strategy which is hedged to an extent by the short sale. The profit is unlimited on a major upside move, yet there is a wider range of potentially profitable outcomes since the trader can also profit to an extent when totally wrong. As with all these plays, this one can be performed with puts when bearish. It should be used when the outlook is for a relatively large move in a volatile market. It generally makes more sense with more time, and it ties up less money than just buying options. The drawback comes with a relatively normal move in the direction anticipated. If the move is not large enough a loss will result.

OK, we've covered the basic ways to trade options, as well as some more sophisticated strategies. In the next chapter, I'll attempt to pull this together to a degree by sharing some of my observations on how to use options to your advantage.

Eight winning option trading rules

The rules

1 Stay away from deep in the money options.

2 Stay away from deep out of the money options.

3 Trade slightly out of the money, at the money, or slightly in the money options.

4 There is a time for all seasons.

5 Covered call writing is a good strategy for what appears to be a bullish environment, and covered put writing is generally good for what looks like a bear.

6 In 'normal' markets, write straddles and strangles.

7 Look for opportunities to backspread.

8 Use options to hedge a profitable futures position.

Now let's look at these rules in more detail.

Rule 1

Stay away from deep in the money options

The key advantages to buying options are limited risk and high leverage. If an option is too deep in the money, it cuts down on your leverage and adds to your risk. You are paying more, and have more to lose, so even though the risk is limited, the risk is higher. You cut down on leverage since you need a bigger move in the underlying asset to generate a significant profit. The whole idea of leverage is to take a smaller amount of money and have the option to exercise an asset worth many times as much. You tie up a lot of money which can be used for other opportunities.

I don't like selling deep in the money options either. You tie up a considerable amount of capital this way (since you need to margin the position) and you have less time value to capitalize on. The biggest advantage to the option seller is time decay, and with less time value you have less to gain the easy way and more risk with the bigger intrinsic value component. So I stay away from deep in the money options when buying or selling. Of course, the objective is to buy an out of the money, at the money, or slightly in the money option and have it turn into a deep in the money. The objective when selling is to avoid having your sale ever turn into a deep in the money. This is a fast way for your wallet to go deep out of money!

Rule 2
Stay away from deep out of the money options

The illusion is that deep out of the money purchases give you a lot of leverage. In reality they give you a lot of hope, promote over-commitments, and offer very little profit opportunity. Yes, they can hit at times, but this is a game of odds, and the odds are certainly against you when buying deep out of the moneys. You have to be realistic. If the premium appears too cheap there is a reason. Sure, you can buy an August 900 soybean call in July when the beans are at 700 and hope for a crop failure. You could probably buy a lot of them because they would be cheap, maybe two pennies or $100 each is all. Yet given recent history, it would be unlikely, not impossible, but very unlikely for beans to rise $2.00 per bushel in four weeks. The odds are just about zero. In fact, the odds are against this kind of rise in four months. It may make more sense to purchase a deep out of the money option if you have a lot of time, but then again you lose some of the leverage because you pay for time. And, sure the odds are greatly in your favour when you sell deep out of the money options, but the expected reward is minuscule in relation to the risk. You could be profitable 99 times out of 100 when selling deep out of the money put options on the stock market, but that crash will come, and when you least expect it. Unless you wish to be 'the house', the one who is capitalized enough to cover that Powerball lottery or Megabucks jackpot, stay away from deep out of the moneys.

> * *Unless you wish to be 'the house', the one who is capitalized enough to cover that Powerball lottery or Megabucks jackpot, stay away from deep out of the moneys.*

Rule 3

Trade slightly out of the money, at the money, or slightly in the money options

The reasons are the opposite of the reasons I prefer to stay away from the deep options. These have a reasonable chance of proving profitable when buying, you gain from the maximum possible time decay when selling, and they are generally the most liquid of the bunch which results in a tighter bid/asked spread which in turn saves on transaction costs. The one variation on this theme has to do with selling options. In this case it is certainly fine, and even advantageous, to sell out of the money options with this one caveat – the premium received must warrant the risk. What price might this be? There are no hard and fast rules. You just need to use good judgement. It is also advisable to use good judgement when cutting losses. This especially involves taking a reasonable or small loss when covering short options which are not working. However, it is also important to cut losses in long options which aren't making you money. It is human nature and all too easy to become complacent when buying options. I've seen too many people play them out to the end when all the indications say the play isn't working. This is just another form of hope and hope is not a recipe for success. The fact that most options expire worthless should be a strong clue to the buyer to sell out prior to the end in cases of non-performance. It is easy to do this, just pick up the phone, and say 'sell'!

Rule 4

There is a time for all seasons

What I mean by this is that you need to have a feel for market conditions prior to implementing an option strategy. I've known traders who have initial success with one or another strategy and think they've found the holy grail. I met a doctor who was lucky enough to turn $5000 into six figures during the bull corn market of 1996. His first trade was a long shot which worked, the purchase of deep out of the money calls for March which were in the money by expiration. He took the profits and rolled them into at the money Mays which eventually went deep into the money, and once again into Julys that worked. He caught the best kind of market for this strategy, and then proceeded to give most of the profits back in a dull period in a variety of flat markets.

I've also seen people win nine out of ten times selling out of the money calls only to fall flat on their face. In the early 1980s a firm called *Volume Investors* became one of the largest option players in the gold pit by selling premium. It worked beautifully for years. It took just one unexpected yet volatile spike to wipe them out – to the tune of $6 million. The lesson is *know your market*. Option writing can be extremely profitable in dull, flat markets. If the tone changes, cover fast, before that catastrophic loss. If option premiums feel too low to give you an adequate cushion of income they probably are. The common wisdom is to 'sell flat markets', but I suggest this is just the time to start thinking about buying. Avoid selling in periods of rising volatility, however. Option purchases will start to become more expensive, but then the rising volatility will work in the buyer's favour. Should volatility reach wild proportions, then think about selling. Just make sure you are adequately margined to take the heat.

Rule 5

Covered call writing is a good strategy for what appears to be a bullish environment, and covered put writing is generally good for what looks like a bear

This is one of the few strategies where you use futures and options together and have the ability to profit on both legs. The strategy works well in a modestly bullish or bearish environment as well. It is not risk free, but is less risky than the outright purchase or sale of futures alone. Furthermore, by using my limited pyramid strategy discussed in the previous chapter, you additionally have the flexibility to capitalize on a major move using covered positions.

Rule 6

In 'normal' markets, write straddles and strangles

Selling puts and calls works in most market environments. It is a good strategy, as long as it is managed properly. 'Normal' is a term which cannot be defined specifically. All I can tell you is, in most cases the premiums received when writing straddles and strangles give an adequate cushion to weather most storms. When the typhoon hits, however, and your margin is starting to feel impaired, run for the exit door.

Rule 7

Look for opportunities to backspread

This is a seldom used strategy, but when used consistently has the potential to make you rich. Recall, this involves selling a call or put at one strike price, and buying a greater number of calls at a higher strike price, or buying a greater number of puts at a lower strike price. Look to establish backspreads for a credit to benefit from time decay, and look only at markets with the potential to move big. This strategy always has a predetermined and limited risk and is one of the few which can still prove mildly profitable (or at least keep your equity together) when you are dead wrong. The profit is unlimited on a major upside move. It is not the holy grail, and there certainly is risk here as well, but I know of one S&P

option trader who traded only backspreads. He held his equity together quite well over a number of years, and was always positioned for a major move in either direction. During the stock market crash of 1987, his bear backspreads worked so well, he is now retired (and still a young man).

Rule 8

Use options to hedge a profitable futures position

If you are a trend following trader, like me, and are lucky enough to catch a major move which is showing massive unrealized profits, the great dilemma is when to cash in. You know you will inevitably have to give up a large part of the paper gain if you wait for confirmation of a trend change. Yet, top and bottom picking are very hard things to do. There is only one top, and only one bottom in major moves of proportion which could unfold over hundreds of trading sessions. Also, many times, the most important leg of a major move comes in the last 48 hours. Why not use put options to lock in a bull-move profit, and calls for the bear-move profits. Commercial hedgers use options all the time. Trading is a business, and this is your prime tool as an individual trader to hedge your profit while still allowing for additional profits.

For example, you own soybeans in a major drought. You're in at $7 and the market is now $9. There is no rain in the forecast, it's mid-July, and another two weeks of this the old rallying call of 'beans in the teens' will become a reality. Options aren't cheap, but this is the type of situation I would buy premium anyway. The $9 August calls are running 40¢. Buy 'em. This is a no-lose situation. Cheap insurance at 40¢, yet you assure yourself a $1.60 profit per contract, $8000 per contract and not all bad.

Plus, this is insurance you hope you never need to use – let the good times roll if the forecasts prove correct. They're not always correct, as I've found out. During the drought of 1988, not one weather service I know of called the end. It was the long 4 July weekend, and when we went home on Friday it was over 100 degrees Fahrenheit with 'no chance of meaningful precipitation for at least two weeks'. Soybeans were approaching $11 with 'beans in the teens' a virtual certainty. It stayed hot and dry Saturday and Sunday with not a cloud in the sky. Then, seemingly out of nowhere, on Monday afternoon, with the markets closed the skies opened. It poured over a wide area, and we were greeted with a multiple limit-down situation beginning with our return Tuesday at the open. 'If I had only' used puts to lock in the significant paper profits. If I did, and it turned out to be a mistake, it would have been the kind of mistake we like to make. On the other hand,

> *** Buying options to lock in profits on futures is the best way I know of to avoid premature profitakingitis. This affects us all at one time or another.**

buying options to lock in profits on futures is the best way I know of to avoid premature profitakingitis. This affects us all at one time or another.

These are wonderful tools, these options: not a panacea, but to a major extent they can offer the best of both worlds. Constantly be on the alert for ways to use them to your benefit!

How to analyze the markets fundamentally

There are two basic ways to analyze the markets: *fundamental analysis* and *technical analysis*. Both the fundamentalist and the technician are trying to solve the same problem – that is to predict future price movement – but they approach this thorny problem in different ways.

Fundamental analysis

Fundamental analysis is the study of supply and demand. The cause and effect of price movement is explained by supply and demand.

For example, if copper new mine production is 300,000 tons, manufacturing demand is projected to be 400,000 tons and 'above-ground' supplies available to the market are 50,000 tons, the fundamentalist will conclude there is a projected supply *deficit* of 50,000 tons.

Therefore, price must rise to 'ration' or diminish this impossible level of demand. Fundamental analysis appeals to our logic. After all, if there is drought in Brazil during the flowering phase of the soybean plant you can rationally explain why bean prices are rising. A good fundamentalist will be able to forecast a major price move well in advance of the technician. However, many fundamentalists have what amounts to 'inside information' (and this is perfectly legal in the futures markets). If Cargill has a scout in Ghana who identifies a cocoa-killing fungus which is devastating the crop, odds are Cargill will be acting on this information long before you or I hear about it.

> *✱ A good fundamentalist will be able to forecast a major price move well in advance of the technician.*

Fundamentalists have the ability to trade the courage of their convictions, and as such will not be shaken out as easily during false market movements. They will be better able emotionally to maximize positions, because fundamentals can take a long time to change. In late 1995, with corn trading in the mid-two dollar range, I read that China (formerly the third largest corn exporter and the largest in Asia) had turned into a corn importer. Apparently their livestock production had grown at a rate that could not keep pace with their reduced crop production of that year. In my mind, this was a significant fundamental which was a major reason why corn prices were able to hit all-time record highs within a six-month period. No doubt, fundamentals can be powerful and will allow a trader to stay with a position longer than he otherwise might. However, they also can prompt a trader to stay with a position longer than he should.

Technical analysis

A technician is concerned with market action only. The basic issue is not that fundamentals move price, the technician concedes this. The technician believes it is impossible to know all the fundamentals that affect price at any given time. Or, by the time the news reaches most of us it is already known by some, or disseminated so widely that it has been discounted in price. Since you make or lose money via price movements, this is what should be studied. Another way of putting it is that the technician believes price is the ultimate fundamental.

In early 1997 corn was back to the 1995 lows in the mid-250 range. It was there because the fundamentals were decidedly bearish. Supply was way up, a 1 billion bushel carryover was projected. The livestock numbers were way down. Exports were falling and, yes, China had once again turned into a corn exporter. However, the market had traced out a technical 'bottom formation', and the commodity funds bought and bought. One day in February they bought 100 million bushels. Many of the commodity funds trade technically. It seemed they all saw the same price action at the same time and acted on it. The 100 million bushel purchase pushed prices higher, the fundamentals aside. The higher prices attracted more technical buying, which hit price stops above the market. Shorts could not meet margin calls and had to cover their positions, which meant more buying. The commercials were selling into the market, but the funds bought more as additional price objectives were hit. In a four-day period, the funds added another 150 million bushels to their initial purchases. Prices soared by 50¢/bushel or over 20 per cent. Farmers started to notice prices were rising and began to hold back on their cash corn sales as they started to get bullish and wait for higher prices. This was a case where a technical move actually resulted in the fundamentals changing (that is a restriction of supply due to less farmer selling). Eventually, the market fell of its own weight, but there is no denying you could have made a nice profit in a case like this by ignoring the fundamentals and just listening to the sounds of the market.

In some ways, technical analysis can be said to include fundamentals. The reverse is not true: a pure fundamentalist does not look at charts. The best fundamentalist will make the most money, but he also will lose the most if he misses something. In the 1970s there was a phenomenal pork belly trader who over time amassed a fortune amounting to several hundred million dollars. When short-term interest rates started their rise from 4 per cent to 10 per cent, he started to short T-Bill futures under the fundamental belief that rates at this level were not sustainable. By the time they reached 18 per cent, he was broke. He was ultimately right, but not before he lost all his money.

Which is the best way to go?

Correct fundamental analysis will make you money; so will a good technical plan. In either case, a good forecaster can go broke if he is not a good trader. A good trader can make money regardless of whether he can ascertain the correct fundamentals or technical tone of the market. It is my belief that a marriage of the two, combined with a sensible money management plan, will produce the best results over time. In my experience, the best trades come when solid fundamentals (as we see them) agree with the technical action of the marketplace. In the following two chapters we will explore the idiosyncrasies of the technical world.

> ✳ Correct fundamental analysis will make you money; so will a good technical plan.

However, since we need to know what it is we're trading (although I know a soybean trader who had not seen a soybean until after he had spent his third successful year in the pit), we'll first delve into a brief overview of the fundamentals inherent in the major markets we will be trading. I am not trying to tell you that this brief introduction will make a good fundamental trader of anyone. I am simply giving the potential speculator background information about the relevant industries as a starting point. I suggest as the next step, you contact the exchange for the market you are most interested in trading. They all provide detailed and in many cases free literature on the markets they list. The exchange internet websites are good too.

There are hundreds of exchange-listed futures contracts in the world, and most of them have liquid options markets as well. We do not have the space to cover them all in this book. Some do not trade very actively, and some are so specialized they should be left to those who know. So we won't be covering cheddar cheese, or tiger shrimp, raw silk or dried cocoon (which is listed on both the Chubu Commodity Exchange and the Manila International Futures Exchange). Rather, I've arranged the major futures markets into four basic groupings:

- financial futures;
- energy;

■ agriculturals;

■ metals.

Financial futures include three major subsets: the interest rate futures, the stock indices, and the currencies. The agriculturals include the grains, the meats and the softs. The metals are classified as either industrial or precious. For any of the markets you have an interest in trading I encourage you to contact the exchange where that particular market is traded and ask for additional information. Your commodity broker can also help.

Financial futures

The highest volume futures and options contracts are not the traditional physical commodities, they are financial futures. After all, money is the ultimate commodity, wouldn't you say?

Financial futures can roughly be broken down into three basic sections: interest rates, stock indices and currencies. Many of the same basic fundamentals that affect one group affect the others. Obviously, interest rates affect stock prices and currency valuations. In fact, interest rates are perhaps the most important fundamental which move stock markets and currencies.

Interest rates

The reason governments allow interest rate futures to exist is so that hedgers can neutralize or shift some of their price risks. A mortgage banker can transfer his price risk to a speculator, just as a corporate comptroller can lock in his cost of borrowing funds. The best way to think of any hedge is to regard it as a temporary substitute for a transaction which will happen at a later time in another market. When talking about interest rates, some hedgers are interested in protecting against higher rates in the future, and some lower. Speculators are trying to profit from the inherent risks in changes in the cost of money.

> ✱ *The best way to think of any hedge is to regard it as a temporary substitute for a transaction which will happen at a later time in another market.*

Of course, in a multinational economy rates can be moving in one direction in Japan and another in the UK. The fundamentals that move interest rates, and therefore interest rate futures, are varied and dynamic. Human emotion is just as important a fundamental, as are credit flows. Below is a list of the major interest rate contracts traded in the world today, and a brief summary of some of the major fundamentals the trader should be aware of. Be aware, whole books have been written on how fundamental factors affect the economy and interest rates. I am not trying to imply my list is all inclusive, and frankly I do not believe any mortal can factor in all the variables which will affect interest rates. Rather, I want to give you a taste for what I have found are the most important factors. If you feel you want to use fundamental analysis to forecast bond or bill futures, you will have a basis from which to delve further.

There are over sixty interest rate contracts traded around the world: everything from one-day swaps, to Euroyen, Euroswiss and Long Gilts. You can speculate and/or hedge interest rates in numerous currencies, lengths of maturities and varieties. Below find the largest and most active of the interest rate futures contracts. All of these have active and liquid options.

Treasury Bonds and Treasury Notes

Futures have been traded on commodity exchanges for over one hundred years. The first interest rate futures contract was introduced in 1975. Today, the two highest volume futures contracts in the world are both interest rate futures, and the top spot most years belongs to the US Treasury Bond (although in recent years the Eurodollar contract has at times captured the number one ranking), traded at the Chicago Board of Trade (CBOT). It can at times account for up to a quarter of all the US futures traded. Treasury Bonds futures are designed to reflect prices of longer term interest rates (such as mortgage rates) and are based on a hypothetical 6 per cent bond of at least fifteen years in length. The contract is based on a security with a face value (par amount) of $100,000; 10-year and 5-year T-Notes futures and options also rank consistently in the top 20 in terms of volume.

Bond prices are a mirror image of interest rates. When interest rates rise, bond prices fall and vice versa. Prices are quoted in 32nds of 100 per cent. A minimum fluctuation is $\frac{1}{32}$, with a full point move ($\frac{32}{32}$) having a value of $1000. Do not confuse a full point move in the T-Bond price with a full point interest rate move. It takes roughly an 8- or 9-point futures move (depending on price) to equal a full percentage point move in the yield of US Treasury Bonds.

Eurodollars

Yields reflect interest rates in various money market investments. It goes without saying that the yield on a short-term instrument will in most cases be dramatically different than longer term 'paper'. You will sooner or later hear the term 'yield curve' which measures the relationship of the yields of various securities against their maturities. The two highest volume futures contracts *in the world* are both interest rate futures contracts. In recent years, it is the Eurodollar contract traded at CME which has been top dog. This is based on a short-term – 90-day – debt issue. Technically, a Eurodollar is defined as any US dollar on deposit outside the USA (generally dollar deposits at London branches of major world banks) which therefore fall outside the reserves and other requirements of the Federal Reserve. Actual Eurodollar time deposits are securities which are available in a short-term maturity time frame for either taking or placing deposits. In reality, this market has become the benchmark for short-term interest rate price discovery for shorter term US rates. The *Treasury Bill* contract is also active, and

> ✳ The two highest volume futures contracts in the world are both interest rate futures contacts.

is a good measure of short-term rates, but is not nearly as liquid as the Euro contract. The T-Bill, an obligation of the US government, effectively has no credit risk, and while it will move in the same direction as the Euro, it will move at a different speed. Alas, we have the TED spread which has been discussed in Chapter 3. Other popular spreads involve the NOB (Note vs. Bond), MOB (Municipal Bond versus T-Bond), as well as the Eurodollar versus T-Bond spread.

The Eurodollar price is quoted in terms of an index. The index is based on the difference between the actual Eurodollar (or T-Bill) yield and 100.00.

> **For example, a yield of 5.00 per cent is quoted as 95.00. If yields rise to 5.50 per cent, the index will fall to 94.50 (the difference between 100 and 95.5). The contract size is $1,000,000 but since we are dealing with a 90-day instrument, 1 basis point is worth $25/contract (0.01 of 1.00 percent). So if yields rise by 1 per cent, price will fall by 100 basis points or $2500 per contract (100 points x $25/point).**

Commercial borrowers have various financing needs, which will dictate which market they will use for hedging purposes. Investors have different objectives that will determine which maturity they will wish to be involved in. If interest rates are *rising*, the investor will wish to keep his cash in shorter term issues because the value (or price) of the shorter term instruments will fall less than the longer. If interest rates are *falling*, cash values will grow to a greater degree in the longer term issues because the price of these will grow more than the shorter. Yields are only half the story, the other half being currency values. If you received a 7 per cent yield in a currency which has lost 7 per cent versus your home currency, your effective purchasing power has grown by zippo. Therefore, in this electronic age, money is zapped between instruments of varying maturities, and varying issuers (both governmental and private) as well as varying currencies.

Bund and Bobl

The Bund is the long-term European (formerly German) government bond (about ten years to maturity). Futures on the Bund are the biggest contract at the totally electronic Eurex Exchange based in Frankfurt, and consistently rank close to or at the largest in volume in the world. Approximately half of all Bunds are held by foreigners. They are traded primarily at the Eurex Exchange, with a contract size of 100,000 Euros. 1 point = 10 Euros. The Schatz is a 2-year product and the Bobl is a medium-term government bond (4–5 years in length) based on a hypothetical 5.5 per cent bond with a EUR100,000 size. The Eurex Bund Futures has a daily average contract volume close to 575,000 contracts. Also the Schatz and the

✳ Approximately half of all Bunds are held by foreigners.

Bobl Futures are two of the world's most heavily traded contracts in the 2- and 5-year segments. The average daily trading volume in these contracts is close to 300,000 contracts.

Notional

Consistently the third or fourth largest in volume (the Bund and Euro Notional Bond trade about equally). Traded at Marché à Terme International de France (MATIF) in Paris (also a totally electronic exchange), based on a 10-year fictional bond, with a size EUR100,000 and a 3.5 per cent coupon rate. The MATIF also lists an active Euro 5-year, 2-year E-Note and 3-month Euribor contract which corresponds to a short-term instrument held 65 per cent by foreigners.

Euribor, Euroyen, Euroswiss, 3-month sterling

Traded on Eurex and Liffe with Tiffe (the Tokyo International Financial Futures Exchange) also having a liquid Euroyen, these are the Eurodollar contracts of Europe and Japan. A typical user would be a company exposed to short-term interest rate risk in a particular currency, as well as banks, speculators, market-makers, issuers and foreign exchange traders. Very active, very liquid, they are based on short-term rates for the other major currencies. In fact, at times the Euro rivals the Bund in terms of volume. The 3-month sterling is also commonly referred to as *short sterling*. The contract size is £500,000; 1 point is also 0.01 of 1.00 percent, but the value of a point is £12.50.

The *long gilt* is the major longer term sterling-based contract, traded on Liffe, with a £50,000 value. The minimum fluctuation is $\frac{1}{32}$, like the T-Bond contract, but since the contract size is half (and in pounds sterling) a minimum tick is worth £15.625. They are based on the standard negotiable bonds issued by the British government, which is now the fourth largest government bond market in the world.

These are the major interest rate contracts of the world. Also of note are the following.

- *Spanish interest rate contracts* The Meff Renta Fija, located in Barcelona, trades a liquid 10-year bond and 90-day and 360-day contracts.

- *Swiss government bond* The most important of the Swiss interest rate futures, the contract has a value of CHF100,000 (Swiss francs). It is traded on the Swiss Options & Financial Futures Exchange (SOFFEX). This Zurich-based exchange trades respectable volume, but the open interest levels are comparatively low, indicating commercial participation which is less broad than some.

- *Swedish interest rate contracts* The OM Stockholm AB is the exchange where the major Swedish contracts, both short term and medium term, are traded.

- *Australian interest rate contracts* The Sydney Futures Exchange is where the major Australian contracts are traded. There are liquid 3- and 10-year bond contracts, contract size A$100,000 (Australian dollars), as well an actively traded 90-day bill contract.

■ *Canadian interest rate contracts* The Montreal Exchange has an active 10-year Canadian bond contract with a size of C$100,000 (Canadian dollars), and a bankers acceptance short-term contract with a face value of one million Canadian dollars.

Major fundamentals affecting interest rates

Due to the thousands of variables, it is somewhat difficult to analyze the fundamentals of any major economy. Basically, the trader has to sort through and prioritize the information available. Each country will have its own fundamentals based on internal politics, infrastructure and economic vitality.

All of the major industrialized countries release regular government reports which form the basis of what fundamental analysts and traders use in an attempt to forecast (or guess) how government policy and economic activity will move the markets. The major ones are listed below, along with other fundamental factors I feel are the most important in trading T-Bonds, T-Notes and Eurodollars.

■ *Unemployment* This is one of the most important reports which affects economic activity, and therefore will reflect credit demand and interest rate expectations. Usually released in the beginning of each month, it shows changes in unemployment for the preceding month.

■ *Inflation* Inflation rates are important in forecasting interest rates because inflationary expectations get built into the price of borrowing money. If you loan money out at 10 per cent for 10 years, and the average inflation rate over this period is 10 per cent, your real return is nothing. If the inflation rate is 5 per cent, you have a real return of 5 per cent. If the inflation rate is now 4 per cent, and the market thinks it will remain that way for years to come, then 10-year notes may be priced at 7 per cent by the marketplace, which would yield a real return of 3 per cent. However, if inflation heats up to, say 6 per cent, and the market thinks this will continue, the yield on 10-year notes may rise to 10 per cent, thus depressing T-Note prices and T-Note futures.

Two major US reports, and similar reports in Europe and Asia, reflect inflation rates. The first is the *Producer Price Index*, commonly referred to as the PPI, which measures the cost of materials at the wholesale or producer level; in other words the cost of raw materials purchased by manufacturers. Since higher costs are generally passed on to the consumer this can be a good leading indicator of inflation at the retail level. The second is the *Consumer Price Index*, the CPI, which measures inflation at the personal or consumer level. The basic rule of thumb is increasing rates of inflation lead to higher interest rates as the cost of money increases, and as the government looks to curb inflation and inflationary expectations. In my experience, these two reports are the second most influential reports to which traders pay attention.

- *Crude oil and gold* Many bond traders closely watch the prices of these two important commodities as indicators of inflation which in turn affect interest rate movements.

- *Housing starts* The entire economy is greatly affected on a trickle-down basis by the rate of home construction. This can be a good indicator of the demand for long-term mortgage money and will affect Treasury Bonds to a greater degree than Euros, or the shorter term contracts.

- *Industrial production* This is the level of factory output which can indicate how economic activity, and subsequently the need for credit, is expanding or contracting.

- *Business inventories* This is a good indicator of the degree of future demand for short-term credit by business. Demand for credit to finance inventories could be a reason for higher interest rates. If inventories are low, and the economic activity is picking up, this could also be a leading indicator of rising rates. This number will affect the shorter term contracts more than the longer.

- *Gross domestic product (GDP)* In the USA, and each of the major industrial countries, GDP measures economic growth rates over the entire spectrum. Changes in this regard affect trader expectations and at times have a profound effect on price. However, at other times this report is virtually ignored.

- *Balance of trade* Released monthly, these reports can have a profound effect on the dollar, and at times interest rates as well. A general rule of thumb is a strong dollar is supportive to bond prices. It draws in foreign buying of domestic securities.

- *Retail sales and car sales* For obvious reasons both of these reports give clues as to consumer confidence and liquidity.

- *Disposable income* This is an indicator of the consumer's buying power, another indicator of general economic activity which affects credit demand.

- *Index of leading indicators* This is a government-constructed indicator which is supposed to provide advance warning of the future health of the economy. It is composed of data such as the average work week, layoff rate, new orders for goods, business formations, building permits issued, stock prices, etc. The basic rule of thumb is a falling indicator indicates a weakening economy which will lead to lower rates, and vice versa.

  The reports listed above are all concurrent or lagging indicators, this one is supposed to be leading or predictive. Its accuracy is in question in my mind. However, this may not matter as the release of an unexpected number here can affect prices *now*, regardless of whether it proves true in the future or not.

▦ *Debt offerings*   As the supply of new securities offerings increases, either by the government's need for money or private financing, the price of all these securities is hurt to a degree. This is generally a short-term factor. The future supply of new issues is published in the *Wall Street Journal* and *Financial Times*.

▦ *Federal Reserve*   The Federal Reserve is the central bank of the USA, and the most influential in the world. The central banks of the other major industrialized nations (such as the Bundesbank in Germany) act in much the same way, and they all have a profound effect on interest rate policy and can move markets. It seems at times that the chairman of the Fed can sneeze and the bond market will fall 16 ticks.

The Fed can purchase or sell government securities. When it sells securities it reduces bank reserves, and therefore the supply of money available for lending. In a roundabout way this reduces the available funds for credit and interest rates should rise as a result. The purchase of securities has the opposite effect.

Traders can read the minutes of the Federal Reserve's Open Market Committee (FOMC). The Committee meets monthly to discuss economic conditions and establish US interest rate policy. One drawback is that these reports are not issued until a month after the meeting; however Fed policy does not usually change on a whim. They gradually affect interest rate movements over a period of time.

The Fed (other major central banks operate in much the same way) can affect interest rate movements in a variety of ways; one of the most important is setting the *discount rate*. The discount rate is the interest rate the Fed charges to banks that borrow from it. A commercial bank that is short on reserves because of high loan demand may need to borrow from the Fed. The Fed can set the discount rate wherever it wants, and by raising this rate it makes it less attractive for commercial banks to borrow. They will in turn raise the rates charged to their customers (consumers and businesses) and as the price of credit goes up, generally the demand for credit goes down. Many times, the market will anticipate a change in the discount rate since the writing is on the wall. I've seen many examples of this in the marketplace. The price of bond futures may be falling for weeks in anticipation of a rise in the discount rate, and the day the news is announced, the bonds will spike down but then close higher on the day. This often confuses novice traders. How can bonds close higher on a day the discount rate is raised? Basically it is already 'discounted' in price.

The Fed (all central banks) will change the discount rate only rarely. However, they are engaged in daily activities which also affect rates. If you trade interest rate futures, you will sooner or later hear the term 'The Fed is doing repos.' Repos are repurchase agreements, which is a transaction involving the sale of a security with an agreement to repurchase at a stated price in the future. In effect, it is a short-term loan. When the Fed is doing repos it is lending money which increases reserves. This is generally a sign of easier monetary policy, or lower rates. Reverse repos are the opposite, where the Fed is in effect decreasing reserves; a sign of tighter money and higher interest rates.

■ *Fed funds rate* This is an interest rate charged among banks for reserves they lend to each other. If the Fed believes this rate is running too high or too low they may enter the market to buy or sell government securities which will affect reserves and therefore the Fed funds rate. The Fed funds rate can change daily, and at times many times in a day. Many traders feel this is one of the most influential determinants of Fed policy and resulting interest rate movements.

■ *Money supply* These figures are released weekly. At times, they are closely watched and an important determinant of futures prices. Other times, they are on the back burner. It all depends on the 'flavour of the week' and what traders seem to be focusing on at the time. M1 measures cheque accounts, cash; basically money available for ready spending. M2 and M3 measure other deposits which are less readily available.

So, which is the most important fundamental to watch? They are all important, and none of them is important. The problem is, no single economic indicator will always dominate the market. They change. At any one time the market seems to focus on certain indicators as the dominant movers, but this changes over time. In the early 1980s, I remember the weekly money supply figures were closely watched and anticipated with glee or dread, as they were certain to move the market in the coming session. Now, they are only looked at by the most die-hard fundamentalists. In the future, perhaps they will rise to prominence again.

Stock indices

There used to be an old Wall Street maxim that went something like this: 'Well, you can't buy the averages.' Well, this just ain't true anymore, now you can. As a speculator, if you have an opinion on the market in general, as opposed to any individual stock, you can buy or short the whole market, or market groups, by buying or selling the futures contracts, or options, on specific indices. As a private investor, there is a way for you to temporarily protect against market declines, or 'lock in' portfolio profits without having to sell good dividend paying stocks that are part of your longer term investment goals. Too many of the 'nouveau stock buyers', that vast group who starting investing in stocks in the early 1980s, at the beginning of the most recent historic rise, are oblivious to one simple fact. The history of markets

> ✳ *There used to be an old Wall Street maxim that went something like this: 'Well, you can't buy the averages.' Well, this just ain't true anymore, now you can.*

has demonstrated that there has never been a bull market which has not come to an end at some point. When the bull falters, the bear will take over and reign supreme for his tenure before the bull rises again.

Stock index futures and/or options can be likened to 'bear market insurance', and this is a classic hedge. I've counted over 70 listed stock index futures contracts on 20 different exchanges. Below is a listing of the major stock indices traded today. All of these have active and liquid options.

S&P 500 Index

This is the daddy of all the stock indices in terms of volume, capitalization and liquidity. Traded on the Chicago Mercantile Exchange (CME), the S&P 500 represents the 500 biggest US stocks which account for about 80 per cent of total US shares traded. It is a weighted index which is composed roughly of 400 industrial companies, 40 utilities, 20 transportation companies and 40 financial companies. It is 'weighted' since a bigger company will carry proportionately greater weight in the index. The value of a contract is 500 times the index. In other words, if the index is trading at 800, the value of the contract is $200,000 (250 × 800 = 200,000). For every 'full point', say a move from 799 to 800, or 799 to 798, the contract will gain or lose $250, as will the buyer or seller of each contract. The S&P is one of the day trader's favourites, since it is *extremely* volatile with major price swings almost every day. As we go to press, the average price swing in the S&P futures is 2000 points, which represents a $5000 average daily move from top to bottom. A volatile day can easily be two or three times this. Due to this volatility, the margin requirements are fairly high to hold an overnight position. Day trading margins are generally much smaller, but you are always obligated for the difference between your entry and exit. This goes without saying. In other words, if you lose, you must pay by the end of the day.

> ✱ *The S&P is one of the day trader's favourites, since it is extremely volatile with major price swings almost every day.*

Value Line

This index, traded at the Kansas City Board of Trade, was actually the first one on the market, introduced in 1982. It represents the 1700 'Value Line' US blue chip and second tier stocks which is considered to be a broader measure of the market as a whole. The problem is this is just about the least liquid of the major indices, with volume running on average less than 1 per cent of the S&P.

NASDAQ 100

This is one of the fastest growing of the exchange-listed index contracts, and is based on the NASDAQ top 100 US stocks, mostly 'hi-tech, bio-tech', dot coms, and the like. Unlike the other indices, the value of this contract is 100 times the index, and a full point is worth plus or minus $100. The index can be volatile, often with a 100-point daily or greater range, and is the most volatile and risky of all futures contracts many days.

Emini Nasdaq and Emini S&P

The Emini S&P and Nasdaq are totally electronic (unlike their big brothers): $\frac{1}{5}$ the size of the big ones, $\frac{1}{5}$ the margin requirements, $\frac{1}{5}$ the risk and two of the fastest growing of all futures contracts.

FTSE 100

The London Financial Futures Exchange (LIFFE) is the world's third largest and fastest growing exchange. The Financial Times–Stock Exchange Index, commonly called the 'Footsie', has a value of £25.25 per index point. For example, at 3000, the value is £75,750. It is based on the top 100 companies by market capitalization, represents 72 per cent of the UK equity market, and is weighted like the S&P.

Bovespa

The volume figures from the Bolsa de Mercadorias & Futuros Exchange (BM&F), Brazil's major stock index, looks huge, but this can be deceiving as the contract sizes are small.

Nikkei 225

This most recognized of all Japanese stock indices trades on the CME, the Osaka Securities Exchange (OSE), and the Singapore International Monetary Exchange (SIMEX). The most liquid is probably the SIMEX (this is where Nick Leeson had his troubles trading for Barings bank), but the other two are definitely tradeable. The contract size is ¥500 times the index.

IBEX35

The Meff Renta Variable, located in Madrid, is the home of the IBEX35, the most important Spanish index.

Swiss Market Index

Traded at the Swiss Options & Financial Futures Exchange (SOFFEX), located in Zurich.

Hang Seng

High volume contract, traded at the Hong Kong Futures Exchange.

DAX

Traded on the Frankfurt-based EUREX, a very liquid electronic exchange that at times has been the volume champion. The DAX option is the most liquid Eurex index contract, with an average daily trading volume of close to 150,000 contracts. The Dow Jones Euro STOXXSM50 and the Dow Jones STOXXSM50 track the European Stock Market. The last two are also traded at the Matif. The Stoxx 50 represent 50 blue chip stocks, over 35 per cent of the capitalization of the Euro zone.

CAC40

Located in Paris, the Marché à Terme International de France (MATIF) trades the very liquid, very active CAC40. The contract size is 200 times the index.

OMX

The major Swedish stock index, the OMX, is traded at OM Stockholm AB (OMS).

EOE

The major Dutch index, it is traded at the European Options Exchange (EOE) based in Amsterdam.

All Ordinaries Share Price Index

The leading Australian index is traded at the Sydney Futures Exchange (SFE). The contract size is Australian dollars 25 times the index.

These are the major exchange listed contracts, but for those interested there are additional exchanges listing both stock index and interest rate contracts in Austria, Belgium, Chile, Denmark, Finland, Hungary, Israel, Italy, New Zealand, Norway, the Philippines and South Africa.

One additional point: unlike many of the physical commodities, the stock index and currency futures are routinely cash settled. What this means is that, at delivery time, there is a cash transaction only. The buyers and sellers trade cash credits and debits in their accounts based on the difference between the 'spot' or index price and the settlement or closing price of the futures contract. There is no need to make or take delivery or a 'basket of stocks'.

How can S&P put options be used to protect a portfolio?
While option prices change and will be different as you read this, as I'm writing, a 60-day S&P *put* option, which allows the buyer to sell the S&P 500 index (500 biggest stocks representing over 80 per cent of the US market) at today's market price (called an 'at the money' put) is trading for approximately $7000. At current values this represents about a 2.3 per cent move in the market. One put protects 250 times the index. In other words, if the index is at 1200, an at the money put will 'protect' a $300,000 stock portfolio (250 × 1200 = 300,000) for a 2-month period. The option gives the buyer the right, but no obligation, to sell the S&P 500. It will increase in value by at least $250 (minus the purchase price) for every point the S&P falls (a point is a move from say 1200 to 1199 – very roughly equal to 10 Dow points). It can be sold prior to

expiration. If prices rise by expiration the purchase price and commission will be lost, but no additional funds would ever be required. Remember, this is a hedge and if you 'lose' on the put, hopefully your stock portfolio rose. If the market falls by about 2.3 per cent, you'll get your purchase price (in this example the $7000) back. In other words you're protecting your portfolio from a fall of *greater* than 2.3 per cent. If the market falls by a greater percentage, you will lose on your portfolio but gain on the put option. If the market falls by 10 per cent the option will be worth, approximately, 120 points or $30,000.

Why not just sell your stocks? For long-term investors cautious of a market dip, this is cheaper and easier. Selling $300,000 worth of stocks would involve numerous and costly commissions. The commission on one S&P option will generally be less than $90. Plus, you need not forgo dividend income on your stocks, pay capital gains on stock sales, and if your portfolio outperforms the market in general you will have a relationship gain.

Major stock market fundamentals

An owner of a single stock participates in the profitability and the risks of that particular company. An index trader is not concerned with the vagaries of any particular company, but the actions of the market as a whole. Mega market moving fundamentals are as follows:

- general economic activity
- interest rates
- inflationary expectations
- political considerations
- investor attitudes

Let's face it, any one thing or any one thousand things could affect the stock market on any particular day: war, a leader's death, an interest rate hike, a major company's earnings. Any and all the factors mentioned above as fundamental considerations for the interest rate markets also will affect the equity markets. The stock markets of the world can move together. However, any one market can certainly move opposite the pack based on internal considerations. One thing seems clear and that is that attitudes and economic trends tend to last for a while. Therefore the major trends of the stock market tend to last for a while. It's those minor trends that can kill you, or make you rich.

> ✳ Let's face it, any one thing or any one thousand things could affect the stock market on any particular day.

Currencies

The very first financial futures contracts were the foreign currency contracts. It should be noted that the spot (or forward market) is much bigger than the futures. The forward market, or Interbank market, is dominated by currency dealers at major global banks. Traded electronically and by telephone, the spot market's volume towers over the listed exchange volume. However, this vehicle is not available to the average investor. The average 'unit' is one million dollars worth. While currencies can be traded at retail-type outlets, the only major leveraged exchange-listed contracts are traded in Chicago at the IMM (International Monetary Division of the CME). Since this book is geared towards the average investor, it is these contracts which we will discuss. They are quite liquid, and the active ones are listed in Table 7.1.

Table 7.1 Major exchange-listed currency contracts

Currency	Contract size
Euro	EUR125,000
Yen	¥12,500,000
Swiss franc	SF125,000
British pound	£62,500
Dollar index	$1000 x index (traded at the FINEX division of NYBOT)
Canadian dollar	C$100,000
Mexican peso	MP500,000
Australian dollar	A$100,000
French franc	FF500,000 (not as actively traded)

Major currency fundamentals

The price of a currency is determined in the same way as the price of any other commodity. Currency users have risks. If a currency depreciates in value, and a manufacturer is to receive this currency in payment for a product he will deliver six months hence, he loses money. If unhedged, his entire profit margin could be wiped out. If the people in the USA demand more Japanese-made goods, the demand for the yen goes up in relation to the dollar, and Americans will have to pay higher prices to induce holders of yen to sell. If interest rates go up in Germany in relation to the UK, the Euro will look relatively more attractive as an investment than the British pound. The major fundamentals are:

- *Trade balances* This is probably the most important determinant of a currency's value. It is imports and exports. If imports are greater than exports there is a trade deficit. If exports are greater than imports, there is a surplus. A shift in the trade balance between two countries will tend to weaken the currency of the country with the greater deficit.

- *Wealth* A country's reserves, in the form of gold, cash, natural resources and the like (basically any factor which will affect a country's ability to repay loans, finance imports and affect investment) will affect the market's perception of its currency and the currency's value.

▨ *Internal budget deficit or surplus* A country which runs a current account deficit will on balance have a weaker currency than one which runs a budget surplus. This is tricky, however, in that the *direction* of the surplus or deficit will affect perceptions and currency valuations as well. Even though the USA continued to run a major 4 trillion dollar deficit in the late 1990s, the US dollar appreciated since the perception was that the deficit was shrinking.

▨ *Interest rates* Funds move around the world electronically in response to changes in short-term interest rates. If 3-month interest rates in Germany are running 1 per cent less than 3-month rates in the USA, then all other things being equal, 'hot money' will flow out of the Euro into the dollar.

▨ *Inflation* In each country, as well as inflationary expectations, this will affect currency values. What good is a 10 per cent short-term rate in some country if inflation is running 15 per cent?

▨ *Political factors* Taxes, stability, whatever affects the international trade of a country, or the perception of 'soundness' of the currency, will affect its valuation.

▨ *Central bank intervention* Intervention to support (or not support) a currency is definitely a market moving factor. At times, a country can move alone to support its currency, and at times there is an orchestrated group effort to support some currency. The central banks are huge, but not always bigger than the speculative community. If the ultimate fundamentals are opposed to artificial support, a currency can still move contrary to the wishes of the central bank. This was demonstrated when Soros was able to break the back of the British pound and successfully challenge the Bank of England in the late 1980s. He profited to the tune of $2billion.

As you can see, some of these factors are subjective, while some are hard to predict in advance. Ultimately, capital flows are the major fundamental which will determine what a currency is worth, and these are determined by the consensus of the traders of the world. Technical analysis, which will be discussed at length later, is in my view a more efficient means of evaluating a currency's worth than the fundamentals, which can be contradictory and confusing at times.

Energy

There are two major energy exchanges. The International Petroleum Exchange of London trades an active Brent Crude Oil and a Gasoil (heating oil) contract. The predominant exchange, however, is the New York Mercantile Exchange based in New York.

When I first entered the business, a part of my training programme at Merrill Lynch was a tour of the exchange floor. The New York exchanges are housed in the same building. After touring the wild and woolly COMEX (where the metals are traded, now a wholly owned division of the NYMEX), we passed a pit with four or five 'traders', not one of which was shouting out bids or offers (in fact a few of them were reading the paper). We were told this was the NYMEX, the 'poor man's exchange', also called the 'Potato Exchange', where platinum was the major contract (we really didn't know what that was at that time), and potatoes were thinly traded due to a delivery default. They also had a 'boneless beef' contract which, on a good day, traded 50 lots. You could have bought a seat for $2000, but then the $100/month dues made this appear to be a losing deal. But they had the foresight and good fortune to register their #2 Heating Oil contract with the CFTC, and start trading it in 1978. Now this is one of the world's major exchanges and you can't buy a seat for under $500,000. (Oh, if we only knew in those 'poor man' days and had picked up a few of those cheap seats.)

Crude oil

Crude oil is the world's largest cash commodity in terms of dollars (the annual value exceeds $500 billion) and volume. In fact, 20 per cent of the world's entire trade is in oil (only money and its derivatives are bigger). The NYMEX has a light sweet crude contract, which in many years is the highest volume non-interest rate futures contract traded. Light, sweet crudes are preferred by refiners due to a low-sulphur content. Most of the world's supply is sour (high sulphur) crude, but since the sulphur content varies widely, the NYMEX contract, based on West Texas Intermediate, has become the pace setter for world oil prices in general. Brent crude, traded on the IPE, is also liquid and active, a bit less than half the volume of the sweet crude. Both are 1000 barrel contracts. Four countries (all OPEC members) – Saudi Arabia, Iran, Kuwait and Iraq – control more than 50 per cent of the world's proven reserves. The USA is the world's second largest producer (after Saudi Arabia), but since it uses over 35 per cent of the world's output is a net importer. The CIS (former Soviet states) is just behind the USA, followed by Iran. Other major producers include (in order of importance): China (also an importer), Mexico, Venezuela, UK (with its North Sea fields), Nigeria and Canada. Prices are quoted in dollars and cents per barrel, with a 1 penny move equal to plus or minus $10/contract. When Saudi Arabia promised to open the spigots, prices fell under $10/barrel in April of 1986. Less than five years later prices topped $40/barrel as Saddam Hussein invaded Kuwait.

> ✳ Crude oil is the world's largest cash commodity in terms of dollars (the annual value exceeds $500 billion) and volume.

Heating oil

The NYMEX heating oil contract is, many times, the second most liquid energy contract, although in recent years it has been overshadowed to an extent by natural gas. It is also known as No. 2 fuel oil and accounts for about 25 per cent of the yield of a barrel of crude. This contract is also used by hedgers of diesel fuel and jet fuel which are both chemically similar to heating oil. There is additionally an active gasoil contract at the IPE. The contract size is 42,000 gallons and a 1¢ move is equal to a profit or loss of $420. When the crude fell under $10 in 1986, the 'heat' (as they call it on the floor) briefly broke the 30¢/gallon mark. When Saddam was in Kuwait, the price broke above $1.00/gallon.

Unleaded gasoline

The major transportation commodity, futures prices may look cheap to you, but they are based on the wholesale price for delivery at the New York harbour. The price you pay at the pump has all those costs on top to get it to the station, not the least of which are all those local and national taxes. This is by far the most important product, and accounts for almost half of the yield from a barrel of crude. The contract size is also 42,000 gallons, with a 1¢ move (100 points) equal to a profit or loss of $420/contract. When crude broke under $10, gasoline futures hit 30¢. Prices briefly hit $1.11 during the Gulf War.

Natural gas

For many years US natural gas prices were subject to government price controls, and it has only been recently that the chains were broken. The contract started trading in 1990 and is now mature and liquid and one of the fastest growing of all commodity contracts. Industry uses about a third of all natural gas produced, with home use a quarter, and utilities the balance. There is a 50-year supply of natural gas under the ground and it is virtually 'free' to tap, except that it costs money to transport and store with middleman profits in between. The contract size is 10,000 MMBtu (Million British thermal units) with price quoted in dollars and cents per MMBtu. Prices were about a dollar in 1992, and above $4.00 during the winter of 1997 when it was freezing cold in both North America and Europe, and again over $4.00 during the hot summer of 2000.

Major energy fundamentals

Twenty-five years ago, seven major oil companies owned 50 per cent of the world's oil reserves and produced two thirds of its crude and products. Today, these same seven own less than 10 per cent, and produce less than a third of the products. OPEC is still a factor, but no longer the major price setter. The major price setter is now the marketplace. The following factors are important and must be considered in any fundamental analysis of the energy markets.

■ *Weather*   Watch the winter weather particularly. The winter of 1989–90 is a classic. In November of 1989 heating oil was trading at 57¢/gallon. The day the January 1990 contract went off the board it hit $1.10. This was the coldest December in a century. The winter of 1996–7 was one of the coldest on record in the Midwestern USA where natural gas is the primary energy source for residential heating. Prices of natural gas soared from $2.00 to an all-time record high of over $4.00 in record time. In 2000 they hit $5.50.

■ *Seasonality*   It gets cold in the winter and warm in the summer, but one of the most reliable seasonal tendencies is not what you might expect. In our research, over 80 per cent of the time heating oil makes a bottom in March, rising in price into May; so does gasoline (which logically makes more sense due to inventory building prior to the peak summer driving season).

■ *API reports*   The American Petroleum Institute (API) releases a weekly report, usually out Tuesday afternoon after the close of the markets, which reports supply and demand figures for crude and the products. They are widely anticipated by the industry and many times will move the ACCESS (electronic overnight markets) prior to next day's open.

■ *AGA reports*   The American Gas Association (AGA) releases a weekly report which measures changes in stock levels for natural gas. These numbers are important for any NG trader.

■ *Politics*   Oil is a strategic commodity, as well as an economic necessity. The Arab Oil embargo, the Iranian hostage crisis, the Iran–Iraq War, and the Gulf War are just four examples of how politics can dramatically affect the price of oil.

■ *OPEC*   While OPEC is not as important as it once was, it still can be at times. The members of OPEC include Saudi Arabia, Iran, Kuwait, Iraq, UAE, Venezuela, Indonesia, Nigeria, Algeria, Libya, Gabon and Qatar. If they collectively make a decision to increase production to meet world demand, or decrease it because they perceive prices to be too low, it will react. In October of 1985, King Fahd of Saudi Arabia said he would increase production, and he did. Prices were then at $31/barrel. Less than five months later they broke below $10.

Agriculturals

Grains and soybeans

Soybeans
Our British friends call and spell them soyabeans, and they were mentioned in ancient Chinese records prior to 2000 BC. Now the USA is the world's largest producer, accounting for about 50 per cent of the world's output. Prior to the 1980s, the USA accounted for 80 per cent, but Carter's grain embargo prompted the

Japanese, who were looking for a more reliable supplier, to fund the Brazilian soybean industry. Now fully 40 per cent of the world's production is grown in South and Central America, primarily Brazil and Argentina, with Paraguay important as well. China accounts for most of the rest of the world's production, but remains an importer of soymeal most years. Called the miracle crop, it is used in thousands of applications, primarily 'crushed' for meal (used as an animal protein feed) and oil (for human consumption and as a cooking oil). This is one of the major commodities traded at the world's largest exchange, the Chicago Board of Trade. It is generally the most volatile of all the grains (although technically it is not a grain but a legume, also known as an oilseed). The contract size is 5000 bushels, with prices quoted in dollars and cents per bushel. So a 1¢ move is worth $50 per contract. There is a limit the price can move up or down in a typical day which is 50¢. There is no limit in the spot month.

> ✱ *Called the miracle crop [the soybean] is used in thousands of applications.*

Soybean meal

The richest protein source of all the oilseeds, soybean meal is a feedstuff suited for cattle, hogs and poultry. One bushel of soybeans weighs about 60 pounds and will yield about 48 pounds of meal. Of US production 70 per cent is used domestically, with the balance exported. A contract's size is 100 short tons (2000 pounds per ton) with prices quoted in dollars and cents per ton. A one dollar move equals plus or minus $100 per contract, and there is a limit up or down which is $20 a day. There is no limit in the spot month.

Soybean oil

The other major 'product' of the soybean, the oil contract is sized at 60,000 pounds. One bushel of beans produces about 11 pounds of oil. This is an edible vegetable oil, and competes in the world market with other edible oils such as palm, peanut, canola, corn, olive, sunflower, peanut and even fats such as lard. Prices are quoted in cents per pound, with a 100 point, or 2¢ move equal to a profit or loss of $1200 per contract. There is no limit in the spot month.

Canola

The major oilseed grown in Canada, this also is the most active of all the contracts traded on the tiny Winnipeg Commodity Exchange. A contract is for 100 tons; however they trade 'job lots' of 20 tons as well. Canola, the oil of choice among the health conscious, will generally move in the same direction as soybeans, albeit at different speed.

Palm oil

This is the world's second most heavily produced vegetable oil, and is traded in Malaysia. Production is dominated by Malaysia and Indonesia. Palm oil competes directly with soybean oil and canola, but generally trades at a discount due to health concerns over saturated fat in tropical oils. Palm oil is attractive to countries with expanding, low-income populations.

Corn

Traditionally the most active of all the grain contracts, corn is the major US grown crop. In recent years in excess of 80 million acres have been planted annually in the USA, producing crops that can exceed 9 billion bushels in a good year, accounting for one-half of the world's production. The USA consumes 70 per cent of its crop domestically (90 per cent used to feed animals) with the balance exported. The limit move is 20¢.

> ✳ *Traditionally the most active of all the grain contracts, corn is the major US grown crop.*

Oats

The oat market is generally a slower moving, thinner market than the other CBT grains. This is the only major crop which the USA imports, primarily from the Scandinavian countries, Argentina and Canada. There are two major varieties of oats – milling quality (used in oatmeal and other forms for human consumption) and feed oats. The contract, also for 5000 bushels, tends to act more like a feed contract based on the delivery specifications which favours delivery of lower quality oats. A 1¢ move/bushel equals plus or minus $50/contract. The allowable limit, like corn, is also 20¢ per bushel. Some traders believe the oats futures are a *leading indicator* of corn and wheat prices; that is oats will tend to move up or down prior to a move in the others.

Wheat CBT

Wheat is the 'staff of life' and grown in over 80 countries. The USA, the CIS, Canada, China and India are the major producing countries. The Chicago Board of Trade contract is the highest volume contract in the world. The deliverable grade is soft red wheat, used for cakes, pastries and cereals. This is grown in the area around Southern Illinois and Missouri. It is interesting to note that the Kansas City and Minneapolis varieties are deliverable on the Chicago contract. However, since they generally trade at a premium price and there are freight considerations, this does not happen very often. However, if Chicago prices ever trade at a greater than 20¢ premium to Minneapolis (the cost of freight from Minneapolis to Chicago), it has not been unheard of for a major grain company to load a unit train of wheat (100 rail cars) and send that train south. The contract size, as it is for all the CBT contracts, is 5000 bushels, so a 1¢ price move equals plus or minus $50/contract. The price limit is variable and starts out at 30¢/bushel.

Wheat KBT

The Kansas City Board of Trade is where hard red winter wheat is traded. This is the most important class of wheat grown in the USA, accounting for half of the production, but the volume here is lower than in Chicago. This wheat is grown primarily in Kansas, Oklahoma and Texas. It is planted, like CBT wheat, in the autumn and harvested in early summer. It lays dormant over the winter, and that's where the name comes from. Hard winter is the bread wheat. The contract size is 5000 bushels, a 1¢ move equals $50.

Wheat MGE

The primary contract of the Minneapolis Grain Exchange is the northern hard spring wheat. This is a high-protein, milling-quality type wheat which is grown primarily in Minnesota, North and South Dakota, Montana and Canada. It is used in specialty bakery products such as croissants, French rolls and bagels. It is planted in late spring (hence the name) and harvested in late summer. Since it is a higher protein wheat, it generally trades at a premium to the Chicago of from 20 to 40¢/bushel, although I have seen it under Chicago (in 1996 they had a very poor winter wheat crop and a bumper spring wheat crop) and as much as one dollar over (in 1988 drought devastated the spring crop after the winter crop was already harvested). The Minneapolis Grain Exchange is a stately 100-year-old building with the trading floor restored to its original elegance. *White wheat*, the fourth major wheat variety, represents 10 per cent of the US crop and is grown in the Pacific Northwest. It used in crackers and pitta bread and is also traded at the MGE, but in relatively thin conditions. The spring wheat contract is very liquid, however, and like the others is for 5000 bushels with a 30¢ limit.

Major grain and soybean fundamentals

- *Supply/demand* For the grains and the soybean complex, fundamental analysts will set up a table and debate where the ending stocks will ultimately be at the end of the crop year. If it looks like stocks are too low, higher prices will be needed to 'ration demand'. If stocks appear too high, lower prices will be the result, as farmer selling overwhelms demand. The supply/demand table for soybeans, as an example, will include the following:
  - *Beginning stocks*: this is what the government says we will carry over from the previous year.
  - *Production*: this is the crop estimate for the current year. During the growing season the USDA releases a weekly 'Crop Progress' report which shows the condition of the crop.
  - *Imports*: since the US is an exporter, this will generally be a small number for the US table.
  - *Total supply*: this is the beginning stocks plus production plus imports.

▓ *Crush* This is the domestic demand by the 'crushers' who buy raw soybeans, and crush them into the products, meal and oil. This figure is released weekly (after the close on Thursdays) for the preceding week.

▓ *Exports, seed and residual* These are the other sources of demand; 3-4 per cent of the crop will be held back for next year's seed use. Export data is released twice weekly by the USDA; there is a Monday report, 'Export Inspections' (after the close), and a similar Thursday report, 'Export Sales' (hits the newswires prior to the open). Exports can also be affected by the strength or weakness of the dollar and other major currencies. If the dollar falls dramatically, it makes these commodities cheaper to foreign buyers and helps to stimulate export demand (and vice versa).

▓ *Total demand* This is the sum of the crush, exports, seed and a 'residual' number for other use.

▓ *Ending carryover stocks* Total supply minus total demand = the carryover, or ending stocks. This is the important number you will hear talked about. A supply/demand table can be set up for a single country, or the world.

 Let's look at a typical one for 1996–7 soybeans (the numbers are in 100 million bushels).

Beginning stocks	183
Production	2383
Imports	4
Total supply	2570
Crushing	1410
Exports	905
Seed	73
Residual	42
Total usage	2430
Ending stocks	140

This table could theoretically be constructed before the crop is in the ground. If production fell by just 100 million bushels, the ending stocks would fall to 40 million which is an unsustainable number. This is perhaps one week's supply. If you knew there were 60 million acres planted, this would be the result of just a 1.6 bushel yield decrease. On the other hand, if yields increased by 2 bushels per acre, due to favourable growing conditions, the ending stocks would rise from 140 to 260 million bushels (which is a comfortable level). So, basically a fundamental analyst will constantly adjust these numbers based on weekly export and crush numbers, and his determination of how the crop is maturing. There are benchmarks for where prices have gone before based on various carryover levels, but every year seems to be completely different.

- *Deliverable stocks of grain* This is a weekly report put out by the CFTC that indicates the quantity and change in terms of bushels of corn, wheat, soybeans and oats which are in the elevators licensed to deliver on the Chicago Board of Trade. It is useful in determining if there is the potential for a 'squeeze', where the shorts will not be able to find the grain to deliver. If all the corn is on the farm and there is very little available for futures delivery, this is short-term bullish (even though the longer term fundamentals could be bearish). If there is a large supply deliverable, and the commercials have no export business, the best place for them to sell may be a futures delivery (to speculators who really don't want the grain) and this is bearish. These numbers are most useful for analyzing the near futures month.

- *Government policy* Government farm programmes can expand or restrict acreage in general or for a specific crop. Price support programmes can pull supply off the market, and 'export enhancement' programmes can stimulate exports.

- *Weather* This is the big one. Nothing affects soybean, corn and wheat prices to a greater degree. There is nothing like a 'weather market', where drought or flooding moves the market. These can be the most emotional of all markets. In spring in the USA, in fact in most of the northern hemisphere, the market will watch the planting progress (for soybeans, corn and spring wheat). In the summer, it will watch the crop development, and in the autumn the harvest progress. In the North American winter it will watch the planting progress and crop development of the South American crops (during their summer). In the spring it will watch their harvest progress. A wet harvest can cause delays and hurt yields. In the winter, the market will watch the weather affecting the dormant winter wheat. The wheat needs 'snow cover' or else it is susceptible to 'winterkill' if the temperatures drop too low without the insulative effect of snow. Weather is so important, that there are services for hire which give weather advice and predictions. (I'm not sure any of them are any better than the USDA which releases its 'Weather Bulletin' every Wednesday after the close during the weather period.) Yet, some of the private forecasters do get hot from time to time.

  > * There is nothing like a 'weather market', where drought or flooding moves the market. These can be the most emotional of all markets.

- *Seasonality* All other factors remaining equal (a bold statement), the grains and oilseeds do exhibit certain seasonal tendencies. Soybeans and corn tend to put in a high in the May–July period, at the height of the 'weather scare' period, and bottom out at harvest time in the October–December time frame.

Cotton exhibits the same seasonal tendency. Winter wheat tends to bottom out in the June–July period (harvest time) and peaks in January–March when supplies are depleted to an extent, but before the new crop is available.

Meats

Live cattle

The USA is the largest producer and consumer of beef. There are four major segments to the beef industry (some consider the retailer where the 'finished product' is sold the fifth). The chicken starts with the egg, the steak starts with the cow/calf operation. This is a breeding operation which uses grazing land, cows and a small number of bulls to produce calves. Calves spend their first six months of life with their mothers, at which time they are weaned. Some are placed in feedlots immediately, but the majority pass through an intermediate stage called backgrounding (or in a 'stocker' operation). Backgrounders place weaned cattle on summer grass, winter wheat or some type of roughage. This phase of the calf's life may last from six to ten months, or until the animal reaches a desirable feedlot weight of 600 to 800 pounds. Once they are ready to be placed in the feedlot, they are termed feeder cattle. Usually feeding will continue until the animal weighs from 900–1300 pounds at which time they are slaughter-ready animals. This is what the CME live cattle contract consists of: 40,000 pounds of slaughter-ready animals. The customer for these animals is the meat packer who buys the livestock and sells the meat and other products such as hides. Prices are quoted two ways, either cents per pound or dollars per hundredweight (hundred pounds), really the same thing. There is a limit the price can move daily which is equal to 150 points (that's 1.5¢/pound or $1.50/hundred pounds) above or below the previous day's close.

> ✳ *The USA is the largest producer and consumer of beef.*

Feeder cattle

Almost all feedlot cattle are steers (castrated males) and heifers (females who have not calved). There are always more steers than heifers since some heifers are retained on ranches to replace cows that are too old. Feedlots can be as small as 100 head or as large as 100,000. Some feedlots are farmer owned and some are commercial operations. The commercial operations (cattle hotels) account for less than 5 per cent of all lots, but 80 per cent of all cattle marketings. The feedlot operator may buy feeder cattle for his own account, or for a fee he may 'custom feed' for farmers or other cattle owners. It is these feedlot-ready animals that make up the CME feeder contract, which has a size of 50,000 pounds. The specifications call for approximately a 750-pound steer, so the contract represents about 60 animals. Prices are quoted in either cents per pound, or dollars per hundredweight. Unlike the cattle contract, the feeder contract is cash settled just like many of the financial futures. It is based on an index, which the contract will equal on the last day, which is complied by the United States Department of Agriculture (USDA) based on a weighted average of feeder cattle cash market sales. The feeder contract also has a 150-point limit. Like oats, some traders believe feeder cattle prices are a *leading indicator* of live cattle prices – they move first. Thus the phrase, 'feeders are the leaders'.

Lean hogs

Like cattle, the pork industry can be divided into segments, but there are important differences. The pre-slaughter phase of hog production is usually combined into what's called the 'farrow to finish operation'. There is no 'backgrounding' phase in the hog industry. In other words, the hog generally stays on the same farm from birth to finish (80 per cent of all hogs are produced this way, with 20 per cent coming from a breeding only operation to the farm). Hogs will be taken to market when they weigh 220–40 pounds, and this takes about six months. Most beef is sold as fresh meat. However, a large portion of pork is further processed and becomes storable as ham, smoked, canned or frozen.

Pork bellies

These are the raw material for bacon, and can be fresh or frozen and stored (the CME contract is frozen) for up to a year. The hog contract represents 40,000 pounds of carcass, and is cash settled based on an index of prices collected by the USDA. A 1¢ move equals plus or minus $400 per contract. The hog contract has a 2¢ limit (200 points or $800/contract) which it can move up or down in a day. The belly contract is 50,000 pounds of frozen bellies; therefore a 1¢ move equals plus or minus $500 per contract. It has a 3¢ or 300-point limit. The pork bellies are notorious for numerous limit moves and volatile, erratic behaviour because the speculative open interest is much higher in this contract than most, often accounting for over 85 per cent of total open interest. Here's a trivia question for you: How many bellies does a hog have? The answer is *wo*.

Major meat fundamentals

■ *Accumulation or liquidation?* During the accumulation phase of the cattle cycle, ranchers are building their herds by holding back cows. This can temporarily create a short supply of market-ready animals, but is bearish longer term. During liquidation (for example, in times of drought which kills off the grazing pastures, or high feed prices) cows are sent to market. This is bearish from a supply and price standpoint in the short run, but bullish longer term. This works the same way for hogs as cattle. During the expansion phase an increased number of gilts and sows (female breeders) will be withheld from slaughter to become part of the breeding herd. During contraction females are culled from the breeding herd and the female portion of the total slaughter rises.

■ *Seasonality* Although this will not happen every year, feeder cattle sales tend to peak in the fall with the end of the grazing season. At the same time, cow/calf operators tend to sell off unproductive cows at this time which increases the total beef supply and depresses prices. Hog prices tend to be the highest in the summer months since the December through February time frame is traditionally a low birth period. Also, the demand for pork tends to peak during the summer months.

■ *Corn and feed prices* The general rule of thumb is that high feed prices will result in liquidation, and low feed prices accumulation. The other variable here is the market price of the finished product. If sale prices of cattle or hogs is high, then more can be spent on feed. In 1996, when corn prices soared to all-time record highs over $5/bushel, many cattle feeders found it more profitable to sell their stored corn and take their cattle to market (including breeding animals). Others could not afford the high feed costs which added to the liquidation. Prices of cattle spiked downward under the weight of the burdensome supply, but this turned out to be bullish for the longer term. The bottom line is that this is pure economics. When it is profitable to raise or feed animals, this is what producers will do; when it isn't, they won't.

■ *Feeder costs* In cattle feeding, the feeder's cost accounts for in many cases more than half the total cost of production. Higher feeder costs lead to lower placements into feedlots.

■ *Weather* Tough winter weather can result in death loss and weight loss. This can reduce supply permanently or temporarily. At times, when the temperatures in the major feeding regions get very cold, cattle eat more and gain less. Animals which were to be ready for market at a certain date are 'pushed back' creating a temporary shortage, with a glut later as they reach market weight. This fundamental is more important for cattle than hogs, since the majority of hogs are now fed indoors.

■ *Consumer tastes* This can be approached in a macro and a micro sense. The per capita consumption of beef or pork and how it changes over time will affect price; this is a macro fundamental. On a more focused approach, hot summer days increase barbecue demand, and holidays increase the demand for hams.

■ *Exports and income levels* When a country achieves a higher level of income, the demand for red meat increases. Exports to Asia have become a much more important factor in recent years, and unexpected new export business can at times result in price spikes.

■ *Substitution effect* Beef, pork, chicken, turkey and fish are substitutable commodities to a major extent. For example, if the price of chicken plummets, sales increase which will take away demand from the other meats.

■ *Cattle on Feed Report* This is an important and much anticipated monthly report released by the USDA. There are three major parts to the report: Cattle on feed (the total numbers in the feedlots); Placements (of cattle into feedlots the previous month); and Marketings (out of the feedlots the previous month). Since a placement of a 700–900 pound animal into a lot will become a market-ready animal in 120–60 days, this report can give a good indication of future market-ready supplies. Marketings out of feedlots can vary based on economic considerations, since cattle feeders can move cattle ahead a bit, or feed them a bit longer at times.

- *Cattle Inventory Report* This is a count of the total numbers of mature animals, as well as the country's 'calf crop'. It is an important report, but only released twice a year, in January and July.

- *Hogs and Pigs Report* This is the most important report for the hog and belly futures. The market often moves 'limit', sometimes for days, after this report is released if it shows numbers higher or lower than expectations. It shows the total numbers (the pig crop); the breeding herd (numbers kept back for breeding); the farrowings and farrowing intentions (the numbers actually bred, and anticipated breeding levels); the market hogs (those intended for market). Weight classes also give clues as to total future supply. It should be noted that while the H&P Report will move the market, it is often wrong. However, this cannot be verified for up to six months in the future when the animals either show or don't.

- *Cold Storage Report* This is released monthly and indicates the amount of meat in the freezers, from beef to chicken to bellies. It has a tendency to move the bellies, more than the others, after release.

- *Out of Town Report* This is a weekly report, released every Tuesday after the close, watched by belly traders who want to see if bellies were put into the freezers (bearish) or removed (bullish).

- *Daily Slaughter Levels* Gives an indication of how many animals are processed by the packers on a daily basis.

Sal tells the story of a successful hog trader who had a brother-in-law also in the pit who was struggling. The successful one wanted to help his sister, who was promised a new house by her husband (the brother-in-law), but he could never seem to come through. The day after a very bullish Hogs and Pigs Report, the struggling trader sees 200 long hog contracts in his account. Thinking it was some sort of error (and not inquiring as to why they were in his account) he proceeds to trade out of them right after the open.

After a $7 run up in hog prices, the successful one goes up to his brother-in-law and tells him to now go and buy that new house for his wife (the successful one's sister). The brother-in-law responds, 'With what?' The successful one says, 'What do you mean with what? Take the profits on those 200 longs I put in your account two weeks ago!'

Softs

Sugar #11

Sugar is grown in over 100 countries around the world with most of it consumed in the country grown and produced under government pricing arrangements. The sugar which is not subject to government restrictions is freely traded among nations, corporations and traders. This free market is typically 15–25 per cent of world production. A 5 per cent change in production can mean a 25 per cent change in free market supply.

There are two main types of sugar grown in the world: cane and beet. Both produce the same type of refined product. Sugar cane, a bamboo-like grass, accounts for about two-thirds of world production. Cuba, India, Thailand and Brazil are the leading cane producers, with CIS and EEC the major beet producers. The largest sugar-exporting nations are Cuba, the EEC, Australia, Thailand and Brazil. The major importing nations are the CIS countries (particularly Russia), EEC, USA, China and Japan.

Sugar is traded in London, but the leading contract is in New York at the Coffee, Sugar and Cocoa Exchange (CSCE). There are two contracts, but the #14 is a domestic contract which reflects quotas supporting the internal sugar industry. The one to trade is the #11 contract, which represents the world free market. A contract is for 112,000 pounds with prices quoted in cents per pound. A one cent move equals a profit or loss of $1120 per contract.

Coffee

This breakfast beverage is traded in London, but the most active contract is in the USA which is also the major consuming nation. It is traded at the CSCE. Coffee is classified into two types: Arabica and Robusta. The Arabica areas produce 60 per cent of the world's output, with Brazil and Columbia accounting for one-third of the world's exportable supplies. The Central American countries of Costa Rica, Mexico, Guatemala, Honduras and El Salvador are also important producers. This contract calls for delivery of Arabica coffee. Robusta is produced in the hot areas of Africa and Asia with flavours generally not as mild as the Arabica. The Liffe contract is a Robusta contract.

> ✳ This breakfast beverage [coffee] is traded in London, but the most active contract is in the USA which is also the major consuming nation.

It takes approximately four years for a coffee bush to produce a useful crop. The fruit is green at first and as it ripens it changes to yellow and then red. It should only be picked when red, and the work is extremely labour intensive. Coffee beans do not ripen simultaneously, even when on the same branch, so it needs to be hand picked in most cases.

At the CSCE, the contract size is 37,500 pounds or roughly 100 bags. A one cent move equals a profit or loss of $375/contract. There is a 6¢ limit, but only in the back months. The front two months can go wherever they want to. It is interesting to note that most of the Central American varieties are deliverable on the contract at par, but if you deliver Colombian you receive a 2¢ bonus, because it is considered a premium product.

Cocoa

The cocoa tree is a tropical plant which only grows in hot, rainy climates. As a result, the major producing countries are (in order) Ivory Coast, Brazil, Ghana, Malaysia and Nigeria. The fruit of the cocoa tree appears as pods on the tree's trunk, which when ripe are cut down, opened and the beans removed. Cocoa butter is extracted from the beans and used in cosmetics and pharmaceuticals, but primarily for the manufacture of chocolate.

Cocoa is primarily consumed in countries of relatively high income. It was first brought to Europe as a luxury drink in the seventeenth century. The leading importing nations are (in order) the USA, Germany, France, the Netherlands and UK. These five countries account for about two-thirds of the world's consumption.

Cocoa trades on Liffe, but the CSCE is also the leading exchange for cocoa. The size of the contract is 10 metric tons of cocoa beans, with prices quoted in dollars per ton. A $1 move in price equals a profit or loss of $10 per contract, with a $100 move equalling $1000.

Cotton

Ever since the US Civil War, cotton has been the major cash crop of the American South, and the USA remains the world's largest producer to this day. However, US production has not grown at the same rate as the rest of the world. Other major producers include China, Russia, Pakistan, Mexico, India and Egypt. The cotton fibre produces fabric, while the seed is used for cooking oil.

The contract calls for 50,000 pounds of US-grown white cotton. A one cent move is equal to plus or minus $500/contract and there is a 2¢/pound daily limit up or down.

Orange juice

Oranges are second only to apples among fruit in production (apples interesting enough are one of the few commodities not traded on a futures exchange).

The USA used to be self-sufficient in production, but a series of killer freezes in Florida created the growth of the Brazilian orange industry. Now up to 50 per cent of US consumption is imported from Brazil.

✷ Oranges are second only to apples among fruit in production.

The contract is based on a US grade of frozen concentrated orange juice. In years of crop problems (primarily a freeze) prices can trade over $2/pound. In years of high production they will trade under $1. This is a relatively thin contract, with a size of 15,000 pounds. A one cent move equals a profit or loss of $150/contract. It is traded at the New York Cotton Exchange.

Lumber

Woods are classified as hard or soft. Softwoods account for 85 per cent of total lumber consumption. Most harvesting of lumber is done by the mill on land leased for timber rights by private parties or the government. The bark is removed and logs move to the headsaw.

The contract calls for construction grade random length 2x4s manufactured in the Pacific Northwest or Canada. The contract size is 80,000 board feet with prices quoted in dollars and cents per board foot. A $1 move equals plus or minus $80/contract. Like orange juice, this is a relatively low volume, thin contract. The limit is $10.

Major soft fundamentals

- *Stocks to usage ratios*   The level of sugar supplies in relation to demand, the stocks to consumption ratio, is the major statistic traders talk about when measuring the degree of 'tightness' in the marketplace. For sugar, a ratio of 20–30 per cent is considered low, and consistent with higher prices. When prices spiked above 25¢/pound in 1980, this ratio was in the mid-twenties. When the ratio rose above 40 per cent in the mid-1980s, prices fell as low as 3¢. Since the free floating supply of sugar is comparatively low, it does not take a big move in the stocks/consumption ration to result in a major price move. Licht, a German-based trade house, is the primary reporting service for sugar statistical reporting. Candy sales are important, as is the price of corn (high fructose corn syrup is a competitor of sugar).

  For cocoa, the 'grind' is the term used to measure consumption. Higher grinds indicate rising demand, and vice versa. From time to time, the International Cocoa Organization will forge an agreement intended to support prices. It is a group of producing nations which will purchase cocoa for their own account and store it to push prices upward. When a shortage develops they will release stocks onto the market.

  Coffee consumption is believed to be more inelastic, with a major price increase needed to curtail demand. However, the sharp rise in coffee prices in 1976–7 was met by a commensurate reduction in consumption. The Americans consume close to double what the Germans drink (they are #2), followed by the French, the Japanese, and then the other major EEC countries. Consumption trends need to be followed closely. In the late 1940s, the USA accounted for two-thirds of world imports, but due to changing preferences this number is down to one-third. However, rising demand in Europe has totally offset the reduced American demand.

- *Crop yields*   Weather, disease, insects, political and economic conditions in the producing countries will affect production rates. As an example, the great freeze in 1994 caused coffee prices to surge from under $1/pound to close to $3.

For coffee, the International Coffee Organization (ICO) can provide useful statistics such as number of bags produced by country. Their web address is aptly named: www.cappuccino.com/ico.html. The International Sugar Association can be reached by email at iso@sugar.org.uk

> When I was a young broker at Merrill Lynch I once heard a commodity broker tell a client that there could be a freeze in Brazil which would hurt the coffee crop. It seemed reasonable to me in that we then lived in Minnesota, and it was well below freezing at the time. Only later did I realize that the North American winter is the South American summer, and there was no way they were going to freeze in the summer.

Metals

Precious metals

Gold

Unique and precious, gold is in effect its own asset class. Prices are quoted alongside securities in the major financial media. It is still a hedge against asset erosion in times of inflation and political unrest, and is becoming increasing popular as an investment vehicle in China (as it has perhaps lost some of its lustre in the West). In 1816 Great Britain, the world's major superpower, backed its currency exclusively with gold which forced other nations to follow its lead. The metal formally entered the world's monetary system in 1944 when the Bretton Woods agreement fixed all the world's paper currencies in relation to the dollar, which in turn was tied to gold. Then in 1971, Nixon cancelled the dollar's convertibility to gold, which probably led to hyperinflation a decade later. Today, many of the world's central banks, particularly in Europe, are divesting themselves of a portion of their gold reserves.

Gold now trades freely in accordance with supply and demand. At times, it acts like an industrial metal (responding to jewellery demand), but it is still its own asset class with money flowing into the metal as a store of value when inflationary expectations heat up. South Africa is the world's largest gold producer, accounting for over 25 per cent of the world's production and one-half of the reserves. Russia, the USA, Canada, Australia and Brazil are the next five major producers in order.

The all-time futures price high was $1026 reached in January 1980 on the October 1980 contract when the spot price reached $875. When the contract was listed in 1976, it came 'on the board' under $100. The COMEX (division of he NYMEX) is by far the world's largest precious metals market, with its 100 troy ounce contract. Prices are quoted in dollars and cents per ounce, with a $1 move equal to a profit or loss of $100/contract.

Platinum

Although an industrial metal (platinum is used in the automotive industry as well as chemical, petroleum refining and electronics), platinum is a precious metal because only 80 tons of new production reaches the world annually. Of the world's production 90 per cent takes place in South Africa and Russia. However, recently there was a major find in North America which is now in the development stage. South Africa still accounts for 85 per cent of the world's reserves, with its two largest production companies, Impala and Rustenberg, setting the producer price.

However, the NYMEX sets the price with its 100 ounce contract, which also is worth $100/$1 ounce move. Platinum and palladium are additionally traded on TOCOM, the Tokyo Commodity Exchange. Like gold, platinum also traded over $1000/ounce in 1980. It now generally trades as a slight premium to gold, and the platinum/gold spread is a popular speculation.

Silver

Silver is truly a hybrid industrial/precious metal. Since many of the world's dedicated silver mines cannot be profitably operated under $8/ounce, much of recent production is the result of a byproduct of copper, lead and zinc mining. Mexico and the USA are the world's largest producers, followed by Peru and Canada. Fourth and fifth in production are Australia and the former Soviet bloc countries. In recent years silver consumption has outpaced new production, with the balance being met by above ground supplies. This probably cannot occur forever without either demand falling, production rising or prices rising.

The major exchange for silver is again the COMEX, where a 5000 troy ounce contract is traded. Prices are quoted in dollars and cents per troy ounce, with a 1¢ move equal to a profit or loss of $50/contract. When the Hunt brothers felt the world would run out of silver and attempted to corner the market in 1979–80, they were able to run prices as high as $50/ounce. Prices were 35¢/ounce during the Great Depression in the 1930s.

Major metal fundamentals

- *Gold* Watch what the central banks are doing. At times they are aggressive sellers, and at times absent from the market. Keep an eye on the global political climate, and how gold reacts to it. In times of instability, gold is considered a store of value. War, or a loss of confidence in traditional investments, can cause a shift of funds into gold. Watch China. As income growth increases there, the potential for gold demand is huge. Most important of all, keep an eye on inflation and inflationary expectations. In the long run the price of gold, and all precious metals, is most sensitive to inflation.

■ *Silver* Watch the price of copper, zinc and lead. Since much of the new production of silver comes as a byproduct of these three metals, if the price of the three is depressed and production curtailed, silver output will suffer as well. The reverse is also true. Watch for alternatives to silver in photography. Since one-third of all silver use is for photographic film, new dry-processing or digital photo technology could curtail silver use. However, widespread use of non-silver film is still a number of years away. Watch Indian imports. Silver is the precious metal of choice in India and a strong economy there increases demand.

■ *Platinum* Watch Japan. In Japan, platinum is the precious metal of choice, with more of it used for jewellery than gold. A strong economy in Japan is good for platinum prices. This is an industrial metal as well as precious and the demand for platinum is somewhat dependent on the health of the automotive, electrical, dental, medical, chemical and petroleum industries (where it is used as a catalyst).

Industrial metals

Copper

The red metal is traded in both New York at the COMEX and in London at the LME. The LME contract trades about six times the volume of the US contract. However, they are both very liquid and active. The LME contract has, at times, held the third spot in terms of volume for non-financial futures, after crude and just after corn. I personally prefer the COMEX contract because I'm not a fan of the LME prompt date offset rules, where you cannot realize your profits or loss until your prompt date.

The LME contract is for 25 metric tons, or 55,000 pounds (prices are quoted in dollars and cents/ton with a $1 move equal to a profit or loss of $25), and the COMEX is for 25,000 pounds or $12\frac{1}{2}$ 'short tons'. The price is quoted in dollars and cents per pound, with a 1¢ move equal to a profit or loss of $250/contract. Copper is the third most widely used metal, after aluminium. The red metal is mined all over the world, but primarily in the USA, Chile, Mexico, Australia, Indonesia, Zaire and Zambia.

Aluminium

The Americans call this one aluminum (al-ou-min-um). Aluminium is the world's second most widely used metal (after iron). The LME lists this very active, very liquid contract which at times can be the fourth highest volume, non-financial future after crude, copper and corn. Some years the soybeans trade more, but it depends on the news and the weather.

The contract size is 25 metric tons, or 55,000 pounds. Prices are quoted in dollars and cents per ton. In the USA prices are routinely quoted in cents per pound. To convert from dollars per metric ton to cents per pound, divide the price by 2204 (the number of pounds in a metric ton). The LME also trades a scrap aluminium contract, the aluminium alloy, which is a 20MT contract.

Zinc

Zinc is used as an alloy with copper to make brass. It is also used with iron or steel in a process called galvanizing, which is the largest use. The former USSR countries, Canada, USA, and Australia are the major producers. The LME lists a 25 metric ton (55,000 pounds) contract, which is also quoted in cents per pound. In 1988 zinc traded as high as 95¢/pound (it was 35¢ just two years earlier).

Nickel

Most of the nickel production is used in stainless steel. It is also used as a coating for such varied applications as helicopter rotors and turbine blades. Nickel is additionally used in coins and rechargeable batteries. The major producers are Canada, the CIS and Australia. The contract is also traded on the LME, in 6 ton lots, with prices quoted in dollars and cents per ton.

Lead

The major uses of lead include car batteries, ammunition, fuel tanks, and as a solder for pipes. The USA is the largest producer, followed by Canada, Mexico, Kazakhstan and Australia. Since it is extremely toxic, there has been a concerted effort to 'get the lead out' of many products in recent years. The USA, UK, Japan and Germany (the common link here is a major automotive industry) are big consumers. In the late 1970s, the price rose above 55¢ and to date has not been there since, averaging 30-40¢ in recent years. Lead is also listed on the LME in 25 metric ton contracts quoted in dollars and cents per ton.

Tin

Tin is manufactured into a coating for steel containers used to preserve foods and beverages and other forms of electroplating. China is the largest producer, followed by Brazil, Indonesia, Malaysia, Bolivia and Thailand. More tin is smelted in Malaysia for export than any other country, however. It can be volatile at times, and in the late 1970s prices soared above 850.00¢/ton. In recent years it has been averaging less than half that. Traded on the LME in 6 ton contracts, prices are also quoted in dollars and cents/metric ton.

Palladium

Palladium is a member of the platinum group used in the automotive, electrical and medical industries. Russia is the world's largest producer with South Africa a close second. The two countries account for about 93 per cent of the world's supply. The all-time high price of $350 per ounce was reached in 1980, a period when all the metals were hot. From its peak, palladium lost almost $300/ounce in only two years. But as new uses were discovered and demand increased, the price has started to rise once again.

Recently, Ford announced that it had developed a catalytic converter which could use palladium as a substitute for platinum at a 70 per cent cost saving.

Palladium futures are traded in 100 ounce contracts on the NYMEX. Every $1 per ounce of price movement results in a $100 profit or loss per each contract purchased. It is a relatively thin market.

Major industrial metal fundamentals

■ *Economic activity* In a word, watch the economies of the major industrialized nations which comprise the prime demand fundamentals of this group. Each of the metals will, of course, have its own fundamentals (zinc and lead are generally mined together, for example), but industrialized demand is the key. If there is the threat of an economic slowdown, this will be reflected in lower prices.

■ *LME stocks* Every day the LME releases its widely watched stocks report, which is a good measure of supply, It lists the stocks in the exchange-approved warehouses for aluminium, copper, zinc, tin and lead.

■ *COMEX stocks* These are released every day for copper. At times there is arbitrage between the LME warehouses and the COMEX, with stocks moving from one to the other.

■ *Mining strikes and production problems*

■ *War* Copper in particular has been called the 'war metal'. Demand traditionally soars for the industrial metals in times of increased defence spending.

■ *Inflation* The industrial metals have at times been called 'the poor man's gold', and will heat up in an inflationary environment.

When I was a novice commodity broker at Merrill Lynch, my biggest client was a retired, former top executive of a major software company. When the company went public his stock was worth over $15 million. In retirement, his hobby was trading commodities. He traded a bit differently than most of us, in that he had the funds available to back his convictions until they eventually worked, and they usually did. I remember he once started to short wheat at $3 a bushel. The market went against him, and he added to the position at $3.50. He added more at $4.00 and more at $4.50. When the crop finally came in, he covered the whole position at $3 – a nice profit. This is not a recommended way to trade, mind you, but it worked for him. He was a strict fundamentalist and never looked at charts.

In 1979 when silver first crossed $8, he started to short the market with a modest position of 5 contracts. His background was as a metallurgical engineer and he had a theory which stated that above $8 the technology was available to extract silver from the slag heaps alongside the mines, and the market would be flooded with supply. You must remember, at this point we did not know the

Hunts and their Arab partners were accumulating silver bullion and silver futures in their attempt to corner the market. Well, at 850 my client shorted another 5 and another 5 at 900. By the time the price crossed 1000 he was short 25 contracts with an unrealized loss of over $125,000. He was determined to keep shorting, 'whatever it takes' until he finally beat this one; this was his style. Well, by the time the market reached 1200 (an all-time high) he was short about 50 contracts with an average price of 1000, and an unrealized loss of $500,000. I was getting very nervous and very concerned, but he was adamant. All we knew at that time was there was a broker from the now defunct Conti Commodity firm who would come into the pit almost daily, purchase a huge position and leave. Many times his buying would put the market up the limit (there was a 50¢/ounce limit at the time). When he left the pit, the market would drift a bit and usually close higher on the day, but not up the limit.

Well, I started to have bad silver dreams at night, afraid my big client would go down with the ship, but I didn't really know what to tell him. At the time, there wasn't a good fundamental explanation which would convince him he was wrong.

I then remembered there was a Merrill Lynch executive who spoke to us at one of the training classes and was also on the board of directors of the COMEX. The next morning I called him, explained I had this big client short silver with a big loss, and he just wouldn't get out. I still remember the call. His response went something like this: 'Look, there's big money behind this market. If you're short, get out. That's all I can tell you, don't call me again!' Then he hung up.

Well, it was about ten minutes prior to the open, and with my heart pounding I called John and told him about this conversation. I must have sounded daft as I told him, the guy says 'If you're short, get out', because he then calmly told me to 'reverse the position at the open'.

I said, 'You mean, not just buy your 50 to cover, but buy 50 more?'

'Yes, that's what I said. If we're wrong to be short, then we should be long.'

Well, now I was really nervous. What if I convinced him to cover and then he buys at the top? He could lose a million and I could lose my best client. But it was too late to do anything but put the order in, and so I did, to buy 100 contracts at the open. And guess what happened? The market opens *limit up*, at all-time high, priced somewhere around 1250. Then it starts to drift down. So he covers his 50 at a loss in excess of a cool half million, and because of my phone call he now owns 50 contracts at what was an all-time record high price. And the market is drifting down!

Well, to make a long story short, the market drifted another 10¢ or so lower, but then reversed up to close that day up at the limit price (so at least he was not showing a loss on the new position at the close that day). The next two to three dollars higher came fairly easily, and when he got his total loss back, plus a modest profit. He got out of the 50 in the $15–$16 range.

Of course, if he held on to the 50 up to the highs, around $50, he could have made about $9 million. Then again, he could still have been there on the descent back to $5. In any case, disaster was averted.

John continued to trade actively until he passed away about three years later, but he never traded silver again.

How to analyze the markets technically

If you work for the multinational commodity trading firm Cargill, or Continental Grain, J.P. Morgan, or Iowa Beef, and you are in the right management position, you no doubt have access to timely, accurate (and probably also expensive) fundamental information. It may not be all you need, but odds are it's better than what the rest of us are getting. Nestlé make it their business to know what the cocoa crop in the Ivory Coast is looking like. We might read a brokerage house report which discusses the 'witch's tail disease' and how it has the potential to devastate the crop, but be assured Nestlé has a man right there in the Ivory Coast, and another one in Ghana for that matter, walking the fields. They have a better feel for just how good or just how bad the crops are than we'll ever have (and they have no obligation to share this information with the rest of us). Let's say the crop is in fact deteriorating. A confidential communiqué will be wired to Switzerland, and those in charge of purchasing get to work. Part of their job is to hedge using cocoa futures in London and in New York. If there's a good chance of the supply dropping, there's a good chance of prices rising once the news hits the wires. That's what a hedge is all about, to protect against future price risk. The Nestlé traders will, as quietly as they can, start to accumulate new crop cocoa futures at the cocoa exchanges long before you or I know what they're up to. But there's a catch, even for them. You cannot accumulate a large position, either on the long or short side, without leaving what I call 'footprints in the sand'. Large, significant, 'informed' volume will move price. This is what technical analysis is all about. Analyzing past and current price action to project future price action.

Does technical analysis work?

Yes, I believe it does. Solid technical analysis is perhaps the only tool which gives the individual a decent chance against the professionals. You do not have the research capabilities of the commercials, or the execution advantages of the floor traders. What you do have is the luxury of moving faster than the big commercial operators, since your trading size will not affect price too significantly. You have one advantage over the 'locals' and that's a better perspective. You are not subject to all the noise and false trend movements which happen on the floor every minute of every day and you are not stuck in one market (which may or may not be moving). You can sit back, relax and look at your 'road maps' in the comfort of your home or office. You can analyze your charts.

> ✱ Solid technical analysis is perhaps the only tool which gives the individual a decent chance against the professionals.

Pure *technicians* believe that the only important factor for analyzing the markets is *price action*. They do not look at crop size, export data, money supply or employment statistics. They don't care if it's raining in Brazil or if the head of the European Central Bank just made a speech and said he's in favour of raising interest rates. They only care about price action.

This is not to say that technicians don't believe fundamentals move the market. They concede this fact. A technician may know that soybean prices are rising because drought is devastating the Iowa crop, but he will also tell you that price will signal when the diminished supply has finally been rationed by diminished demand. This could happen long before the drought has broken.

The technician believes that all the pertinent fundamental information, which could include thousands of bits of data impossible for any mortal to assimilate, will be reflected in price and price action. In essence, the price action will reflect the consensus of the market players far better than mainstream fundamental information available to the trader.

Is this the best way to go?

Well, I personally feel a *mix* of fundamental and technical makes the most sense. However, as I will demonstrate later in the book, certain technical approaches can be more important, in my opinion, than the fundamentals. I do know many successful traders, people who consistently take money *out* of the markets, who are purely technical. (This may be something you should look into.)

Charts

The **price chart** is the road map, the primary trading tool of the technician. Charts come in different flavours, from point and figure and Japanese candlestick to the most popular, the **bar chart**.

Most of you are no doubt familiar with bar charts. They are fairly easy to construct and read. They are not always that easy to analyze for maximum profitability however; we will attempt that later. The bar chart can be in any time frame the trader prefers. A five-minute one might be used by the day trader, while a monthly would be consulted by the long-term 'position trader'. They are all constructed in the same way, the most popular being the ***daily bar chart***. Each day is plotted as a vertical line (or bar), with the range of the day's trading represented by the length of the bar. In other words, the top point of the bar is the day's high, the low point, the day's low. On a standard bar chart, the horizontal axis measures time, the vertical axis measures price. A small horizontal flag (or 'tick mark') is plotted on each daily bar 'waving' to the right to indicate the closing price. Some bar charts also reflect the open via a small horizontal flag (or 'tick mark') plotted on each daily bar waving to the left.

For example, if on 9 May, July sugar opened at 1104, proceeded to trade down to 1080, then up to 1142 with a close, or 'settlement price' near the highs at 1138, the daily bar for July sugar for 9 May on the horizontal axis of time would be the length of the range, in this case 1080 to 1142. This bar would be positioned to correspond with the vertical axis of price from 1080 to 1142. The flag representing the open would be a 'tick' placed waving to the left 'looking towards' 1104 on the vertical price scale, with the closing flag waving to the right of the bar 'looking away' from 1138 on the price bar.

Look at any chart for a few minutes and you'll pick up how they're constructed fairly easily. A picture is worth a thousand words, so we'll get on to the pictures shortly.

There are many good charting services available for purchase via mail or electronic means. Most of the professionals in the business subscribe to at least one real time data service which updates their charts automatically. However, I know of more than one person who trades for a living and still prefers the old-fashioned method. These folks have graph paper and a pencil. They chart each market they are interested in daily and *by hand*. They tell me it is the only way to get a real 'feel' for the price action. I even know of a couple of floor traders who chart ticks right in the trading pit, not an easy thing to do. Even if you decide to subscribe to a commercial charting service, I highly recommend you do some charting by hand. This hands-on approach will give you an interesting perspective.

How to use price charts

I buy the technical approach because I have been able to use it successfully in my trading. Success in trading equals making money. Yet, even if you are a sceptic, and it appears to you charting is no more than 'crystal ball gazing', you should still make yourself familiar with technical analysis. It will help you be a better fundamental trader. Most of the fundamental analysts I know still look at the charts. The reason they do this is because so many of today's market participants use the charts that, in effect, it has now become a fundamental. At times, a particular chart movement or pattern will become self-fulfilling. So many traders are looking at the same thing that it's very existence encourages them simultaneously to make a move which influences prices and in effect can make the projected move happen – a self-fulfilling prophesy. At other times, certain price actions on the charts will create temporary, 'false' moves which give the fundamentalist an excellent opportunity to enter or exit a trade. Without a working knowledge of technical analysis, the fundamental trader is at a disadvantage to those who know what to look for.

In this chapter I will touch briefly on some of the more popular and significant chart patterns. In subsequent chapters, I will go into depth concerning a specific technical approach I use in the markets. What's presented below should give you a good basis for additional study, but I do not mean to imply that the price patterns discussed are the gospel. Far from it. Every one of these will provide you with false signals at times. In a way, this can be useful too, since even false signals are useful signals, if you know what to look for and how to react.

The trendline

The trendline is perhaps the most popular of all chart tools. I've mentioned numerous times in this book that if you can determine the trend of the market, you'll make money. This is what the trendline is designed to do: determine the trend of the market and then keep you with the trend until it changes.

Trendlines come in two basic flavours; the up-trendline and the down-trendline. In an uptrend, the market will tend to make higher lows and higher highs. A downtrend is characterized by lower highs and lower lows. This is valid and significant advice and is what the trendline is attempting to show. You can prove to yourself that markets move in trends simply by picking up a diversified chart book and doing an 'eyeball'. Note how the moves of significance are characterized by series of higher highs/higher lows, or lower highs/lower lows.

As with all else here, hindsight is 20/20. It is not always easy to know just what the trend is in the thick of the battle or if you can determine the trend, how long it will last. This is where the trendlines come in (Charts 8.1 to 8.3).

A trendline is drawn on the chart you are analyzing along the tops or bottoms of the price bars in the direction of the then significant trend. In a bull or rising market, the trendline is drawn by connecting a straight line which connects higher lows. At least two points are necessary, but I recommend a minimum of three to add validity. In a bear or falling market, the line connects two, preferably three or more highs.

The more points connected, the more 'valid' the trendline. But here's the rub. The more valid the trendline, the more price data you have to use, so by definition the older the trend the closer it is to its conclusion. When a trendline is broken (price action moving below an up-trendline, or above a down-trendline), this a danger signal that the trend has reversed. This is how technicians use trendlines. When an up-trendline is broken, longs should liquidate and go short. Shorts should do the opposite when a down-trendline is broken. Many will place

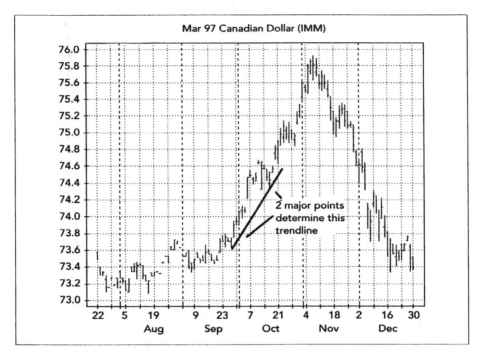

■ **Chart 8.1** Two major points determine this trendline

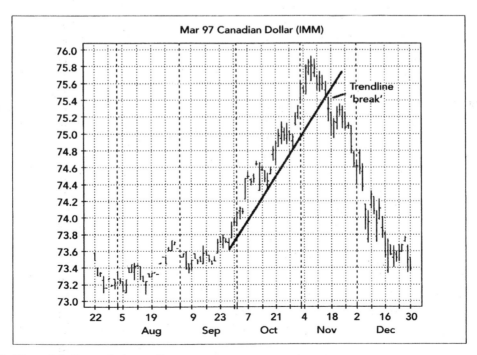

■ **Chart 8.2** Extended trendline

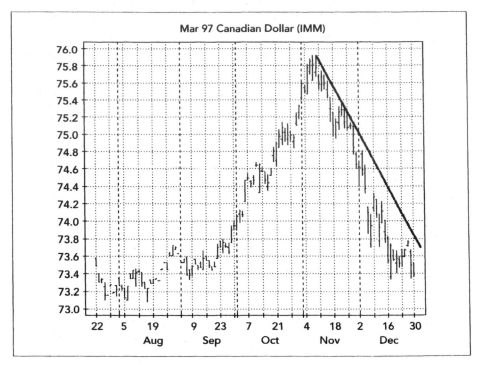

Chart 8.3 Down-trendline

stops just under an up-trendline, or just above a down-trendline to exit positions. If a trend is of significant duration a *trailing stop* can be used, where the risk is gradually reduced daily as the stop loss is moved in the direction of the prevailing trend. In this way, the first risk is the greatest risk. Over time, a break-even is achieved. Then if everything goes according to plan a modest profit is 'locked in'. Then additional profits are 'locked in' until the trendline is finally broken. The best and most reliable trendlines will be older and therefore longer.

The problem in using trendlines is that they are not always all that orderly in practice. A straight line assumes some sort of symmetrical series of higher lows and highs, or the reverse. In the real world, markets can act this way for a time but, human nature being what it is, there will be sharp and meaningless reversals in trend which in the long run will generate false trendline reversal signals. False trendline reversal signals are more likely to occur when the trendline is too steep. Steeper trendlines are generally those of shorter length, therefore shorter duration, and by definition most likely to be violated.

Once a trendline is broken, it certainly is a danger signal, but what do you do if the market then resumes back in the direction of the major preceding trend? Well, you can construct a new trendline using the new significant low or high (Chart 8.4).

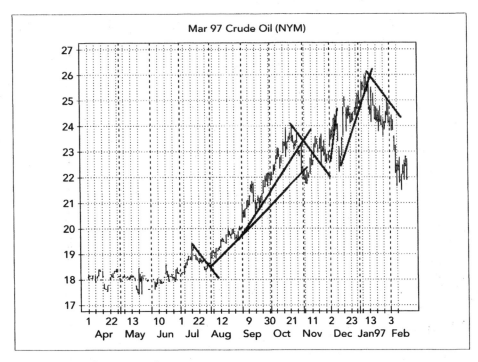

Chart 8.4 Redrawn trendlines

When trendlines are repeatedly broken and new trendlines drawn, the chart will tend to look like a fan. There will be a series of trendlines, all starting out at the same point, all moving in parallel. This fan effect will either indicate the major trend is still intact (albeit less steep), or the major trend is actually changing. This is where good interpretation and analytical tools come into play. Some traders have a sixth sense here. Some need to rely on a completely mechanical approach. Bottom line, it is best not to become too reliant on any one technical tool. Trendlines are helpful, but I do not believe you can make money using them alone. Not all markets trend well, and markets do not trend all the time. In these cases trendlines will not work well at all. Nevertheless, they can indicate the basic tendency of a trending market, and can also tell you when the trend has exhausted itself. However, combine trendlines with other chart patterns, plus some of the more powerful tools we'll discuss shortly, and you have yourself a winning combination.

Channels

In the most typical of all trends, if there is such a thing, prices will tend to trade roughly within a channel. A channel is identified by constructing a parallel line to the major trendline (Chart 8.5). If a market is trending higher, and a standard up-trendline has been constructed, the top line of the channel is drawn by connecting progressive highs. In a downtrend, a parallel to the down-trendline is drawn connecting progressive lows. Presto, a channel is born. As long as the market remains for the most part within the channel, the market is behaving as it normally would during a trending-type period. Nimble traders will look to buy on the trendline, and sell towards the upper channel line (assuming we're in an uptrend). Extremely active traders look to actually reverse at the channel lines, but this is not recommended since you would be fighting the trend.

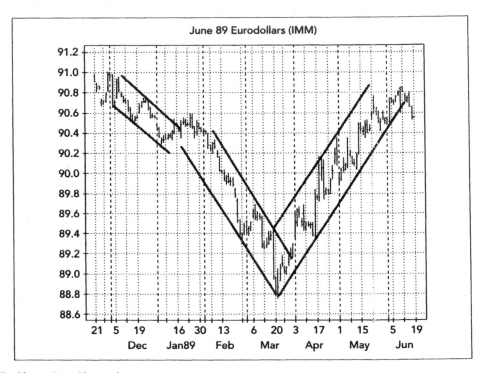

Chart 8.5 Channels

There will no doubt be times when the market will trade out of the bounds of the channel and this is something to look for as it can be a significant clue to subsequent market action. *The general rule of thumb is when a market trades above the upper channel line (in an uptrend) or below the lower channel line (in a downtrend) the odds have increased that the market is entering an accelerated phase.* A significant change in the normal supply/demand balance has taken place. With bona fide breakouts of channels, the market will tend to move faster and price action will become more dramatic. Stops can be tightened, positions can be pyramided and your 'antenna should be up' for any sign of subsequent trend reversal. The accelerated phase of any market can be the most profitable, most exciting time to play, but it can also be the shortest. Don't fight it, go with it, but be alert. If acting right, once it has broken out, the market should not fall back into the channel. This would be the place to exit and re-evaluate.

Support and resistance

As soon as you start trading for real, you will repeatedly hear these terms bandied about. Support and resistance levels are neon signs along the avenue which can clearly indicate at what prices the demand or the supply for a particular commodity is located. Think of them as floors and ceilings. Simply put, *support* is a significant area where buying interest develops, has developed, or is expected to develop based on past history. Support becomes evident on a price chart, as the market 'bounces off support' or 'holds support'.

If copper trades up to 99¢, bounces down to 95, back up to 97, back down to 9490, up to 100 then back to 9510 where it again starts to move in an upward direction, it can be said 'support is around 95'.

This is an area where the buying interest, whether it be commercial copper users, or fund buyers or bargain hunters (it actually doesn't matter who), has either placed resting buy orders, or it shows up when the market trades at or close to the level. It might also be an area where a big short, or perhaps many shorts, look to cover their positions to take profits or exit a losing position. It doesn't matter what the reason is that the price holds at this level, this is a level at which buying comes out of the woodwork, and as a result it is termed a support level.

Support levels can be plainly seen by looking at price charts. Support is basically where buying interest has shown before, and therefore the expectation is that it will be there again should the market trade back there. If it doesn't hold on a return run, say, in our example copper breaks down to 94 the fourth time, this is called *breaking support*, and is a bearish sign. Those traders who previously had supported the market at around 95 are either gone (or all the significant shorts have covered), or if they were new longs they are weaker this go around than the new sellers.

> **✱** *Support and resistance levels are neon signs along the avenue which can clearly indicate at what prices the demand or the supply for a particular commodity is located.*

The mirror image of support, the ceiling, is called *resistance*. This is a level which a market has trouble getting above, or has a hard time moving higher when it gets close to. If copper rallies to 100, then tails off to 97, back up to 9995, and does this more than once, this is the level, at least temporarily, of resistance. It is an area where the selling interest is greater than the demand.

Support and resistance levels can be drawn graphically by using a horizontal line on the bar chart connecting the *floor* points, in the case of support, and *ceiling* points in case of resistance (Chart 8.6). These are important levels which indicate the areas you would expect a market to hold or to fail. Like trendlines, traders are very cognizant of where support and resistance levels are. As a result, they can become a self-fulfilling prophecy, at least in the short run. If a market

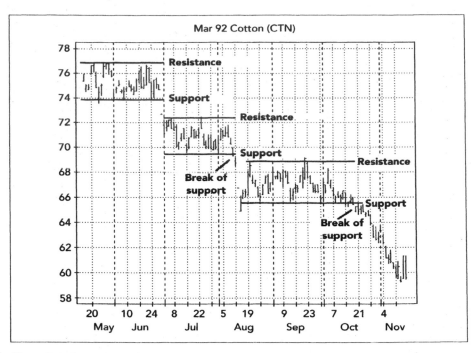

Chart 8.6 Support and resistance

continues to fail at a certain resistance level, the sellers become bolder every time that price is reached, and the buyers assume this is the place to exit.

For example, for years corn prices were unable to trade above $4.00, give or take a few cents either way. This was considered a ceiling price in years of big demand and drought years. In 1996 when the Chinese turned from a corn exporter into a major importer, corn prices broke the $4 'glass ceiling' (and didn't look back until they hit $5.50).

It didn't take all that long either. Once the resistance was taken out, the path of least resistance was north.

Extended periods of support and resistance both holding simultaneously can lead to one of the more powerful of all chart patterns, the 'breakout from consolidation'.

Breakouts from consolidation

A market bouncing off support is like a ball bouncing off the floor. If the floor is a deck four storeys off the ground, it will bounce as long it falls on the deck, but if it falls off the deck, watch out below. Alternatively, once a glass ceiling is smashed, the birds are free to fly away.

Support and resistance levels are very important to traders. The reason they develop at all is because the markets are human creations. Human beings remember what has happened before, and this prompts them to repeat certain actions in the future. When a market is in a relatively flat range, holding at support *and* failing at resistance, this is termed *consolidation*. Consolidation is nothing more than an inability by either the bulls or the bears to win the battle.

When the market holds at some level, rallies and then again retreats to that same level it will appear cheap. Those bulls who missed the first rally feel like they have a second chance at 'cheap' levels and step up to the plate. The shorts, especially those who are scalping and sold at higher levels, see the market start to bounce and are induced to cover their shorts before their paper profits disappear. This additional buying, this short covering, adds fuel to the bull move.

> ✳ *Once a glass ceiling is smashed, the birds are free to fly away.*

The reverse occurs when the market rallies to the level of previous failure, the resistance point. Some of the longs, who purchased at support, may feel the market is looking expensive and cash in. Bears, who missed selling the last rally, will consider this a 'second chance' and start to become active. The market starts its retreat, and other longs who do not wish to see their paper profits disappear, sell out, thus adding fuel to the bear fire. This type of action can continue for minutes, hours, days, months or years, depending on the market and the price level. As long as a market fails at resistance and holds at support it is establishing a consolidation area. *The longer a consolidation area remains intact the stronger it is.* This is important, because when a market breaks out from consolidation this can be a powerful indication of a change in market character.

If a market fails at a resistance level on numerous occasions, and over a significant period of time, and then one day trades above that level, this is a sign that the bears have lost the battle – at least temporarily or perhaps significantly and for a long time. The buying interest was finally strong enough to overwhelm the selling interest, and the defensive ceiling built by the bears has been shattered. The opposite is happening if a support level is broken. The bears have overrun the bulls and, instead of the equilibrium which had previously existed, the bulls are on the run. *As soon as you can see a bona fide breakout from consolidation, it is time to act.*

If you are long, and the market breaks support, exit your longs immediately. You may or may not want to go short at the same time. You may want to wait a bit and watch to see how the market reacts, but you shouldn't continue to stand on a floor which appears to be collapsing around you. I have seen many occasions where a breakout from a consolidation range has marked the beginning of a move of *major* proportions. It can be the first signal of a major shift in the supply/demand balance of some commodity, and this shift will be there to see in plain view for anyone looking at the chart (who knows what to look for).

> ✳ *As soon as you can see a bona fide breakout from consolidation, it is time to act.*

Charts 8.7 and 8.8, are good examples of breakouts from long consolidations which marked the beginnings of major moves. I particularly remember the oats move of 1988. This is a true story.

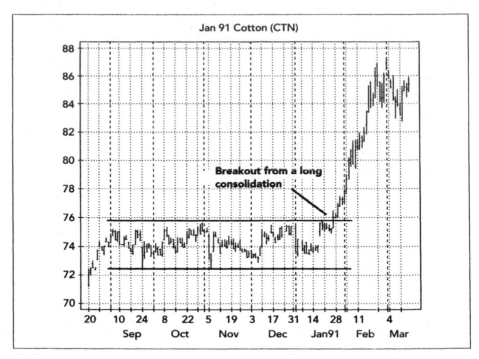

■ Chart 8.7 Breakout from consolidation (cotton)

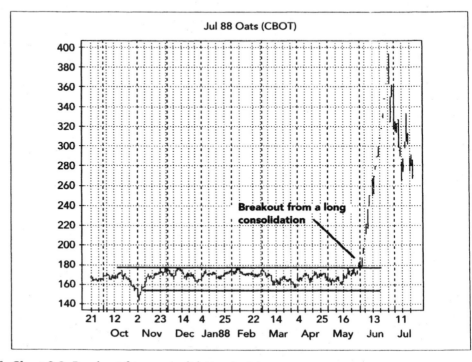

■ Chart 8.8 Breakout from consolidation (oats)

I had a large client who had money, was stubborn, gutsy and would not get out of his March oats because he felt they were too cheap. He had 2 million bushels (the limit an individual could own), and I told him if he didn't get out he would get delivery. No problem, he told me, even though when delivery happens you are required to put up the full value of the contract. You are no longer on margin.

So, he took delivery of the 2 million bushels at about $1.60/bushel in March. He wired in the $3,200,000. From that day on, my job was to be on the lookout for a good bid to sell the oats to a processor in the cash market, but none of the big boys (neither General Mills nor Quaker Oats) seemed interested. Well, the market traded in the consolidation range for a few months and then it got hot and dry.

The drought of 1988 is history now, but let me tell you how this all worked out. The oat crop in the Dakotas was devastated. The futures traded up to about $4/bushel. On 28 June, the all-time record high day for oats, I got a call from one of the large processors. When he asked if the oats were still for sale, and I told him yes, he offered $4/bushel for the entire 2 million. I called my client who told me to offer the whole lot at $4.40. When I called the processor back, he said 'Sold!' My client sold 2 million bushels of cash oats over 40¢/bushel higher than the futures and as far as I know the all-time record price oats have ever been sold at. The client cleared a cool $5 million.

When I later asked the grain man why he was so quick to buy the oats (remember these are oats he didn't want at $1.60) at $4.40 (which was obviously too high), he told me this 'I had the choice of closing down the mill and putting 500 people out of work because I didn't have any oats to make oatmeal, or I paid a little too much and bumped the price of a box of cereal by 10¢. What would you have done?'

Support becomes resistance and vice versa

An interesting characteristic of support and resistance is that upon penetration one tends to turn into the other.

For example, if copper was in a consolidation between 95 and 100, then blasts through 100 to trade up to 103, the assumption is now the 100 level will offer new support. The reason for this again has to do with human nature. The first blast through resistance most likely came with new money which created new demand. Those longs, having completed their initial purchases are satiated; done for the time being. The market starts to drift back on profit taking from those bulls who have not recognized the change in trend and now see a chance to cash in with profits at levels not seen for a while. New shorts are established by uninformed speculators who perceive these new high levels as expensive. Meanwhile, there are those shorts who had successfully sold at the 100 level many times in the past, and this time they were caught behind the eight ball. If the market is able to drift back to their break-even level they are relieved since they are able to liquidate (cover their shorts, which is just like buying) without much pain. Meanwhile new bulls, who can clearly see the breakout, view the 100 level as an excellent place to establish new positions. The 'strong arms' who know what's going on, also look at any break as a buying opportunity. Markets are made by human beings and this is why support when broken becomes resistance and vice versa (Chart 8.9).

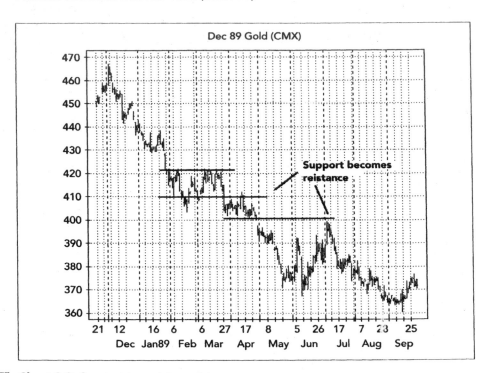

Chart 8.9 Support turns into resistance

False breakouts

Now at this point, I should digress a bit. This stuff is good, and I do believe it works more times than not, and that's why we are going to spend more time on technical analysis than just about any other aspect of trading. However, you didn't think this would be that easy, now did you? Unfortunately, it isn't.

When I first studied technical analysis, I saw the profitable examples in the books and thought this trading thing would be a piece of cake, but unfortunately it doesn't work all the time. There will be false breakouts from consolidation. Many traders are well aware of how powerful a tool these patterns can be and look for these breakouts. Many technicans will place stops just under support: (a) to limit losses; or (b) to establish new short positions. Floor traders know intuitively just where these stops are. There is nothing sinister about this. They can surmise where the stops are just by looking at a price chart. After all, they look at the same charts everyone else does.

> ✳ You didn't think this would be that easy, now did you? Unfortunately, it isn't.

If a market has held numerous times at, say, 95, and it approaches that level again, what's to stop a floor trader, or group of floor traders, from offering the market down to, say, 9490. The objective is to uncover the sell stops. Recall, a sell stop is a resting order to sell at some predetermined level. If the stops are actually 'resting' there at 9490, and they could be held by numerous commission house brokers representing hundreds of traders from various unrelated firms, the selling starts. At times, this action can feed on itself. The brokers with sell stops at 9490 immediately begin to offer to sell. Remember, a stop is nothing more than a market order to sell at the next best price prevailing at the time. The resting orders to buy at 9490 are filled, so the brokers offer lower, 9480, 9470, 9460, but everyone seems to be selling. All on stops. The floorbrokers love this, especially in a quiet or thin market. They will come back in and bid at, say 9450, and 9440 and cover their shorts at a quick and tidy profit. Since there was really no fundamental substance behind this price action, the market quickly bounces back above 95 as the shorts are covered, and commercial traders and bargain hunters step in.

As a speculator, getting caught in a false breakout is frustrating. Seeing your stop hit and knock you out of a good position, only to see the market quickly reverse in the direction you thought it was going in the first place, will make you mad. All I can tell you is that this will happen to you if you trade long enough, so keep your cool. Place your stops carefully, *where you don't think everyone else's stops are.* Breakouts from consolidation are such powerful indicators of potential trend changes that you cannot become complacent when they occur, just because false breakouts exist. The six rules for trading breakouts from consolidation should help.

> * *Place your stops carefully, where you don't think everyone else's stops are.*

Six rules for trading breakouts from consolidation

Rule 1

The longer the time it takes to form a consolidation, the more significant the breakout, and the bigger the expected move to follow. Look at different time frames. A breakout on a daily chart is more powerful than a 30-minute, and a breakout on a weekly chart is more powerful yet. A breakout from consolidation from a yearly chart is the most powerful of all, signifying a major fundamental change in the supply/demand balance of that market.

Rule 2

Once the breakout occurs, the market can retrace back to the breakout level, but it probably shouldn't trade back into the consolidation zone. If it does, the odds of a false breakout increase.

Rule 3

The breakout should remain above the breakout level for a significant amount of time. Once above the resistance, or below support, you really should not be in much trouble if you went with the breakout. If profits are not forthcoming in a fairly reasonable amount of time, be wary. A *quick* failure is a symptom of a false breakout.

Rule 4

Watch the volume on the breakout day. A true breakout is often times associated with a sharp rise in the daily volume. False breakouts are associated with modest volume.

Rule 5

Never place your stops just under support, or just above resistance. This is what all the amateurs are doing, and they become bait for running the stops. It is generally better to take a bit more risk and place your stop at a slightly greater distance. Just like the three bears' porridge, there is a delicate balance here. If you place the stop too far away, your risk is too high. I cannot give you any hard and fast rules for where to place your stop. This is an art as much as a science and experience helps here.

eg   **To give you an example, I've noticed over the years, in silver they tend to run the stops by 2¢ and that's it. If the market held at 500 four times, I wouldn't put my stop at 498. I would place it at 496.5, which would be a more significant breakout, but not that much additional risk. If I sold short at 496.5, I would sit through a rally back to 500, and perhaps even 502, just into the consolidation zone. However, if the market traded back to 503 I would start to assume this was a false breakout. On the other hand, if the market quickly moved down to, say, 480, I would consider the breakout significant and place my protective buy stop at, say, 502.5. My risk is now low in relation to the profit potential. If the market subsequently rallied back up to 494 and then broke under the 480 level, I would move my stop down to 496.5, thus assuring no more than a loss of commissions plus some slippage. If the next rally took the market to 489 and failed, I would move my stop to 491.5, therefore assuring a modest profit on the trade. As the market continued to go my way, making lower lows and lower highs, I would continue to trail the stop downward, locking in more and more of a profit until the market took me out.**

Never be afraid to call your broker to move your stop as often as necessary. This should not be an inconvenience to him; it's his job and his business. By the way, this is part of the service and costs you nothing.

Rule 6

The count – a 'basic' rule of thumb, which truly does work (more or less, you need to use some judgement here), is that when a market breaks out from consolidation, it will move roughly the distance up or down equal to the horizontal distance of the consolidation phase. To determine the count, you would take a ruler and measure the horizontal distance of the consolidation, and then measure upward from the resistance breakout, or downward from the support breakout, to give you an indication of the price objective for the coming move (Chart 8.10).

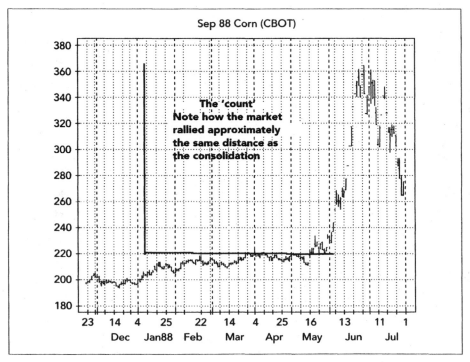

Chart 8.10 The count

Classic chart patterns

Technical Analysis of Stock Trends is often referred to as the 'Bible of Technical Analysis'. It was written by Edwards and McGee and first published in 1948. It is still available in bookstores, I'm not sure at this point what printing it's in. The basic premise of the book was that prices of stocks and commodities move in repeating and identifiable patterns. The patterns are the result of the ebb and flow of supply and demand. Some of the concepts presented in the book at that time were new, with others around since the turn of the century. Markets may have changed dramatically since the 1940s, but human nature has not. Many of the patterns presented by these two groundbreakers are still valid today. Chart patterns fall into two basic groups:

- those patterns which signal a reversal in trend;
- those which signal a continuation in the prevailing trend.

Reversal patterns include the *head and shoulders, double tops and bottoms, rounding tops and bottoms*, and *reversal days*. Continuation patterns include *flags* and *pennants. Gaps* and *triangles* are hybrids which can signal either or both. Presented below are the major 'classic' patterns that I feel still remain valid today and which you should be aware of in your daily trading.

Head and shoulders

This is perhaps the most famous of all the classic chart patterns and is probably one of the most reliable. It is a reversal pattern – one which signals a major top or bottom is forming. When you see a head and shoulders, it is time to get out and take your profits, cut your losses and/or establish a new position in the new direction. An interesting characteristic of the head and shoulders is that it not only tells you a market is making a top or bottom, but will tell you how far the ensuing move will go. It does not actually pick *the* top or *the* bottom, but gives you the sign after the top or bottom is in place.

Since a picture is worth a thousand words, let's start with one. Chart 8.11 illustrates a head and shoulders pattern.

The head is a price peak with another peak lower than the head to the left (the left shoulder) and another peak lower than the head to the right (the right shoulder). The line connecting the lows of the declines from the left shoulder and the heads is termed the *neckline*. In a classic head and shoulders, the neckline is horizontal, very much like a support line. However, it need not be. It can also be upsloping, like an up-trendline, or downsloping (in our wheat example), like a down-trendline. This is where your detective skills come to play. Many of the best head and shoulder patterns are mutants, which resemble the original but in a strange way.

You can see a head and shoulders developing when the left shoulder and the head are in place, and the market starts to rally from the 'neckline'. If it fails at a lower high than the major high, the right shoulder is in formation. A classic H&S will have a right shoulder of the same size and duration of the left, but once again it need not be. It can be lower or higher, longer or shorter, but its peak will ultimately end up to be lower than the head. *The pattern is not complete until the right shoulder is completed*, and the decline from the right shoulder's peak breaks under the neckline. When that happens, the supposition is that the top is in place. It is time to exit longs and go short. As with breakouts from consolidation, the best signals occur accompanied by higher than average volume. Many times, after the initial breakout below the neckline, the market will rally back up to approximately the neckline. Many times this will be an excellent and low-risk shorting opportunity.

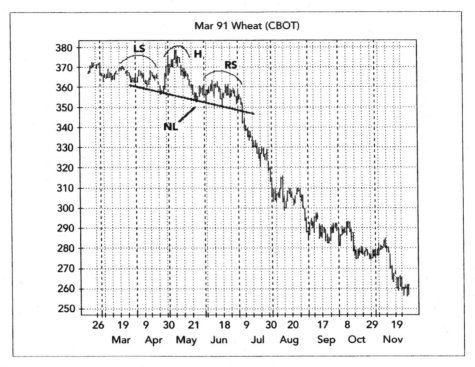

Chart 8.11 Head and shoulders top

Alas, H&S patterns can also provide false signals. A false signal should be suspected if the market can again rally back above the neckline. This will not happen with the best H&S signals. However, the pattern is still intact as long as prices remain under the peak of the right shoulder. Should the market again be able to trade above the peak of the right shoulder, you can safely assume all bets off; this one isn't 'right'.

With that said, I have included the H&S here in the book as one of the most important technical indicators precisely because it is generally one of the most reliable of all chart patterns. Plus, there is a bonus that comes with the H&S. It gives us a target, generally reliable and more precise than most technical techniques. If you measure from the top of the head to the neckline, and bring this measurement down starting from the neckline, you have a *minimum* target for where prices should subsequently end up. The market can certainly move farther than this count, but it gives you a minimum objective which could prevent exiting prematurely (Chart 8.12).

Head and shoulders occur at major bottoms as well, and they look like the mirror image of those that form at the top. Some traders call these *inverted head and shoulders*, or *reverse head and shoulders*. In this variety, the head is at the lowest point, with two higher shoulders at either side (Chart 8.13). Other than the fact that these are the mirror image of the tops, you trade them the same way. Volume should increase with the breakout above the neckline, and the measurement

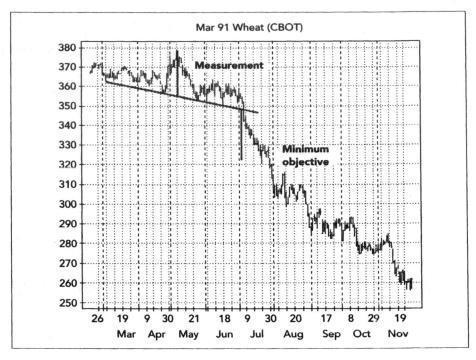

Chart 8.12 Head and shoulders target

works the same way, only it measures from the neckline up for a *minimum* upside target (Chart 8.14).

Ten rules for successfully trading the head and shoulders

Rule 1 Never anticipate
After I first discovered H&S patterns I had a very good trade. All of a sudden I started finding them everywhere. I would start to sell after a right shoulder and a head developed, only to lose money. I would see complete H&S patterns develop and take action *prior* to penetration of the neckline, only to have my head handed to me. My best advice to you is to look for these, but not too hard. As Yogi Berra says, 'It's only over when it's over.' Wait until the pattern is completed before you trade off it.

Rule 2 The bigger the H&S pattern and the longer it takes to develop, the bigger the subsequent resulting move

Rule 3 The count is a *minimum* measurement
Odds favour the move carrying much further. However, a warning here as well. As with all chart patterns we are not dealing with a certainty here. If your count says the market will fall 400 points and it falls 380 and starts to reverse, it would be a shame to let all your profits evaporate for a lousy 20 points.

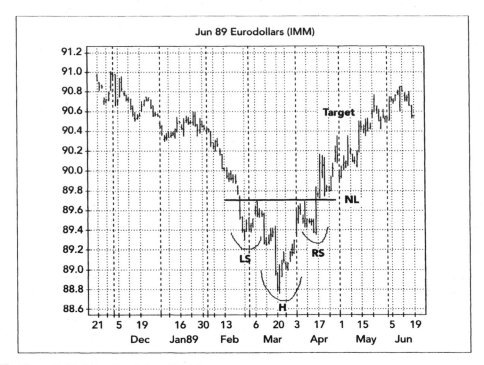

■ Chart 8.13 Head and shoulders bottom

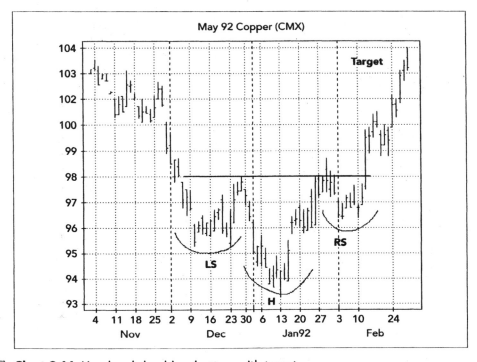

■ Chart 8.14 Head and shoulders bottom with target

Rule 4 Once the market breaks the neckline, watch for the return move, back to the neckline
They occur in at least half of all valid cases, and offer a place to enter with a close stop.

Rule 5 Watch the slope of the neckline
Downward sloping necklines with an H&S top increase the odds for a more powerful bear move to follow. Upward sloping necklines for inverted H&S bottoms increase the odds for a more powerful bull move to follow.

Rule 6 Be volume cognizant
The most valid neckline breakouts are accompanied with higher than average volume. In retrospect, there have been times when I've seen the highest daily volume days of the year associated with head and shoulder patterns. This rule is more important with tops than bottoms.

Rule 7 Watch for the head to also form an 'island'
This combines two very powerful patterns and geometrically increases the validity of the signal. (Islands are discussed later in the chapter.)

Rule 8 When the pattern is completed, it should act the right way
These are fairly reliable, and do not deviate from their true purpose, that is unless they are false. How can you tell if they are false? One good indication is your margin account will start to show a loss. Don't place so much faith in this, or any technical signal, that you freeze when it's not acting right. When in doubt get out. Be suspicious if the pattern occurs on low volume. Remember, the market can retrace to the neckline. This is normal and a good place to position, but if any good the retracement really shouldn't go much further.

Rule 9 If a false signal, look to reverse
This is another one of my rules, never talked about by Edwards and McGee. I've found that many times a classic H&S failure offers an excellent opportunity to get back in sync with the major trend. If the market again trades above the right shoulder's top (or below the right shoulder's bottom for a reverse H&S), odds favour, at the minimum, one last thrust to a new high or new low. I would buy the market at this point, with the objective of a new high, risking to under the neckline. For an inverted H&S failure, sell the market under the low of the right shoulder with a minimum objective of a new low, risking to above the neckline.

Rule 10 After a false signal is confirmed, watch the market action closely as soon as new highs or lows are registered
This is also one of my rules. I've noticed a head and shoulders failure will ultimately lead to a new contract high or low, but many times this will be the final high or low (Chart 8.15). In other words, the H&S was telling us we are close to the top or bottom, but the bulls or bears were able to make one final thrust to a

final climax. If the market cannot show much follow-through after this climactic top or bottom following an H&S which didn't work, be ready to move. A major top or bottom is in place.

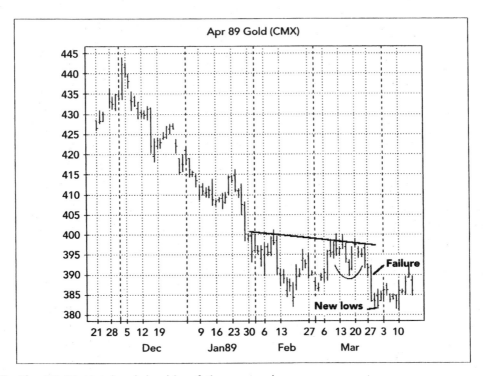

Chart 8.15 Head and shoulders failure = new lows

Double tops and bottoms

I like double tops and double bottoms. They are reversal patterns and many times will be associated with *major* tops and bottoms.

Double tops occur when prices rally to an area close to a previous high, but then the market fails without being able to decisively continue into new high territory. I'm trying to be careful here in my choice of words, since many novice traders (and one major newsletter which looks for these exclusively) believe a double top is only valid if a market fails under the previous top. I've found in practice many times double tops are formed when a market just nicks and at times moves slightly above the previous high, then fails. Think of this as an M, with the right mast at times a bit lower than the left, or at times a bit higher (Chart 8.16).

Double bottoms are the mirror image of the tops. Think of them as a W. The market makes a major bottom, then rallies, fails and holds slightly above or slightly below the previous bottom, then it reverses (Chart 8.17).

The only problem with double tops and double bottoms is that they don't always occur at the top or the bottom. Many times you'll see them in the middle

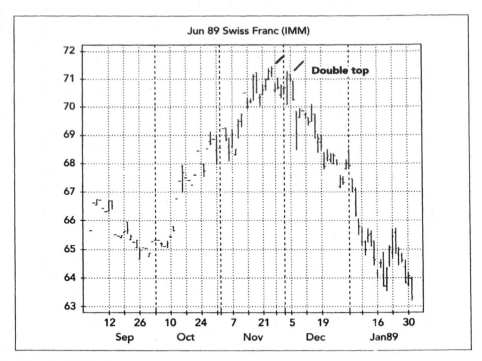

■ **Chart 8.16** Double top

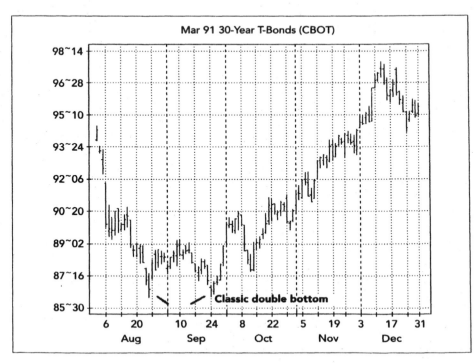

■ **Chart 8.17** Double bottom

of moves (which obviously doesn't help us in identifying a top or a bottom), so you have to be careful here. As I've stated before, and will again, there is no holy grail. All we can hope to do is place the odds in our favour and then use good money management to cut the losses on the ones that don't go according to plan. To avoid false signals, it is important to wait until the pattern is completed. This removes some of the profit potential, but also improves your odds. Make sure you look for double bottoms and tops *only* after a *major* top or bottom is made, and then wait for the market to test the low/high and then rally/break significantly enough to increase its validity. How much is significant? Unfortunately, there is not a number I can give you, but after you have been doing this a while, and after studying hundreds of charts, you'll get a feel for it in different markets.

Rounding tops and bottoms

These are often reliable reversal type patterns (sometimes referred to as saucer bottoms. Charts 8.18 and 8.19 give examples.

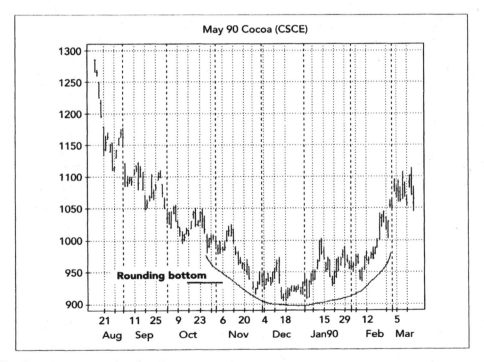

■ **Chart 8.18** Rounding bottom

These patterns are usually a long time in the making, and quite reliable. However, they're increasingly rare and difficult to find. Once again, it is important to wait for the pattern to be totally completed. False rounding tops or bottoms when they do occur (evidenced by a higher high or lower low) many times just precede the final top or bottom (somewhat like a false H&S).

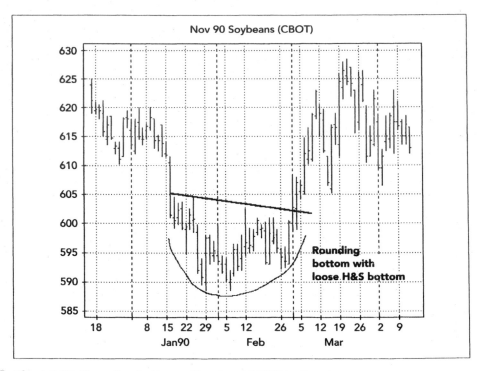

Nov 90 Soybeans (CBOT)

Rounding bottom with loose H&S bottom

Jan90   Feb   Mar

Chart 8.19 Rounding bottom with a 'loose' H&S bottom

Flags, rectangles and pennants

These are three common continuation patterns. They generally occur in the beginning or the middle of moves and can be good formations to pyramid positions from. They also give you the ability to use fairly tight stops.

Rectangles, at times called 'boxes', are formations where the market pauses and trades in a tight range. It is something like a consolidation, but much smaller in length, and unlike a consolidation, occurs after a move is underway and not at a top or bottom. It is generally a price movement which is contained between two horizontal lines as illustrated in Chart 8.20.

The upper line of the rectangle is your resistance line, and the lower line is the support. The plan is to go with the flow. In an uptrend buy on the break of resistance, and in a downtrend sell on the break of support. Rectangles basically represent pauses in the major trend. The market remains fundamentally bullish or bearish, but has to undergo a 'healthy' round of repositioning or profit taking before resumption of the move. Volume generally *dries up* during this box-like formation, and increases on the breakout. Just like the neckline of the H&S, many times the market will return to the breakout level after it occurs. They provide an excellent time to pyramid a winning position. I look to add to profitable positions after the breakout, moving my stop on the *total* position to below the opposite boundary of the box.

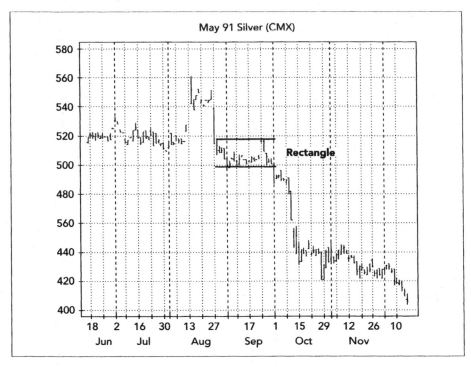

Chart 8.20 Rectangle

The drawback of these is that they are continuation patterns which at times can revert into reversal patterns. So once again, be warned, keep an open mind, and be nimble.

A *flag* is a rectangle whose boundaries slant up or down. The boundaries are parallel, like a rectangle. The 'flagpole' from which it flies is usually formed on large volume since this is the major trend. The 'flag' is, again, a pause based on profit taking, a rest stop before the train once again rolls out of the station on the way to the next station (Chart 8.21).

As a general rule of thumb, the slant of the flag runs *opposite* to the direction of the major price trend, not always however. In fact, contrary to popular belief, I've found that many powerful moves out of flag congestions come from those which slant *in* the direction of the major trend.

Pennants work just like flags and rectangles, the basic difference being that the boundaries are not parallel (Chart 8.22).

With all three of these continuation patterns, they work best when they are tight, quick, fast and neat and formed on relatively light volume. Be wary of moves which don't meet your expectations quickly.

Triangles

Triangles are congestion patterns which can signal either continuation or reversal. They come in three distinct varieties.

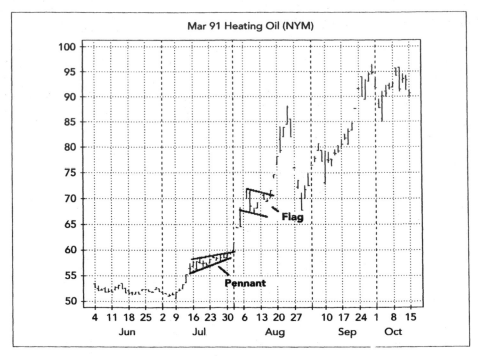

■ Chart 8.21 Flag

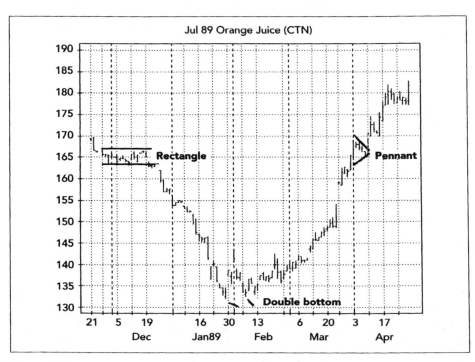

■ Chart 8.22 Pennant

The *symmetrical triangle* has an upper line (looks like a down-trendline) which slopes downward and a lower line (looks like an up-trendline) which slopes upward. They converge at a point. Like all congestion patterns, there is a war going on here between the bulls and the bears. Within the triangle they are fairly evenly matched, neither side winning. However, at some point, as time goes forward one side is going to win. The market will break out of the triangle, and this is the time to act. The breakout signifies the direction of the next major move (Chart 8.23).

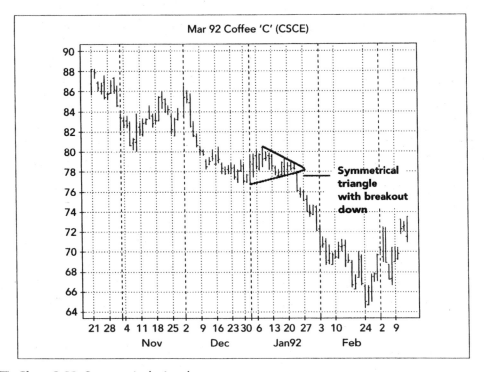

Chart 8.23 Symmetrical triangles

The general rule of thumb is that the most valid signals will come when the market breaks out prior to reaching the end, or the apex. The best breakouts generally come approximately two-thirds of the length of the triangle. Also, as with most of these patterns, volume should increase on the breakout. You know you're caught in a false move, a 'trap', when the market trades back into the triangle after the breakout, and all bets are off when it moves over to the other side.

Ascending triangles and *descending triangles* are like their symmetrical brethren, except they work towards a breakout in the direction of their respective names (Chart 8.24). The ascending variety has a flat upper boundary with a rising lower boundary which can be defined by an up-trendline. The bulls are able to support the market at successively higher lows, the bears are making a stand at the upper resistance level, and the result is more likely to be a breakout to the upside. This is generally a continuation pattern, and will most likely be seen during a major uptrend. The descending variety is the mirror image, with a lower horizontal support line and successively lower highs which can be connected by a down-trendline.

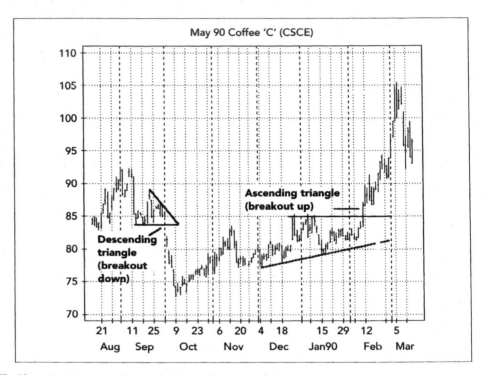

Chart 8.24 Ascending and descending triangles

Volume characteristics match the other patterns. It should jump on the breakout. The bigger the triangle, the odds are the bigger the move to follow. Watch out for false breakouts.

Reversal days

There are occasions in which the market reverses direction in the same day. Prices rise to a new high for the move, and end up closing lower on the day. Alternatively, prices fall to a new low for the move, and rally at the end to close up for the day. They may signify a temporary halt in the prevailing trend, but my experience has been that they are seldom very valuable other than for a day or two at the most. Many traders place far too much emphasis on common reversals.

Of greater significance is the *key reversal*. A key reversal occurs when a market makes a significant new high during the trading session, but ends up closing *lower* than the previous day's *low* (Chart 8.25). A key reversal to the upside occurs when a market hits a new contract low, or significant low for a move, and ends up closing higher than the previous day's high. If they are associated with very high volume they become more significant. They are more likely to indicate a genuine top or bottom, but once again not always. The rule is to go in the direction of the reversal, with your stop above the high (or below the low) of the reversal day. A false signal occurs when the key reversal high or low is able to be violated within a few trading days.

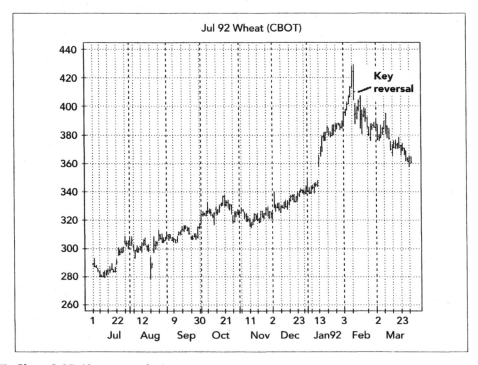

Chart 8.25 Key reversal

There is one circumstance where I have found reversals to be a most significant and important indicator.

George's reversal rule

The third reversal (after two previous reversal failures) will work more often than not. I usually ignore the first and second reversals and rely on other indicators to identify a reversal in trend. However, I've found it pays to take notice on that third consecutive reversal. The third doesn't have to occur over any particular time period. It can be short or long. Even better, if the third reversal is a *key* reversal. (This was the case on Chart 8.25. Can you find the first two reversals?) Try to enter on the close of the reversal day, place your stop at the extreme of the day, and keep moving it as the market moves your way. The move will, on balance, be greater when the market gaps in your favour on the opening of the following session, which leads nicely into our discussion of gaps.

Gaps!

A gap occurs when a commodity opens at a price higher than the high of the previous day, or lower than the low of the previous day. By definition, the gap remains intact if not 'filled' during the trading session. In other words, on a gap up day, the market never traded low enough to equal or exceed the high of the previous day on the downside. On a gap down day, the market was never able to trade high enough to equal or exceed the low of the previous day on the upside. They are easily identified on the daily bar chart by a space. There are four major flavours of gaps: common, breakaway, measuring and exhaustion.

Common gaps

Most gaps are more likely to be filled sooner rather than later. Most daily gaps are filled during the same trading session. Of those that aren't, more are filled within a day or two, than not. Since these are the most common variety, they are known as common gaps. They may occur as the result of a government report, for example, but the news, whatever it is, is usually not strong enough to change the major trend. As such the gap is quickly filled. Common gaps are seen often in thin or low-volume markets and are rarely significant. The trick is to be able to differentiate the common variety from the other three. The others are important technical tools which have powerful forecasting abilities.

> ✱ *Most gaps are more likely to be filled sooner rather than later.*

Breakaway gaps

Breakaway gaps occur at a beginning of a new move. An *upside breakaway gap* occurs when prices jump up from a bottom, generally from some sort of congestion area. A *downside breakaway gap* occurs when prices jump down from a top, generally from some sort of consolidation. A breakaway gap is significant because it signals a change in the supply/demand balance. The pressure to push a market to the next level up or down is so great that the market literally has to leapfrog to this new level, effectively trapping many market participants on the wrong side. Those trapped on the wrong side will eventually add fuel to this new fire as they liquidate. The shorts trapped under the upside breakaway gap are all at a loss and will eventually need to find some place to cover. Some of them will hope for a break to cover, but it doesn't come. Alternatively, numerous longs will be trapped above the downside breakaway gap, and at some point will be selling out. The result is more downside pressure.

> ✱ *How can you tell a breakaway from a common gap?*

How can you tell a breakaway from a common gap? A number of ways. Common gaps are filled fairly quickly. Breakaway gaps will not be filled for a long time, if ever. A breakaway will generally be open for weeks, or more likely months. This is the start of a new and major trend move. They will begin near a consolidation or blowoff highs or lows. The breakaway day will be accompanied by larger than normal volume, usually at least 50 per cent greater than the average volume of the preceding two weeks. These are significant and powerful tools which you should constantly be alert for. Particularly watch for them when a market appears that it could be basing for a major bottom, or climaxing for a major top. I can testify, they've served as a wake-up call for me on many occasions.

Measuring gaps

These are found at approximately the mid-point of a powerful trend move. They show up one day, many times on news and, unlike a common gap, the market continues on its way *without* filling the gap. Once again, volume should be large. It serves to trap many players who are still on the wrong side even more deeply in the muck, and these traders will provide some of the fuel for the next leg up or down. The interesting thing about these is that many times they occur when a move is just about half over. So if the breakaway came at 100, and the measuring at 140, you can project this move will run to about 180. I have seen, at times, more than one measuring-type gap in very powerful moves. Perhaps one at 33 per cent of the move and another when the move is about 60 per cent. So, the measurement rule is certainly not written in stone. However, these can help you determine approximately where you are in the move, and so can exhaustion gaps.

Exhaustion gaps

An exhaustion gap comes close to the end of a move. In a major uptrend, the market will gap up to new highs, generally on very bullish news. In a major downtrend, the market will gap down to new lows, maybe on new bearish news, sometimes based on final panic liquidation. In both cases, these many times follow limit-type moves, and the exhaustion day may even trade at the limit at some point in the direction of the major trend. Unlike the other gaps, however, this is the beginning of the end. The market has run out of steam, even though most do not realize it on that day. The day of an upside exhaustion gap, the last of the weak shorts has thrown in the towel and covered, and the last of the uninformed longs jumps in believing this market still has a long way to go. However, the news is always the most bullish at the top, and the market is satiated. High prices are starting to ration demand, and supply is beginning to come out of the woodwork. With a downside exhaustion gap, the last of the under-margined longs has given up. Many times panicky conditions prevail as the red ink flows. Yet, this too is the beginning of the end as low prices have started to beef up demand.

> **✱** *Keep your antenna up when a market becommes wild eyed after a long run up, and panic stricken after a long run down.*

How can you tell an exhaustion gap? Most importantly, unlike the breakaway or measuring, it will be filled fairly quickly. Sometimes the next day; many times the market will churn for three to five days; but it will be filled fairly quickly. Second, many times, the high of the exhaustion top day will not be exceeded, and with a downside, there will be no lower lows. Volume will be high, but it was probably high the days preceding the exhaustion day as well. Like the breakaway, these are powerful indicators. Keep your antenna up when a market becomes wild eyed after a long run up, and panic stricken after a long run down. Watch for a final-type gap. Remember, it is always darkest before the dawn, and brightest just before the sun starts to recede.

Islands

Islands are made by gaps, and can be formed in part by either exhaustion or break-away gaps. An island bottom is formed by a gap down, some price action at a basing level, and a breakaway gap up. An island top is formed by a continuation or exhaustion gap up, some price action at new highs, and a breakaway-type gap down. They are easy to spot, in that they look like islands in the sky (or the sea). They are rare, but powerful. You'll know one when you see it!

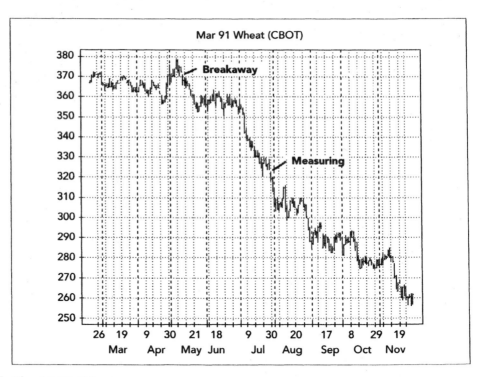

Chart 8.26 Wheat gaps

On Chart 8.26, March wheat, there was a well-defined breakaway gap, just days from the high right above the 370 level. A week later it was still not filled, so if you originally considered this a common gap, you had to re-evaluate by then. Also note the high day was a reversal day, plus this formation eventually turned into a head and shoulders top with a down sloping neckline (additional evidence of a major top). Once the market broke out of the rectangle below 350 there was no doubt, from a technical standpoint, this market was done for. Note the measuring gap at approximately the 325 level. Measuring from the top at about 375 we could project a move down another 50¢ to minimum 275 (a level it reached and eventually exceeded.)

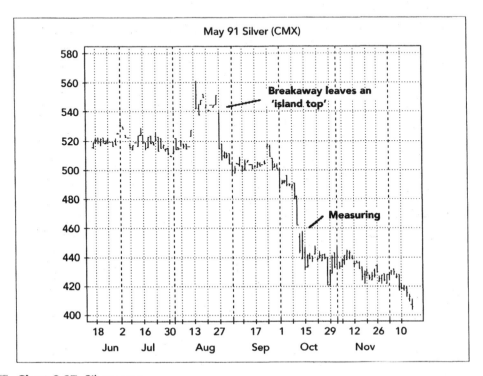

Chart 8.27 Silver gaps

Chart 8.27, May silver, shows a breakaway gap on the top which left an island top on a wide-ranging, high-volume day which closed on the lows. It looked technically weak on that day, but there should have been no doubt of the weakness after the market broke the downside of the rectangle below the psychologically important 500 mark. If we had identified the gap at 460 as a measuring gap, the objective would be another 80¢ lower, or 380. The silver market actually did reach this objective by the end of January, about a month past the chart as presented.

Chart 8.28 shows March pork bellies. Bellies are a thinner market, so we need to be careful to avoid labelling common gaps as significant. The upside breakaway in mid-September was not filled a week later, and therefore marked a major bottom. The large early October gap was formed by a very bullish Hogs and Pigs Report which pushed the market 'limit up' for three consecutive days. Apparently, the 'smart money' who originally had a hand in forming the breakaway knew something bullish was about to happen. If we take the approximate

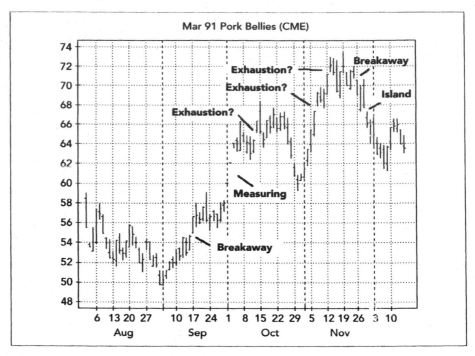

■ **Chart 8.28** Belly gaps

mid-point of the measuring at 61, this would project an ultimate objective of approximately 68–70. There was a gap a few weeks later that could have falsely been labelled an exhaustion (since it was filled quickly after a reversal), but the measurement did not seem right. However, this did lead to a significant correction of over $8. It might have been prudent to take profits and look for a sign of the resumption of the uptrend. Note, on the correction, the measuring gap was unable to be filled totally, a bullish sign. I labelled two possible exhaustion gaps, and actually they both would have helped you identify a top formation, even if you labelled one falsely. Note, after the final exhaustion gap, which was filled quickly, the bulls were able to mount one last rally which briefly took the market to new highs. This was the final gasp, however, which quickly failed, leading to a downside breakaway gap which did come very close to the top. Three days later, this gap was not filled, and led to another downside gap which formed an island top. If you wanted to label this second gap (the one which formed the island) a downside measuring gap, it projected a move to about the 62–63 level. This was reached in less than two weeks!

Five rules for successful gap trading

Rule 1 Most gaps are common gaps and will be filled
Do not look for significant gaps at non-significant times. If a market gaps on minor news, low volume, or what doesn't appear to be a major top or bottom,

assume it will be filled. Short-term traders can fade these common gaps, and look to take profits when they're filled. If a gap is not filled fairly quickly, within two to seven trading days, begin to treat it as a significant gap (either a break-away, measuring or exhaustion, depending on where the market is in its cycle).

Rule 2 When a market is forming a long base, place a buy stop above the base to catch a breakaway-type move

Many times, the breakaway gaps will occur when least expected, and at times on no news. I've observed on breakaway-up days, the lows are generally registered right at the open. If you are stopped into a new long position in this way, place your sell stop at the low end (the fill) of the gap. If any good it should not be filled, and if good you are in close to the lows for maximum potential profitability.

Rule 3 Measuring gaps offer an excellent place to pyramid a position

If you spot one, and you are already in on a base position, this is time to double up and move your stop loss on the entire position to the fill of the gap. Your average price should still be better than the market, and your risk on the new 'add' is minor. When they work, you have a lot of room left to profit on the new, larger position.

Rule 4 Never anticipate exhaustion gaps, wait for them to be filled to take a new position

These occur in the final stages of a major move. This phase is almost always volatile, and it is extremely difficult to pick a top or bottom. It is only after the exhaustion gap is filled that you can define what your risk is and that it truly was an exhaustion. I have seen occasions when a market is so bullish it will form an exhaustion but still be able to work higher for days or weeks before it's filled.

Rule 5 When you see a significant gap (a breakaway, measuring or exhaustion) don't wait!

This is the time to act and be aggressive. If you wait you'll be left holding the bag. Significant gaps generally offer good reward to risk since you can define fairly close to the penny what your risk should be.

Volume

I've discussed volume repeatedly in this section because it adds evidence to other technical signals. The one recurring theme you may have noticed is that significant days are generally associated with larger than average volume. Gap days, breakouts from consolidation, neckline penetrations are all associated with larger than normal volume. To know what larger than normal is, you need to know what average volume is for the market you're trading. COMEX copper, for example, trades about 8 to 13,000 contracts on an average day. 20,000 plus is a significant day. Yet CME live cattle trade 25,000 on an average day, with 35,000 a big day. Crude oil may trade 80–100,000 on a normal day. They are all different and you'll need to know.

Many charting services graphically chart volume on the bottom of the bar chart in histogram form so you can get a feel for what a significantly greater than average day looks like. You will want to use total volume and not volume by contract, which can fluctuate randomly for the thinner 'back' months.

There is a philosophical question we can ponder at this point: does price change trigger volume, or is it volume that moves the price? I think both. George Soros once said, 'Price is the ultimate fundamental.' How profound! Whenever you see volume pick up, ask yourself 'Who's in trouble?' This will give you a strong clue for the move to come.

> *** Does price change trigger volume, or is it volume that moves the price?**

Three major volume rules

Rule 1

In a major uptrend, volume will tend to be relatively higher on rallies and lower on declines and trading ranges (consolidations).

Rule 2

In a major downtrend, volume will tend to be relatively higher on declines and lower on rallies and trading ranges (consolidations).

Rule 3

Volume will tend to expand dramatically at major tops and bottoms. Major bottoms can be characterized by climax-type selling. Blowoff tops can come with climactic buying.

Open interest

Open interest is the number of contracts outstanding; the total number held by buyers or (not and) sold short by sellers on any given day. The open interest number gives you the total number of longs and the total number of shorts, since in commodity futures the short interest is always equal to the long interest. Each long is either willing to accept delivery of a particular commodity, or to offset his (her) contract(s) at some time prior to the expiration date. Each short is either willing to make delivery or to offset his (her) contract(s) prior to the expiration date. With this in mind, you can plainly see that open interest is a measurement of the willingness of longs and shorts to maintain their *opposing* positions in the marketplace. It is a quantitative measurement of this difference of opinion.

Open interest numbers go up or down based on how many new traders are entering the market and how many old traders are leaving. Open interest goes up by one, when one new buyer and one new seller enter the market. *This act cre-*

ates one new contract. Open interest goes down by one when a trader who is long closes out one contract with someone who is already short. Since this contract is now closed out, it disappears from the open interest statistics. If a new buyer buys from an old buyer (who is selling out) total open interest remains unchanged. If a new seller buys back or *covers* from a new seller entering the market, open interest also does not change. The old bear had to buy to cover, with the other side of this transaction being a sell by the new bear.

Let's look at a typical example. If one day heating oil has a total open interest of 50,000 contracts, and the next day it rises to 50,100 this means 100 new contracts were created by 100 new buyers and 100 new sellers. Or perhaps 10 new net buyers and sellers of 10 contracts each, or whatever it takes net to create the new 100. Of course, during that day many people closed out, many entered, but the net result was the creation of new open interest. 50,100 shorts and 50,100 longs at the end of the day. Theoretically, one short who had 100 contracts sold could have taken the opposing side of 100 others who each bought one, but the short and long interest are always the same on any particular day.

Open interest figures are released daily by the exchanges, but they are always for the previous day, so they are a day old. You can chart open interest on a price chart, and the direction it is changing can tell you some interesting things.

Open interest statistics are a valuable tool which can be used to predict price trends as well as reversals. The size of the open interest reflects the intensity of the willingness of the participants to hold positions. Whenever prices move, someone wins and someone loses; the zero sum game we've talked about before. This is important to remember because when you think about the ramifications of changes in open interest *you must think about it in the context of which way the market is moving at the time*. An increase in open interest shows a willingness on the part of the participants to enlarge their commitments. Let's say the market is moving lower, and open interest is increasing. You can assume that some hurt longs have left the party, but they are being replaced by new longs and many existing longs are still there. If they were liquidating en masse, open interest would drop. Or, if the short holders were on balance taking profits and leaving the party, open interest would also drop. However, since the open interest is increasing, and the price is dropping, you can assume the bulls are losing money, but many must be hanging in there and/or they are recruiting buddies at an increasing rate. What are the ramifications of an open interest decline? It is a sign that the losers are in a liquidation phase (it doesn't matter which way the market is moving), the winners are cashing it, and new players are not entering in sufficient numbers to replace them.

> ❋ *Whenever prices move, someone wins and someone loses; the zero sum game we've talked about before.*

Six rules for analyzing open interest

Rule 1 If prices are in an uptrend and open interest is rising, this is a bullish sign
The bulls are in charge. They are adding to positions and making the money, thus becoming more powerful. There are undoubtedly shorts who are being stopped out, but new sellers are taking their place. As the market continues to rise, the longs get stronger and the shorts get weaker.

Rule 2 If prices are in a downtrend and open interest is rising, this is a bearish sign
The bears are in charge in this case. They are adding to their positions, and they are the ones making the money. Weaker longs are being stopped out, but new buyers are taking their place. As the market continues to fall, the shorts get stronger and the longs get weaker. Another way to look at rules 1 and 2: as long as the open interest is increasing in a major trend, it will have the necessary financing to draw upon and prosper.

Rule 3 If prices are in an uptrend and open interest is falling, this is a bearish sign
The old longs, the 'smart money' (after all they have been right to this point) are taking profits, they're liquidating. They are replaced to some extent by new buyers, who will not be as strong on balance, but the declining open interest is an indication the weak shorts are also bailing. They will be replaced to an extent by new shorts who are stronger than the old shorts were.

Rule 4 If prices are in a downtrend and open interest is falling, this is a bullish sign
This is the mirror image of rule 3. The smart money, the shorts are covering or liquidating. They will be replaced to a degree by new shorts not as strong as they were, but the declining open interest indicates the weakened longs are throwing in the towel to a major degree. They will be replaced by fresh longs who were not as weakened by the lower prices as the old longs were. Another way to look at rules 3 and 4: when the pool of losers is depleted, the party will be over.

Rule 5 If prices are in a congestion range and open interest is rising, this is a bearish sign
The reason is that the public generally plays the long side. Rising open interest in a trading range affair assumes the commercials and professionals are taking the short side, and the uninformed public will most likely lose out in the end.

Rule 6 If prices are in a congestion range and open interest is falling, this is a bullish sign
The reason is that the professionals, who are more likely to be short, are covering. The weak hands are throwing in the towel.

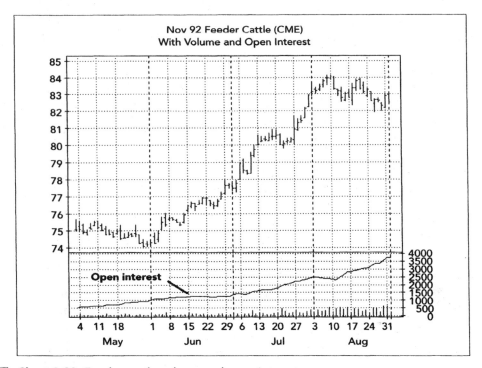

Chart 8.29 Feeder cattle volume and open interest

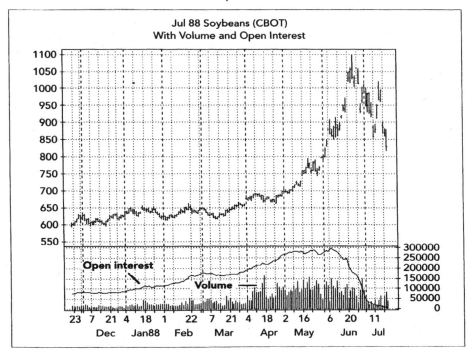

Chart 8.30 Soybean volume and open interest

Look at Chart 8.29. This is a nicely trending market, trending up, and open interest has been building the whole time. As long as open interest continues to climb in a bull market, the bulls are in charge. Chart 8.30 was the drought market of 1988. Note how open interest and volume rose dramatically on the bull move from April until end of June. Volume remained high, but open interest started to collapse as did the market. Once the last weak short was out, and the smart money was long gone, the new folk took it down in a hurry!

A few more points about open interest. Open interest is our best indicator of market liquidity. I only like to trade high open interest markets and, unless I have a specific reason (I want to be in new crop beans, for example), the highest open interest contract of any market I'm trading. The simple reason has to do with slippage. It is easier to find a seller for my buys and a buyer for my sales since there are more participants. The bid/offer spreads are tighter, and you give much less away when getting in and out.

Second, combining your volume rules with your open interest rules can provide you with additional fuel for your profit engine. For example, when prices are going up, volume is increasing and open interest is increasing, this is quite bullish. The capital is there to sustain and accelerate the move. Alternatively, when prices are going down, volume is increasing and so is open interest, this is a very bearish sign. Finally, it is important to note that chart patterns are, on the whole, more reliable with higher volume and open interest than with lower of either.

Oscillators

Relative Strength Index (RSI)

There's a group of technical indicators call *oscillators*. They work in a similar manner and are popular with traders as *overbought* or *oversold* indicators. The most commonly used is the Relative Strength Index (RSI). It was originally developed by Welles Wilder in the late 1970s. You'll hear the words oversold and overbought touted by your broker, advisory firms, newsletters, etc. Here's what they're talking about. Markets do not go straight up or straight down forever without corrective moves. There comes a point where the market is ready to turn, either temporarily or for good. Overbought basically means the market is too high in the respect that it's running out of buyers; in effect about to fall of its own weight. Oversold is the antonym. The market is too low, running out of sellers (at least for the current time period) and ready for a bounce. It is not a very scientific term and is bandied about somewhat arbitrarily. The RSI attempts to quantify the degree of oversoldness or overboughtness (spellcheck wants to discard these two words, but I'll leave them in; I think you get the idea). For you mathematicians, the formula is as follows:

> ✱ *Overbought basically means the market is too high in the respect that it's running out of buyers; in effect about to fall of its own weight. Oversold is the antonym.*

RSI = 100 – (100/[1 + RS])
where RS = Average of net up closing changes for *N* days/Average of net down closing changes for *N* days

The number of days is selected by the trader; 9 is the standard or 'default' in most programs.

To calculate the 9-day RSI you would need to average the change of the previous 9 up days, and divide this number by the average of the change of the previous 9 down days. Just about all the technical software programs, and many commodity brokers, will calculate the daily RSI for you.

The RSI will range from just above 0 to just under 100, but it is extremely rare to see a number close to either of these extremes. The RSI spends most of its time fluctuating between 30 and 70. At extremes, it will move under 30 or over 70. These are the 'standard' oversold (<30) and overbought (>70) areas. Many traders like to use 20 and 80 to indicate oversold or overbought.

How do you use it? When this number gets too small or too big it is theoretically time to put your antenna up. The market is getting close to a reversal point. There are traders who attempt to buy when the RSI wanders into oversold range and sell in the overbought. My opinion is, if you attempt to do this, you had better have deep pockets. At times, (trading range type markets) this *can* be an excellent way to pick tops and bottoms. However, in the major moves and at extremes (the most profitable time for the trend follower) the RSI can remain in the extreme ranges for a long time and for quite a few points. (And, hey, it's 'only' points, right?) This is the major drawback of the RSI. It will work in normal markets, but when the market is in the blowoff or panic stage it can remain in overbought or oversold territory for a while and become quite costly.

I do think this can be a useful tool, but only when used in conjunction with other indicators. You need to know what type of market you are in (trading range or trending, young or mature). If you can determine this, the RSI can help you identify what point in the life of the market you're at. RSIs do tend to get high in the mature stages of a bull market and low in the mature stages of a bear, but there is no magic number which signals the bottom. In fact, I've found it is better practice to watch for the RSI to turn up *after* it falls under 30 to signal a bottom, and vice versa for the bull. Yet even this tactic tends to lead to numerous false and money losing signals, since the RSI is a *coincident* indicator. It moves with price. A minor upswing has to turn the RSI up (Chart 8.31).

The best way to use RSI

The best way to use RSI (and you will hear this phrase if you trade for a while) is to look for *divergences*. These occur when the RSI doesn't make a new low with the market, or doesn't make a new high with the market.

For example, let's suppose coffee rallies from 128 to 158; the RSI registers a high for the move of *83* at 158 (so it is in overbought territory). The market then falls back to 152, a normal correction, and the RSI falls back to *71*. Subsequently, the coffee market continues its bullish ways and reaches a new high of 161. Up until this point, the RSI has moved with price. Every day coffee registered a new closing high for the move, so did the RSI. However, on this occasion the RSI only moved up to *79*, a lower high. The market made a new high, the RSI made a lower high; this is classic divergence.

I've found the best signals come from RSI divergence (Chart 8.32). And the very best signals come from triple divergence, where the market makes a third higher high, or third lower low, while the RSI makes a third lower high, or third higher low. And yes, I've seen quadruple divergence and even more divergences. This can be another dilemma when using RSI. Double divergence can be seen many times just before a turning point, but in the most powerful moves (the ones we really want to be on) there is nothing to say the market cannot keep going in the direction of the major trend. Bottom line, this is something to look at daily because it can give you some useful information, but I would use RSI as a confirming indicator only, not as your primary indicator. Never use it as a stand-alone trading method.

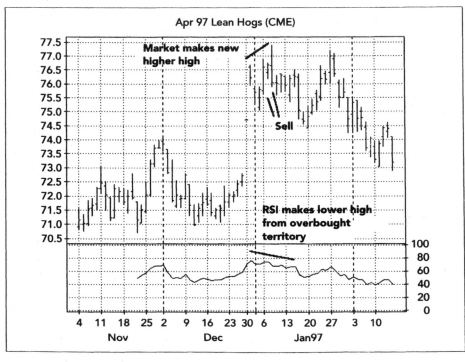

■ **Chart 8.31** Relative Strength Index (RSI)

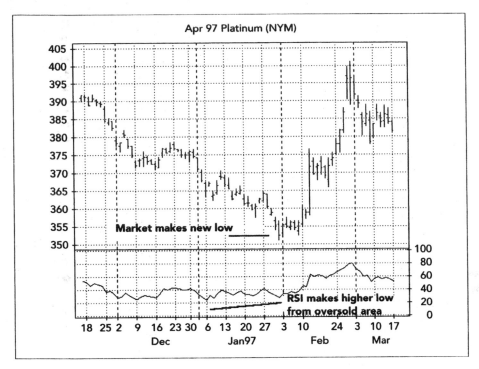

Chart 8.32 RSI divergence

Stochastics

Stochastics are another popular oscillator, developed by George Lane and also available on most software programs. The stochastics formula is a bit more complex than RSI, and readily available for those who want to see the mathematics. I won't go into it here (you can let the computer figure it out for you like most traders do), but I will go into the basics of how to interpret stochastics data. What the formula does is to measure how the close impacts the trend. The theory is, in bull markets the close will more likely be near the day's high, and in bear markets the close will more likely be near the day's lows. The way the market *closes* will determine how the stochastic trends. In essence, stochastics are a measurement of how the most current close relates to where prices have been during the period under study.

> ✱ *In essence, stochastics are a measurement of how the most current close relates to where prices have been during the period under study.*

Stochastics (Chart 8.33) consist of two lines, the %K, which is more sensitive, and the %D which is slower moving. Like the RSI, the trader can choose the number of days for the formula. Shorter term (5 days is popular) are very sensitive, will act quickly, but lead to many more whipsaws. Longer term (14 days is widely used) identify longer term moves and eliminate some of the whipsaws of the shorter variety. If you plan to work with stochastics, the computer will plot the 'fast' stochastic and the 'slow' version. I've found the slow is a better way to go, since it is smoothed to eliminate many of the whipsaw and false signals of the former.

The stochastic's values will range between 0 and 100, just like the RSI, and overbought is generally considered to be a value in excess of 80, oversold less than 20. They can be used like the RSI this way, but they tend to give better signals when they diverge from price (just like the RSI). *Divergence can precede the market*. Bullish divergence is when prices hit new lows, but the stochastic makes a higher low than its previous low. Bearish divergence is when prices hit a new high, but the stochastic makes a lower high. Both of these occurrences can give strong indications of market tops and bottoms. Traders also look for the stochastic lines to *cross* to exit an existing position or enter a new one. *The best signals come when divergence is present, and then the %K line crosses the %D line which confirms the divergence.*

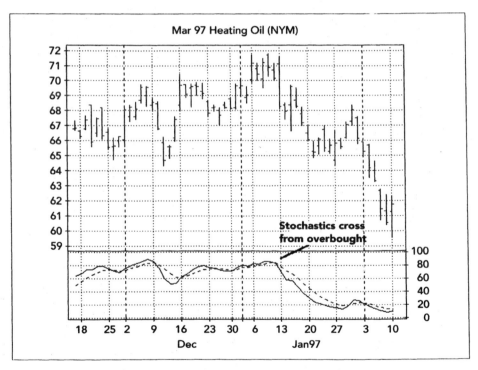

Chart 8.33 Stochastics

Elliot wave analysis

I'm including Elliot wave since many traders do swear by it. Ralph Elliot was an accountant who developed his theory on market cycles in 1939. Some believe his theory is based on an ancient Japanese trading method.

Basically, Elliot believed there is a 'natural order' to the markets and they travel in predictable cycles. He believed the stock market (and the theorists say this can be transferred to commodities) rallies in five waves when in an uptrend, and falls in three wave corrective moves. When in a downtrend the main trend is five waves down with three-wave corrective up moves. This five-wave pattern is made up of three odd-numbered waves, 1,3, and 5 which are connected by two corrective waves, 2 and 4. Each major odd-numbered wave can also be sub-divided into five waves, and corrective waves can be broken into three parts (the abc correction).

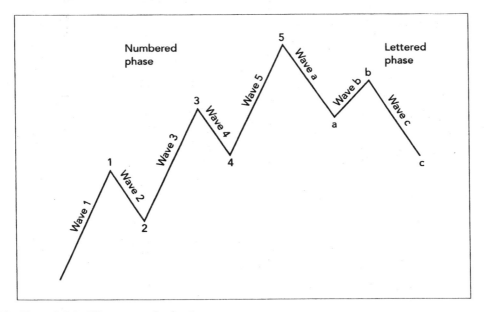

Chart 8.34 Elliot wave: the basic pattern

At times, I have looked at longer term charts of major trends and been able to see exactly what Elliot was talking about. However, other times it just doesn't happen. The main problem I have personally had with Elliot wave is that I find it difficult, if not impossible, to determine what wave the market is in during the thick of the battle. If you delve deeply into Elliot wave analysis, you'll find numerous rules which explain away every wiggle on the charts. There are sub-sets of subsets of waves, and when an Elliot wave theorist misses the count, he will revise his analysis to say wave 3 was actually not wave 3, but a sub-wave 4 of major wave 3, and this is why we had an abc correction, which he didn't expect. I'm not trying to be critical here, because I do believe there is real validity to some of Elliot's stuff. I have just had trouble using it. Every trader must use what works for him. Two traders can have entirely different approaches, and still

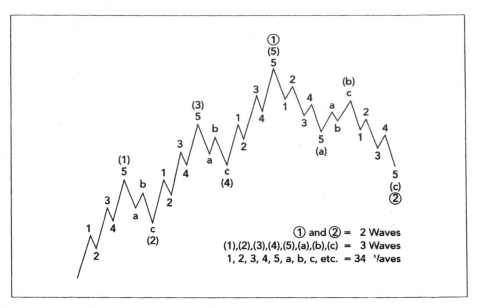

Chart 8.35 Elliot wave with sub-waves

both make money. There are many good books and a few computer programs on Elliot (Robert Prechter is considered the modern expert on Elliot wave) and you may wish to pick one up if this appeals to you.

Point and figure charts

The point and figure is another flavour of price charting which ignores time. Time is irrelevant, only price matters. Price signals are indicated by Xs and Os (Chart 8.36). The point and figure chartist uses Xs to illustrate rising prices, and Os for falling prices. As long as the price is rising, Xs are added. Os come into play when they are dropping. The decision to start a new column of Xs or Os is based on the market making a price change of a certain amount designated by the technician. This would be a 'box'. The technician must also designate (in addition to the size of each box) what determines a *reversal*. For example, a popular reversal size is 3 boxes. So, if you use a scale of 10 points for cattle, a reversal size would be 30 points. The values for the box and reversal are arbitrary depending on how sensitive the trader wishes his point and figure chart to be. The larger the box size and reversal values the less sensitive the chart will be, and vice versa. A 1¢ box for wheat will obviously be more sensitive than a 10¢ box. If the chart is too sensitive, the boxes too small, you increase the chances of being whipsawed by insignificant fluctuations. If too large, you will miss out on significant portions of some moves and be taking too much risk.

I personally do not use P&F charts, but know some very successful floor traders who do. This is why I wanted at least to mention them in the book, so the serious student who wants to pursue the P&F can do some of his own research. Since I don't use them, I really can't help you in determining the correct values to use as price increments. However, like many technical tools, there is no magic answer here. It is mainly a function of trial and error and depends on the market and price volatility. P&F traders I know tell me they generally like to use price reversals of a 3- to 5-box move. The box varies by the time frame of the trader.

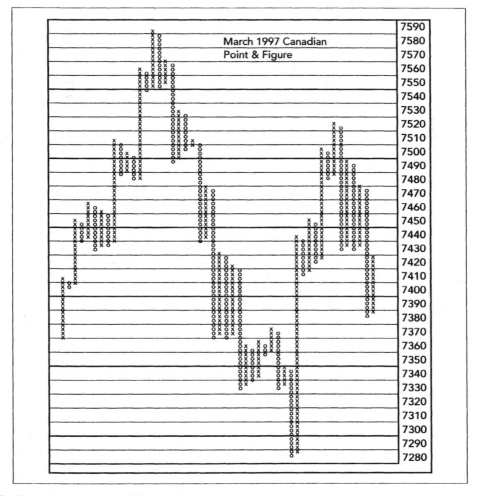

■ **Chart 8.36** Point and figure chart

Let's look at an example: you are a cotton trader and want to use 20 points (or $\frac{1}{5}$ of a cent per pound) as your box with 3 boxes or 60 points as a price reversal. A point in cotton is worth $5 (1¢/pound, or 100 points = $500 because it is a 50,000 pound contract) therefore the 20-point box represents $100 per contract.

The 60-point reversal represents $300 per contract. A price movement of, say, 100 points or a penny per pound would be charted on the P&F using 5 Xs if rising, or 5 Os if falling. For every 20-point rise in the price of cotton, the chartist would add one X on top of the previous X in the same column. He would start a new column (move over one column to the right) only when the market fell 60 points from the high. Then he would start a new column of Os and continue to add Os, one under another, for every 20-point down move. When using the 60-point reversal, he would only get started using Os when the market fell at least 60 points from the previous high. A fall of 55 points would never be recorded as long as the market recovered and made new highs above the previous high. However, in this example, no new Xs would be recorded until the market makes a new high for the move by at least 20 points.

This is how the P&F user determines what the trend is. As long as Xs are being recorded – it doesn't matter how much time this phenomenon takes – the trend is up and the long side is the way to play. When Os start to appear, this is an indication of a new downtrend; longs should be reversed and the short side probed.

Japanese candlestick chart

Candlesticks are the third major charting method and were used by the Japanese before charting ever became popular in the West. Rice futures were active in Japan as early as the 1700s, and the traders of the day developed this earliest form of technical analysis. Bar charts use bars, point and figure charts use Xs and Os, candlestick charts use rows of candles with wicks on either end. The body of each candle is the distance between the opening and closing prices. If the closing price is higher than the open, the body is left empty (or white, or it could be one colour like blue). If the closing price is lower than the open, the body is filled in (black, or another colour like red). The upper wick represents the high, and the lower wick the low. The wicks are not as important as the body. In other words, candlestick chartists are not as interested in the day's high or low as they are in the *relationship* between the open and the close.

I've studied candlesticks and have decided they do not fit my personal style. However, there are a number of interesting patterns that do appear to have some validity to them. They have colourful names as well. Candlestick chartists refer to 'hanging men', 'tweezers tops' and 'dark cloud covers'. In my studies, I didn't find most of these to be preferable to the more traditional bar charting patterns, with the possible exception of the engulfing patterns. They seem to be able to identify tops and bottoms better than standard reversal patterns. The engulfing line can be seen at major tops and bottoms and they can also be continuation patterns seen in the midst of a major trend. In many cases they do signal the end of a correction within a major trend.

The *bullish engulfing line* consists of a white (empty) body which totally engulfs, or covers, the previous day's body In other words, the high of the body is higher than the high of the previous body and the low is below the previous low. The white body is formed by a low opening met by strong buying which will push price to close above the previous candle: a very bullish indicator, and often seen at major bottoms.

Bearish engulfing lines are the mirror image seen at tops: a long black candle that totally engulfs, or covers, the previous day's candle. This is often seen at a blowoff top. A powerful signal for candlestick people (Chart 8.37).

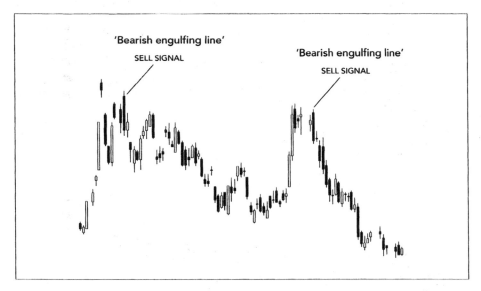

Chart 8.37 Japanese candlesticks: engulfing lines

As with Elliot wave, there are entire books written only about candlestick trading. If you are interested in delving further into this arcane subject, the information is out there.

Why technical analysis makes sense

Some pure fundamentalists dismiss technicians as merely 'chartists', the insinuation being that this is black magic. I should point out that charts are an integral part of most sciences – from engineering to medicine. The reasons technical analysis makes sense are fourfold:

1   'Footprints in the sand': the smart money (who are generally the big players since they are the ones making the money) cannot hide. They may be better informed, but their buying or selling will have to show up in price, volume and open interest.

2   The market *discounts* all fundamentals *in* price.

3   History does repeat, and if you don't learn from it you are bound to fail.

4   Markets do move in trends and these trends are more likely to continue than not.

In the next two chapters we will delve into a technical method which I use for determining and profiting from trends.

The most valuable technical tool (TMVTT)

When trading futures and options there is no sure thing. I've seen the advertisements, I've tested many of the systems, but no matter what the ads say there aren't any which win 95 per cent of the time (or even close). Let's put it this way; if there is a holy grail, I've not found it.

In fact, one of the most important lessons I can teach you is this; there is no single pattern, system, method, or indicator which will work all the time, or work in all markets. The best you can hope for is to find a tool (or tools) which can put the odds in your favour. If your winning percentage is favourable, and/or if your wins on average are bigger than your losses, you will make money. The good news is, as we discussed in Chapter 8, there are many good technical tools available which will put the odds in your favor.

> ✳ *There is no single pattern, system, method, or indicator which will work all the time, or work in all markets.*

There is one specific set of technical tools which I've found work better than most (at least for me). They are *moving averages*. While not new, I have personally found moving average systems to be 'the most valuable technical tool' (let's call them TMVTT for short). I've used them successfully in my own trading and I plan to show you how I do it in the pages to come.

Because I find moving averages to be such a useful tool, we will devote the next two chapters to the subject. This chapter will discuss the basics: what they are, how they work and how to use them properly in your own trading. In the next chapter, I will present a specific trading approach using certain averages, which I believe could greatly enhance your bottom line profitability.

Bottom pickers vs. trend followers

There are traders who say they are able to pick tops and bottoms with a fair degree of accuracy. There are certain indicators (the RSI for example) and various patterns (the 'key reversal', 'engulfing lines' in candlestick charting) which are designed to do just that. There is no doubt that the trader who can pick tops and bottoms with any degree of success will make the most money. However, I've found in practice that this is a very, very difficult thing to do over time. Anyone who trades long enough will no doubt be lucky at times and catch a major top or bottom. I can remember two cases in my career where I've been lucky enough to catch one (this is over thousands of trades) – one in soybeans and one in copper. I'm not talking about a daily high or low here, or even a weekly high or low, but a *major* top or bottom. I'm talking here about the *contract* high or low published in the paper. The price that sticks on the historic price charts as that extreme number. This is a very lucky, almost impossible thing to do since in hundreds of trading days every year, there is only one major top and one major bottom. Even minor tops and bottoms, daily and weekly highs and lows, are hard to get since they are the exception. Over a two-week period every market will have its top and its bottom price, but how many thousands of other trades took place even in this fairly short period of time? There's an old commodity trading adage which goes something like 'Bottom pickers get their hands slapped.' As W.D. Gann has taught us, no matter how cheap or how expensive a market may appear, it is never too cheap to sell, or too high to buy.

I've found it much easier, and ultimately much more profitable, to take a chunk out of the middle of a move, and this is what moving averages are designed to do. Moving averages are *trend following* tools. This means they do not anticipate the market they *lag* it. They are designed to help us determine two things: what the current trend is; and when the trend has turned. However, they can only tell us this after a trend is in place. By definition, this will be after the move is already underway. Therefore, it is impossible to pick tops and bottoms using moving averages. I wouldn't worry about missing a portion of any move however. Too many traders feel that if they haven't picked a top or bottom it is too late to take a trade, and this is one of the reasons the majority do not make money. Gold may have fallen $100/ounce in the past year and have already made its low, but then after it has rallied $10 off the bottom, it doesn't look that cheap to most people any more. This is because most people have short memories, and recent history is the history remembered first. The previous $90 down was a tremendous short, anyone looking at a chart could determine that. Looking back (and hindsight is always 20/20), so what if you missed the first $10 of *that* move? Or what if you were trying to hang on to a long position for the previous $100 down? In that case, I bet you wished you had left that top $10 on the table (to save the grief and financial devastation the remaining $90 brought).

Remember, we are just trying to identify the major trend here, and if we can do this with any degree of accuracy we will make money. Never worry about missing the first part of a move. The second part can be very profitable. Also you should know that there are scores of legendary traders, Richard Dennis and his 'turtles' come to mind, who use trend *following* techniques, and have taken hundreds of millions of dollars out of the futures markets.

Moving averages

Moving average techniques have been around for over a century. The modern father of moving averages is recognized to be Richard Donchian, an executive with Shearson when I started in the business in the late 1970s/early 1980s. He developed specific moving average trading methods, and successfully managed money using them for over 20 years. They were useful then, and are just as useful now. This is because the markets still move in *trends*, and *if we can accurately identify the trend of the market, we will make money*.

A moving picture

You might agree with me that any one price is sort of like a snapshot in time. It can never tell us the trend. It does tell us something, but it hardly tells the whole story. When you take ten photographs in rapid succession, you get a better picture of the whole story. If the story is the market, you get a better feel for the real trend of prices looking at the last ten, as opposed to looking at just one. When you put together a series of, say, 20 blocks of ten photos each, you have a movie which will be even more informative than a photo or two. This movie is analogous to a *moving average line* which can be plotted right onto a price chart. It can give you a sense of who is stronger at the time, the bulls or the bears, by just looking at the strength of the move, and the direction the line is moving. *If the bulls become stronger than the bears, the moving average line will appear to move up and the current price will move above the MA, and vice versa*. The tough question when using MAs is how many prices give us the best feel for the trend. If we use too many, the old data can tend to put the real trend out of focus. Too few, and we cannot really tell what it is we're looking at.

> * If we can accurately identify the trend of the market, we will make money.

It's important to remember that when we utilize any trend following method, we are not trying to forecast exactly when a market move will be over. Rather, we are using a totally technical approach, which relies on a specific type of indicator, to tell us what the trend is. We also want this indicator to alert us, with some degree of reliability, when the trend has changed *before* we give back too big a chunk of our paper profits, or *before* our unrealized losses become serious.

Moving averages will tell you when the trend changes. More importantly, they will keep you on the major portion of a major trend, *and this is where the big money is made*. However, nothing worthwhile is ever easy. In trendless markets, moving average techniques will generate false signals, and there could be strings of smaller losses. At times, strings of smaller losses can add up to big losses. In the next chapter I will share with you a technique hopefully designed to save you some grief here. But be forewarned: there will be drawdown periods and you are required to be well enough capitalized to ride these out. Finally, when using moving averages, it will be extremely important for you never to lose your winning qualities of patience and discipline – especially when the bad strings come. This is the key to success.

A moving average primer

Moving averages come in various flavours. They range from simple, to weighted, to smoothed and exponential. Traders use them alone, or in combinations as crossovers, even triple crossovers. They use them in oscillators as moving average convergence/divergence, and in bands. The basic underlying assumption here is that markets move in a trending fashion more often than not. I should mention that not everyone believes this is a true statement. There is a contingent of academics that feels market movements are random in nature (the 'random walk theorists'). I think you can fairly easily prove to yourself that 'random walk' is bunk. Just look at any chart of any commodity of at least six months in length. You will see the trends unfold before your eyes. (Just keep your eye peeled since that's when they taste best!) When demand for a particular commodity or financial asset is stronger than supply, prices (and therefore the market) will move in an uptrend. When supply is overwhelming demand at any particular point in time, the market will trend downward.

Markets will trend up or down, but they can at times move sideways as well. An erratic up/down type affair, a trendless market, will wreak havoc temporarily with any trend following system. These are the periods you need to use your discipline and patience to persevere. The good news is, I've found markets are engaged in up and/or downtrends for longer periods of time, and more often, than they are in sideways trends. This is why moving average techniques put the odds in your favour. Incidentally, it is easy to determine trends after the fact by looking at a chart (Charts 9.1 and 9.2, for instance). It is not all that easy in the thick of the battle. The news, the fundamentals, will not help you at all, since the news is always most bullish at the top and bearish at the bottom.

The simple moving average

The simplest moving average is fairly simple to construct and it's called (surprise) the simple moving average (SMA). It can come in any number of days, selected by the trader. Here's the formula:

$$SMA = \frac{P_1 + P_2 + P_3 + ...+ P_N}{N}$$

P is the price of the commodity being averaged
N is the number of days in the moving average.

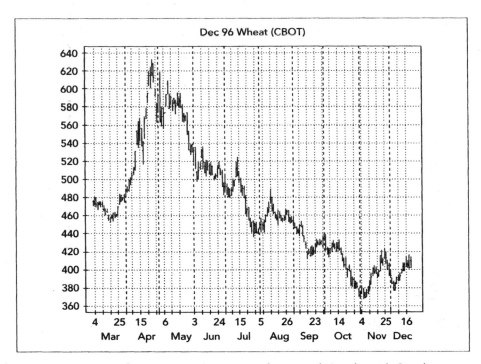

■ **Chart 9.1** Uptrend first two months – *major downtrend* May through October

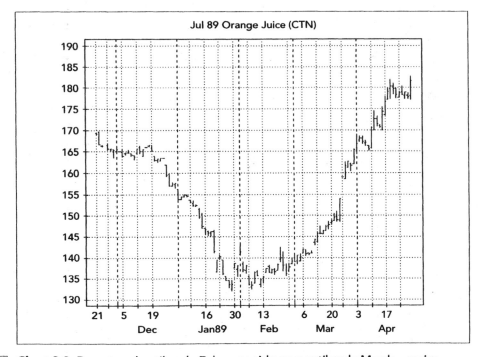

■ **Chart 9.2** Downtrend until early February, sideways until early March – *major uptrend* March through end of April

The value of an SMA is determined by the values that are being averaged and the time period. A 10-day SMA shows the average price for the past 10 days. A 20-day SMA, the average price for the last 20 days, etc. Moving averages can be calculated based on opens, closes, highs or lows, and even the average of the day's ranges. I recommend only using the *close* or the *settlement* price for each day. I feel this is generally the most important price of the day, since this is the price used to calculate margin calls. If the market closes on the high, or in the high range, most of the short players, unless they shorted right at the high(s), will have funds transferred out of their accounts. This money will be placed in the long's accounts. This makes the shorts a bit weaker and the longs a bit stronger, at least for the next day.

Let's construct a 5-day SMA of crude oil based on the closing prices. Assume the closes the past 5 days were 2105, 2110, 2115, 2120, 2125. The 5-day SMA is 2115. If on the sixth day the market closes at 2155, it will cause the 5-day SMA to rise to 2125, the average of the last 5 days divided by 5.

$$5 \text{ SMA day } 1 = \frac{2105 + 2110 + 2115 + 2120 + 2125}{5} = 2115$$

$$5 \text{ SMA day } 2 = \frac{2110 + 2115 + 2120 + 2125 + 2155}{5} = 2125$$

You always drop the oldest closing price and add today's closing price. In other words, when using the 5-day, you would always drop the sixth oldest day. With a 10-day you drop the eleventh oldest day, etc. The direction of the trend is determined by the direction in which the SMAs are moving and by comparing today's settlement price with the moving average. In the simple example above, the trend is up since the close on day 2 (2155) is higher than the SMA (2125). On day 1, the close was 2125 and the SMA was 2115, so the trend is up and we are long. On day 2 the close was 2155, and the SMA 2125, so the trend is up and we stay long. *When the average turns down and under the closing price, it generates a sell signal.*

> ✳ *When the average turns down and under the closing price, it generates a sell signal.*

You can connect each day's MA value on a chart and this produces a line. You can chart this line right onto a price chart to generate trading signals. As long as the line on any particular day is *under* the closing price, the trader would stay long; the trend is up. Once the line *crosses over* the closing price, the trader would go short; the trend has turned down. If long, and the line crosses over the closing price, the trader would reverse the position by selling double the amount of contracts owned. The problem is, if you do this every time the line crosses price, especially when using shorter term averages, you can get whipsawed (bounced back and forth with small losses and commissions eating you up). Many times a market will trade in a wild range, moving up wildly and down in the same session but, as I've mentioned before, I believe the closing price is the most significant.

As a simple rule when using MAs, I suggest waiting for the *close* to penetrate the MA to generate a signal. Even better, you should wait for a 'two-day close' (two consecutive days of penetration of the MA on the close), to signal a change in trend and therefore a change in position. Of course, by waiting for the close you do take on additional risk, since in a volatile market, or a wide-ranging day, the price at the close could be far under or above the MA. If you waited for the close on Black Monday (the day the Dow closed 500 points lower than Black Friday), you were in deep water. This is why it additionally makes good money management sense always to use an ultimate down and out point for any position (in other words a stop). You should do this when using any technical system, or fundamental for that matter. When using a MA, place your stop at some point away from the MA to create an approximate maximum percentage loss for those few abnormal moves that happen each year.

> ✳ *Rule 1 is always to avoid the catastrophic loss (that's the one so big it renders us unable to continue trading).*

Abnormal moves are quite rare, but they do occur, and these are the ones which have the potential to cause a catastrophic loss. Rule 1 is *always* to avoid the catastrophic loss (that's the one so big it renders us unable to continue trading). By the way, option strategies can also help here. Use puts to protect long positions, and calls to protect short positions. However, most markets are normal, and in normal markets here is the general rule of thumb:

- On the close, if the market price has fallen *below* the moving average line, a sell signal is generated.
- On the close, if the market price has *risen* above the moving average line, a buy signal is generated.

The signal can be taken at either the close of the signal day, or the open of the next day. I prefer the close the day of the signal, since it has been proven that when a market closes at an extreme of a day's price range (which many times will create the signal) it will follow through in the direction of the close the next day. So you need to know on a daily basis exactly where the average is coming into the close, and then use a 'stop close only' order. Alternatively you can place a 'market order' just prior to the close. Make sure your broker is ready for this and has good floor communications.

There will be times when the violation of the MA could be a close call. On days like these, I would opt to wait one more day, rather than risking taking a false signal.

How many days should you use in your MA?

The length of the MA will greatly impact trading activity and therefore profitability. Some traders use 5-day MAs, some 10-day, some 20, some 50. With very long-term traders, particularly stock market investors, the 200-day MA is popular. The length is an arbitrary decision, but the sensitivity of any MA is directly determined by its length. It is the length which determines how much time an MA has to respond to a change in price. It is a matter of 'lag time'. Very simply, shorter moving averages are more sensitive than longer moving averages. A 5-day is more sensitive than a 10-day, and they are both more sensitive than a 20-day. The more sensitive an MA, the smaller the loss will be on a reversal signal. However, there will a higher likelihood of a 'whipsaw', where a false reversal signal will cause a trader to reverse a trade too soon. A false signal occurs when a minor movement, which ultimately does not change the major trend, is enough to push the MA in the opposite direction of the settlement price, therefore resulting in a false change in position. It is false simply because the trader will subsequently need to reverse once again when the true trend reasserts itself.

Bottom line, it's important to use an MA which is long enough so it is not overly sensitive. On the other hand, if the MA is too long, the trader will tend to take too big a loss (or give up too big a portion of unrealized paper profits) before he or she is even aware of a trend change. A longer MA will keep you in a trade longer, thereby maximizing paper profits, but it can eat into realized profits because it moves too slowly. So, just like the story of the three bears, the MA cannot be too hot or too cold; it needs to be 'just right'. 'Just right', however, is not always that easy to determine, and can certainly change with market conditions. Voluminous studies have been done to determine which length is right for which market, but I believe these are useless simply because market conditions change for all markets. The silver market of the Hunt era is not the same silver market of today. Soybeans in a drought market act far differently than a normal weather market. In the next chapter I will share with you just which moving averages I use, and how I use them, but first let's discuss the different varieties of MAs.

> ✱ *So, just like the story of the three bears, the MA cannot be too hot or too cold; it needs to be 'just right'.*

Disadvantages of the SMA

Most of the traders who use moving averages use SMAs, because they are simple. They are easy to calculate since all you need is a calculator, or pencil and paper – but I don't recommend them. This is because the oldest price has the same influence as the newest. Generally, the newest reflects current market conditions better than the oldest, but with the SMA they are weighted equally.

eg **For example, suppose wheat is trading between 490 and 510 and the simple 9-day SMA is about 500. However, there is one day of data when the price was 475. When this low number becomes 10 days old and is dropped, the SMA jumps. This could generate a buy signal indicating a new major uptrend. However, the market tone may not have changed at all.**

In other words, when one old piece of oddball data gets dropped, it has a tendency to jump the SMA. This jump many times can be an overstatement.

Better MAs

Remember any one price is just a snapshot in time. It tells you something about price, but it hardly tells the whole story. Ten photos in rapid succession gives you a better picture of the story, and 20 blocks of ten photos each, an even better picture. If you are looking at a movie composed of 200 snapshots, the last 20 will most likely tell you more about what's likely to come next than the first 20. This is where exponential and weighted moving averages come in. They place more weight on the newest prices, which are generally more valid than the older prices.

Exponential and weighted moving averages (EMAs and WMAs)

The exponential and weighted moving averages assign greater weights to more recent events. The WMA increases the importance of the most recent price by a factor equal to the period used.

eg **For example, with a 5-day weighted, the fifth day will be given a factor 5 times greater than the first. To calculate a 5-day weighted average, multiply day 5 by 5, day 4 by 4, day 3 by 3, day 2 by 2, and the first or oldest day by 1, then divide by 15.**

The EMA also weights recent events more than the distant, but it smoothes out the average for a more consistent result. The smoothing factor (SF) is determined by dividing 2 into the moving average plus one of the SMA you wish to weight and smooth.

eg **For example, if you wish to smooth a 5-day SMA you divide 2 by 6. The result, 0.33, is the smoothing factor. For a 10 day, the SF is $\frac{2}{11}$ = 0.18, for a 20-day the SF is $\frac{2}{21}$ = 0.096.**

The SF is a fixed weight which is applied to the current price, with the balance applied to the most recent moving average value itself. This should become clearer when we look at a specific example.

eg Let's calculate a 5-day SMA, and a 5-day EMA for wheat. Remember, we need at least 5 days of data to produce our starting point for the SMA. Suppose the closing (settlement) prices for 11 consecutive days of wheat prices are as follows:

Day	Price
1	440
2	446
3	461
4	446
5	463
6	458
7	472
8	470
9	464
10	476
11	481

We can see from the above that the trend was definitely up during this 11-day period.

However, hindsight is always 20/20, and it is not always that easy to know just what the trend actually is when we're in the thick of the battle. This is where moving averages are supposed to help.

eg The SMA is calculated as follows:

Day	Price	Calculation	SMA
1	440		
2	446		
3	461		
4	446		
5	463	(440 + 446 + 461 + 446 + 463)/5	451.2
6	458	(446 + 461 + 446 + 463 + 458)/5	454.8
7	472	(461 + 446 + 463 + 458 + 472)/5	460.0
8	470	(446 + 463 + 458 + 472 + 470)/5	461.8
9	464	(463 + 458 + 472 + 470 + 464)/5	465.4
10	476	(458 + 472 + 470 + 464 + 476)/5	468.0
11	481	(472 + 470 + 464 + 476 + 481)/5	472.6

If you used the 5-day SMA to generate buy or sell signals, starting on day 5, you would have been a buyer at the closing price of 463 (since the price was *above* the SMA). You would have stayed long on days 6, 7 and 8, but on day 9 the price fell under the SMA and you would have sold and reversed (gone short) the position at the closing price of 464 for a marginal trade. Now you are short at 464 and would have to reverse again on day 10 at 476 for 12¢ loss. This is a classic whipsaw. You got jerked out of what was a good trade in an uptrend when one low-ball price (the oldest) is dropped out of the equation.

Now let's look at how the 5-day **EMA** performed over the same time period.

 To calculate the smoothing factor for the 5-day you divide 2 by 6; 6 is used because it is 1 more than 5: 2 divided by 6 = 0.33. You multiply this smoothing factor of 0.33 by today's price, and add this to 1 minus the smoothing factor, which is 0.67, times the EMA.

Day	Price	Calculation	EMA
1	440	start	440.00
2	446	[(0.33 × 446) + (0.67 × 440.00)]	441.98
3	461	[(0.33 × 461) + (0.67 × 441.98)]	448.26
4	449	[(0.33 × 449) + (0.67 × 448.26)]	448.50
5	463	[(0.33 × 463) + (0.67 × 448.50)]	453.29
6	458	[(0.33 × 458) + (0.67 × 453.29)]	454.84
7	472	[(0.33 × 472) + (0.67 × 454.84)]	460.50
8	470	[(0.33 × 470) + (0.67 × 460.50)]	463.64
9	464	[(0.33 × 464) + (0.67 × 463.64)]	463.76
10	476	[(0.33 × 476) + (0.67 × 463.76)]	467.80
11	481	[(0.33 × 481) + (0.67 × 467.80)]	472.15

The results show the price remained above the EMA during the entire period, even day 9, so no whipsaw resulted. The trader would remain long from 446, and still be long on day 11 at 481.

Yes, you can still get whipsawed using the EMA in a choppy market, but overall I've found WMAs and EMAs to be superior moving averages with fewer whipsaws!

Most of the trading software programs on the market today will calculate the WMA and the EMA for you automatically. If you have access to real time quotes they will calculate these averages in real time.

I should mention that popular these days with many computerized traders are moving average systems with a percentage band which uses an exponentially smoothed moving average plus a band above the EMA and minus a band below the EMA by the same percentage. A signal occurs whenever the closing price breaks outside the band. Exit occurs when the price recrosses into the band. Some traders like to trade within the bands, which is more like top and bottom picking. They sell at the top band, and buy at the bottom. The risk point is set at some percentage outside the band. I believe there is some validity to this, but since I personally find it difficult to pick tops and bottoms (I'm more of a trend follower), I will leave this to those who are inclined to trade the other way.

Bottom line

Moving averages are not all created equal and they are not the holy grail. However, if used systematically and consistently they will keep a trader on the right side of the big moves. They are a totally technical approach (rely on price only) plus it doesn't matter what market you use them on. They work in bull and bear markets, but will whipsaw the trader in a sideways or trendless market. This isn't as big a disadvantage as it may appear on the surface, since my experience says markets will spend more time trending than not trending. However, at times I have been involved in choppy, whipsaw-type markets that last for many weeks. If not properly capitalized, or if not disciplined, a trader can be 'wiped out', or at the very least become demoralized and abandon the system. Usually he or she will quit just before the big move starts. Remember, you need to catch the big moves when using a moving average system or you won't win.

In the next chapter we will go into greater detail of how to use TMVTT and I will share with you how to combine moving averages of varying lengths, and a specific method I've found useful.

How I use TMVTT

When constructing an MA, I recommend using the *closes* and *weighted* averages. I've found either the WMA and/or the smoothed and weighted EMA superior to the SMA. The real dilemma, the one which directly affects the bottom line, is what length to use. Shorter term averages are more sensitive. With a more sensitive average, the losses will be smaller, but the whipsaw factor increases geometrically. A long string of small losses is no better than a small string of big losses, and this latter problem can surface when using too long an average. Losses will be larger with a longer term average, and more unrealized profits will left on the table. However, the big money can only be made in the big moves, and a longer term average will keep you in for the big swings with a lesser tendency towards whipsaw.

So what's the answer? I've found a reasonable and profitable compromise is to use a *combination* of various moving averages. To follow is my two-step approach.

Step 1

Use the 30-day WMA to determine the longer term trend

The 30-day WMA is an excellent indicator of the major trend. I've found that many fund managers use the 20-day, and those with a longer term perspective use the 50-day. Since I don't know of any funds which use the 30-day, I've found this one a good tradeoff.

Here's how I use it. At our office we have live quotes feeding into our trading computers. The computers use a software program which calculates the 30-day WMA real time. (However, if you want to calculate it by hand, it's not all that hard; consult the previous chapter.) I have the 30-day WMA plotted over the price chart of the market I'm trading.

If the market is trading (on the close) above the 30WMA line for at least 2 consecutive days, the long-term trend is designated as *up*. It has to close 2 consecutive days below the line to signal the long-term trend *down*. Once it has closed 2 consecutive days under the 30WMA line, the long-term trend is designated as *down* until the market again closes two consecutive days above the line.

Just using the 30-day alone in this way all by itself can be a powerful tool.

Look at Chart 10.1 of live cattle. This is the entire trading period for the October 1996 contract, a particularly volatile year. Just eyeballing the chart, I would say the trend was sideways for November through January, then dipped down, trended higher from February into mid-April, sharply lower, then basically trended up through the balance of the year. Again, hindsight is 20/20 and at any point in time how would you know what the trend was? How would you know when the trend had turned?

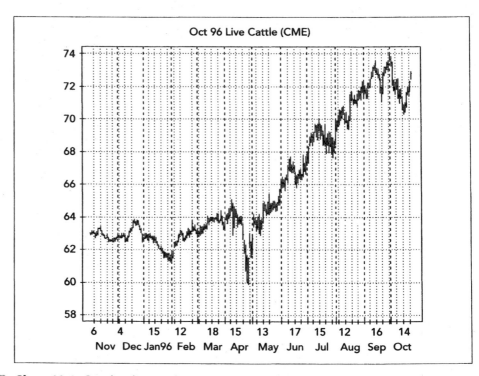

■ **Chart 10.1** October live cattle

Now look at the same chart with the 30-day WMA superimposed (Chart 10.2). A sell signal is generated when the market closes 2 days under the 30-day WMA. A buy signal is generated when the market closes 2 days above the 30-day WMA. Using this simple rule, for this contract we can see 5 sell signals and 4 buy signals (Chart 10.3).

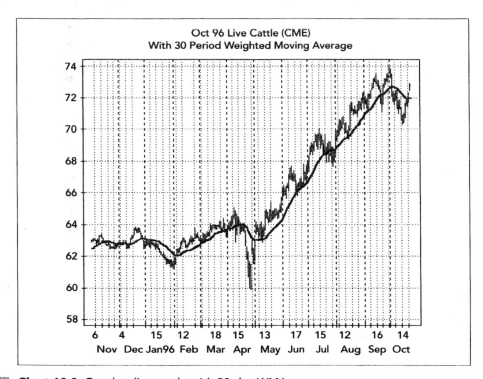

Chart 10.2 October live cattle with 30-day WMA

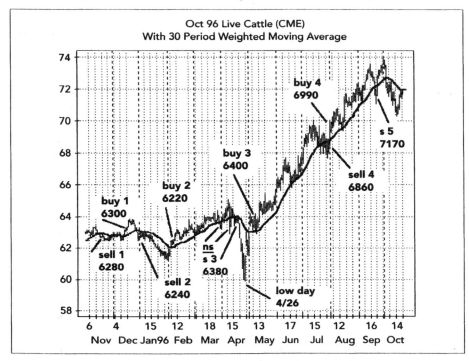

Chart 10.3 October live cattle with 30-day WMA and signals

If you took every sell signal, and then reversed every time a buy was signalled, then reversed again on a new sell, this is how you would you have fared.

Signal	Price	Points	Net profit/(loss) ($)*
Sell 1	6280		
Buy 1	6300	(20)	($180)
Sell 2	6240	(60)	($340)
Buy 2	6220	20	($20)
Sell 3	6380	160	$540
Buy 3	6400	(20)	($180)
Sell 4	6860	460	$1740
Buy 4	6990	(130)	($620)
Sell 5	7170	180	$620
Total		590	$1560

***assumes $100 fee/trade**

This result, a profit of $1560, is based on one contract only. A $100 fee per contract is deducted to cover commissions and slippage. Note, at times the market closed below or above the 30-day WMA, but no signal was generated (ns). The market has to close 2 consecutive days above or below the moving average to generate a signal.

As the above example illustrates, this simple program can be quite profitable *all by itself*. Don't take my word for it, prove this for yourself by using historic data on any market you wish to test.

This is one of my primary indicators, but I do not use it alone – I use it in combination with two other averages. I've found the 30-day alone is an excellent indicator of the longer term trend. It will catch a portion of the big move. In this particular case, Sell #4 was the big move which made our year. You needed to be consistent, however, so you were there for that move. The drawdowns were reasonable. However, at extremes, too much is left on the table.

For example, look at sell 3 and buy 4. Sell 3 came at 6380, about a week before the major low. This was a time of panic liquidation in the cattle market. Record high feed prices were causing farmers to dump cattle on the market at *any* price. The near month, the June, was actually trading at historic lows, about 54 at this same time. The market was actually setting the stage for a significant low, since the dumping of cattle now created shortages in the future. The actual contract low came on 26 April (see Chart 10.3) in this market and this was the start of a major uptrend for the remainder of the year (and into future years as well). However, in the thick of the battle, it was impossible to know when the panic liquidation of cattle would end. The day before the low, the market closed 'limit down' and it was impossible to sell at any price at the end of that day.

Now, from the sell signal 3 to the low, a trader using the 30-day WMA as I suggest herein, would have up to 400 points, that's $1600/contract, *unrealized* profits in his account. By the time the next buy signal, 3, came, the trade was actually a small loser. On the other hand, I am not an advocate of 'bottom picking', since I believe this is fairly impossible. Who knew when the actual bottom would arrive?

So, I use a second step, described below, which I have found overcomes this problem to an extent. If you used this second step you would have covered sell 3 at about 6170 (instead of 6400). The result would have been a net profit of 230 points, that's $920, instead of a loss of $180, a huge difference in the bottom line. Using the second step upped the total profit from $1560 to $3860.

So what's the second step? It is illustrated in Chart 10.4, and explained next. I use the 30-day WMA to determine the market trend, but not the buy and sell signals.

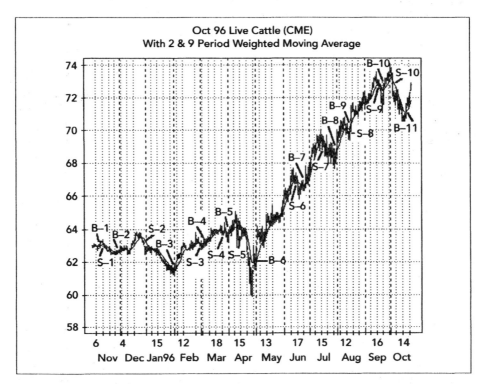

Chart 10.4 October live cattle with 2-day and 9-day WMA superimposed and signals

The rules are as follows:

Rule 1

When the market trend is designated as *up*, sell signals (short sales) are ignored: only buy signals (longs) are accepted

Rule 2

Whenever the market trend is designated as *down*, buy signals (longs) are ignored: only sell signals (short sales) are accepted

Now, how do we get our buy or sell signals?

Step 2

Use the 2-day WMA with the 9-day WMA (simultaneously) to generate buy and sell signals

Many traders use a combination of moving averages *together* in the *crossover* method to determine the trend of the market. The trader must monitor the relationship between the averages. A buy signal is generated when one average *crosses* the other.

The shorter term average will be the one to cross the longer term average because it is more sensitive. After experimenting with various combinations of averages, I've found the 2-day WMA (a very, very sensitive average which closely mirrors the current market), and the 9-day WMA (an intermediate term average), to be the best combination. This combination will keep you in all the major moves, but will also tend to generate false signals in choppy markets.

Rule 3

When the 2-day WMA crosses the 9-day WMA in an upward direction, a buy signal is generated: the trade is accepted if the long-term trend is up (rule 1)

Rule 4

When the 2-day WMA crosses the 9-day WMA in a downward direction a *sell* signal is generated: the trade is accepted if the long-term trend is down (rule 2)

We only accept new buy signals *if* the market is designated as *up*, as indicated by the 30-day WMA. Conversely, we only accept new sell signals *if* the market is designated as *down* as indicated by the 30-day WMA. So for rule 3 to take effect (the buy signal), rule 1 must be met. For rule 4 to take effect (the sell signal), rule 2 must be met.

So if we are in a long-term uptrend (as indicated by the 30-day WMA), *and* the 2-day crosses the 9 to the downside, we have a sell signal but will not go short. We will liquidate the long position and remain on the sidelines. If rule 2 is subsequently met (down designation, with the market under the 30-day at least 2 consecutive days), we then go short. If we are in a long-term uptrend *and* the 2-day crosses down (rule 3), with rule 2 simultaneously met (2 days under the 30-day WMA) we then *reverse* the position and go from long to short.

In other words, it is possible to have a sell signal and no short position and vice versa. A position is only entered if rule 1 and rule 3 are met simultaneously, *or* rule 2 and rule 4 are met simultaneously.

This is a compromise which in many respects melds the best of both moving average worlds. It locks in some additional profits on the more dramatic up/down or down/up moves, but prevents whipsaws to an extent. This is a mechanical system which is designed to let profits run in major trends, yet cuts losses short when there is an indication of trend reversal.

Look at Chart 10.5 of December 1996 wheat. This was a period of severe weather which hurt the US winter wheat crop. The March into April trend was decidedly up. April 26 was the high day, a day the May contract traded up the limit at over $7. Nobody could tell this would be the high day for years to come. The forecasts were for more severe weather the coming week. The market basically trended lower for the remainder of the year.

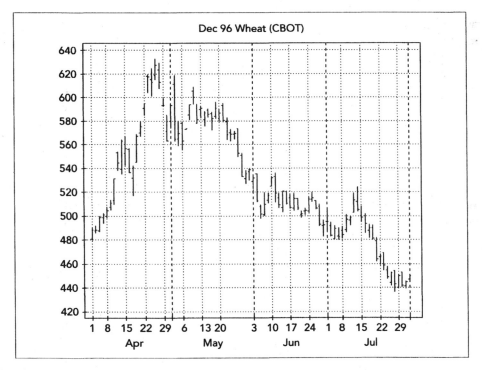

■ **Chart 10.5** December wheat

Chart 10.6 shows the same contract with the 30-day WMA and signals according to our rules.

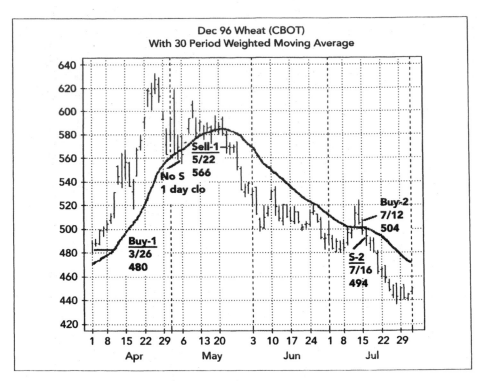

Dec 96 Wheat (CBOT)
With 30 Period Weighted Moving Average

Chart 10.6 December wheat with 30-day WMA and signals

30-day WMA signal	Date	Price	Gross profit/(loss)	Commission	NET profit/(loss)
Buy 1	26 March	480			
Sell 1	22 May	566	86¢	(2¢)	84¢
Buy 2	12 July	504	62¢	(2¢)	60¢
Sell 2	16 July	494	(10¢)	(2¢)	(12¢)
Total					132¢

We deducted 2¢/trade ($100) for commission and slippage. This was a nicely trending period and the net result was good, $1.32 per contract. Since a penny in wheat is equal to $50/contract, this was a net profit of $6600.

Now, let's look at the same period with the 2-day WMA, and the 9-day WMA superimposed over the wheat chart (Chart 10.7). The 2-day is very sensitive and follows the short-term trend of the market very, very closely. The 9-day is a more intermediate term average, less sensitive than the 30-day, but more than the 2-day.

Crossovers generate signals. If the 2-day crosses the 9-day to the upside at the close a buy signal is generated. A sell signal flashed at the close if the 2-day crosses the 9 to the downside. This system of crossovers alone can be used as a trading program. As a stand-alone program, net profits (assuming $100/contract commissions and slippage) were 57¢, or $2850. Note the best profit was $1.21 or

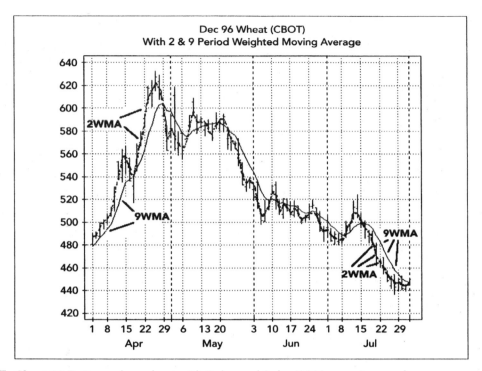

Chart 10.7 December wheat with 2-day and 9-day WMA superimposed

37¢ better than the best 30-day trade. This is because this system uses shorter term averages and is more sensitive. It captures more of the profits on the big swings after the turn. However, since there were a greater number of false signals (whipsaws), the total net profit during the period was smaller. This is the tradeoff. There are also circumstances where the 2/9 will outperform the 30. These are periods with higher and/or lower swings which turn direction more quickly. They are generally periods which trend better. However, in trendless or sideways markets the longer term averages will produce fewer whipsaws.

2/9 signals	Date	Price	Gross profit/ loss	Commission	Net profit/ (loss)
Buy 1	25 March	470			
Sell 1	29 April	593	123	(2)	121
Buy 2	10 May	600	(7)	(2)	(9)
Sell 2	17 May	574	(26)	(2)	(28)
Buy 3	22 May	594	(20)	(2)	(22)
Sell 3	24 May	580	(14)	(2)	(16)
Buy 4	10 June	534	46	(2)	44
Sell 4	13 June	508	(26)	(2)	(28)
Buy 5	10 July	498	10	(2)	8
Sell 5	16 July	487	(11)	(2)	(13)
Total					57

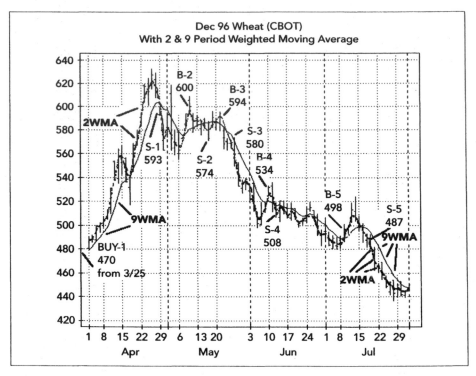

Chart 10.8 December wheat with 2-day and 9-day WMA and signals

What happens if we combine the two. In other words, if the 30-day the trend is up (rule 1) we accept 2/9 buy signals (rule 3). If the 30-day indicates the trend is down (rule 2) we accept 2/9 sell signals (rule 4).

2/9 signals	Date	Price	30-day	take?	Gross profit/(loss)	Commission	Net profit/(loss)
Buy 1	25 March	470	B	Y			
Sell 1	29 April	593	B	N	123	(2)	121
Buy 2	10 May	600	B	Y			0
Sell 2	17 May	574	B	N	(26)	(2)	(28)
Buy 3	22 May	594	S	N			0
Sell 3	24 May	580	S	Y			0
Buy 4	10 June	534	S	N	46	(2)	44
Sell 4	13 June	508	S	Y			0
Buy 5	10 July	498	S	N	10	(2)	8
Sell 5	16 July	487	S	Y			0

145

Net results improve with the combination, versus the 30-day alone and the 2/9 combined. This has been my general experience.

Charts 10.9, 10.10 and 10.11 show the results for the full period until contract expiration.

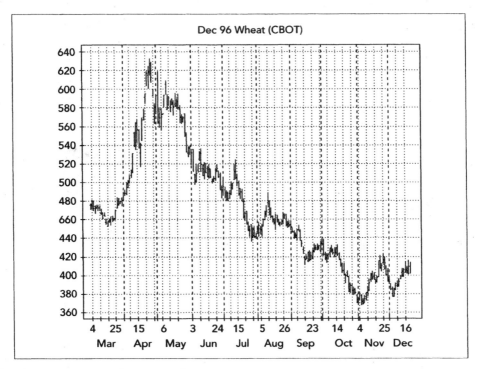

Chart 10.9 December 1996 wheat

That's it! For maximum profitability, however, I suggest a few additional rules:

Rule 5

Diversify into a minimum of three unrelated markets: these should be broad and liquid to allow for 'market orders' to be used with a minimum of slippage

This is a recommended rule only, not written in stone. I believe you can make money using this system trading one market, or two, but it might take longer and may require greater patience (if you just happen to start at the wrong time). The greater the diversification, the greater the chance of catching a major move *somewhere* and more quickly. At any point in time, one market may be in a major uptrend, one in a major downtrend, with a third trendless. The whole theory of this system is that the major moves will be profitable enough to offset minor losses which are inevitable in a choppy market. Our odds of catching major moves increases with the number of markets traded. One caveat: *they must be unrelated markets*. While the Swiss franc and the euro can move in opposite

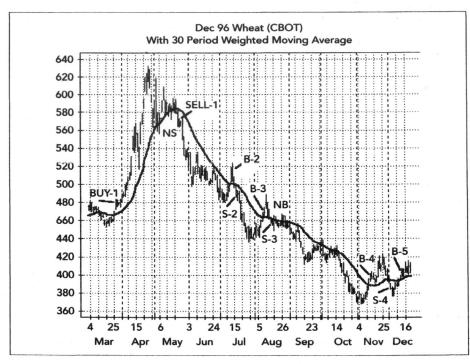

Chart 10.10 December 1996 wheat with 30-day WMA

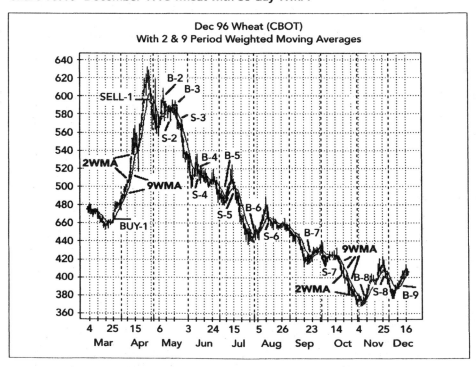

Chart 10.11 December 1996 wheat with 2-day and 9-day WMA

directions at times, they generally move in the same direction (albeit at different speeds) in relation to the dollar. Hogs and pork bellies can move in opposite directions, and they have, but since they are directly related products they generally move in the same direction (albeit at different speeds).

I personally like markets which have the tendency to be more volatile, rather than dull, since the more volatile markets have big enough moves to overcome the inevitable costs, commissions and slippage. For example, I prefer soybeans to corn, silver to gold, and the Swiss franc to the Deutschemark due to the increased volatility of the formers. I like markets with good volume and major commercial participation. The commercial interests have deeper pockets, and tend to stay with their positions longer. They can be a valuable ally for the big moves, and these are the moves we're looking for.

I will generally trade up to four unrelated markets. More than that number I've personally found too hard to follow. Fewer do not provide the diversification required. I always like to be in one currency. I usually trade the Swiss franc, but any of the major currencies will do nicely: the euro, the Swiss franc, the British pound, the dollar or the yen. The currencies tend to trend well in most market conditions. The Mexican peso and the Canadian dollar also appear to trend nicely. I do not recommend trading two of the European currencies in tandem, but the Japanese yen can be a good diversification with a European currency, or a North American currency. I also do not recommend trading two Western hemisphere currencies concurrently as they all (the Brazilian cruzerios, the peso, the C$), tend to be tied to the dollar to one extent or another.

Second, I like to trade a grain or oilseed, and personally prefer the soybeans (and/or the products, the meal and soybean oil), since they can trend nicely and possess sufficient volatility.

I round out my portfolio with either a meat (I like the cattle), most often a metal (copper and/or silver are both good), and/or an energy product. The crude oil is a liquid market which tends to trend nicely. I personally prefer it to the products (heating oil and gasoline) since the latter tends to be more erratic.

Other markets which are deep and liquid, allowing for easy entry and egress are the US Treasury Bonds and many of the other global interest rate futures products. Aluminium, traded on the LME, is a good metal to trade, as are gold on the COMEX, many of the stock index futures (if you have deep pockets), sugar, coffee, cocoa and hogs.

Again, this program theoretically works if used systematically on any market. My experience has been that some markets do not have the tendency to trend as nicely (lumber comes to mind). Others are too thin and the fills can be disappointing (orange juice and pork bellies are like this at times).

Additional rules for maximum success

Rule 6

Watch for breakouts from consolidation

If you can identify a period of consolidation, be patient. This is the one time you do not want to trade the system. Wait until the market breaks out of consolidation to take the next trade. Then trade the system for maximum profitability. The reason for this is the best trends *come out of consolidation*. Consolidation patterns are generally formed at major bottoms and (to a lesser extent) at major tops. If we can enter close to a major top, or bottom, our odds for success increase.

Consolidation is nothing more than an inability for either side (the bulls or the bears) to prevail. It is where the battle is being waged, but the war is not being won by either side. It is also termed a trendless or sideways market. During these periods, the system will not work, so we save ourselves money and grief if we can spot this type of pattern. It is not always easy to identify these periods, but it is possible. The odds you will accurately identify a consolidation period will increase when you do not have an opinion or position.

Pick up a chart book with a variety of markets illustrated and as you leaf through it you will undoubtedly find some. These are your potential targets for the best future trades, so start to monitor these types of markets daily, looking for the breakout.

The general rule is: *the longer the period of consolidation the bigger the move to follow*. Also, there will be fewer false signals after the breakout is completed from a longer consolidation. Basically, when a market breaks out of a trading range, it means one group (either the bulls or the bears) has prevailed. The longer the period of sideways action, the greater the number of participants on the wrong side of the market. The greater number on the wrong side, the more fuel available for a move in the direction of least resistance: the more shorts to panic in a bull move, and the more longs to panic in a bear. Certainly, there can be false breakouts. However the longer the period of consolidation the less likely a false result.

> ✳ *The general rule is: the longer the period of consolidation the bigger the move to follow.*

My experience has shown consolidation periods for most major commodities generally do not last more than four weeks. Periods of six to eight weeks do occur at times, however, and they generally result in the best moves. Periods of sideways action lasting greater than eight weeks are rare.

Footprints in the sand

Take a look at Chart 10.12. This was to be an historic market, but few knew it at the beginning of the year. The fundamentals were bullish in the early part of the year, demand was outstripping new mine production and scrap copper was in short supply. The market started the year consolidating in the 105 to 110 range

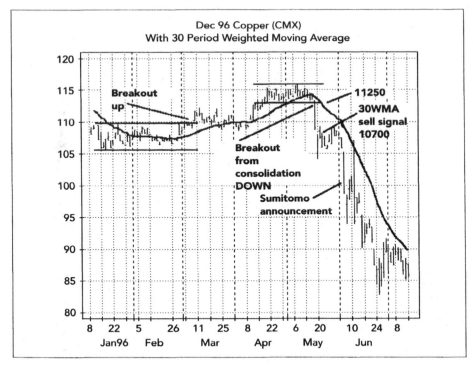

Dec 96 Copper (CMX)
With 30 Period Weighted Moving Average

Chart 10.12 Copper, breakout from consolidation

from January to early March. It broke above the 110 upper barrier of consolidation decisively in March, and began to trend higher, up to the 115 range. Then the market started a new consolidation, quite evident, between 113 and 115 for the 5-week period from mid-April to the end of May. At this time, we had no idea one of the most infamous of all scandals was about to be announced, the Sumitomo affair. This turned out to be the largest financial loss in history, $2.6 billion.

The news (a rogue copper trader from the international trading firm, Sumitomo, had 'secretly' racked up these huge losses in copper over a 10-year period) would not hit the wires until early June. However, someone knew what was going on weeks earlier, and left their footprints in the sand. Despite bullish news, the market broke out of the consolidation to the *downside* at about the 112.50 level. The news services attributed this to sell stops being hit and fund selling. The news still appeared bullish on the surface, at least according to the published fundamentals. However, the charts were telling us something was wrong with this market. In fact, a 2/9 sell signal came a few days *prior* to the downside breakout at 113.90 (see Chart 10.13). So, if we were following TMVTT we should have been out of all longs before the breakout was even completed. The 2/9 gave us an excellent early warning sell signal.

The breakout down was the second bearish clue. Finally, a 30-day WMA sell was registered the second day *after* the breakout at 107.00 (see Chart

10.14). Even though this was about 800 points below the recent highs, it still was plenty high enough to ride the trend down. There was another 2700 points to come before the 30-day WMA would flash the next buy signal.

To recap, the first 2/9 from the top came approximately 2900 points from the bottom, or $7250 per contract. The breakout from the consolidation began about 2750 points above the bottom, or $6875 per contract, and the 30-day WMA sell came in approximately 2200 points above the bottom, or $5500 per contract. The whole down move took place in just a little over a month.

This one market would have made your year if you saw the footprints in the sand and went short. Incidentally, after the collapse, the market consolidated for a few months, and eventually started back on a beautiful uptrend which recouped all the losses. The basic bullish fundamentals took hold again.

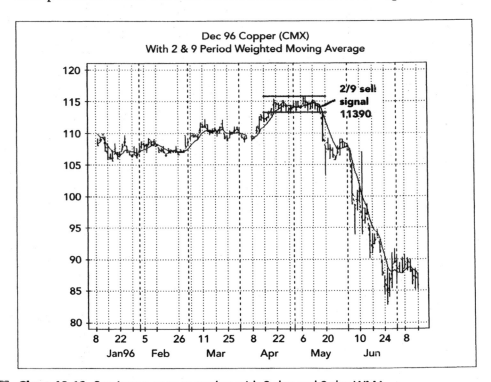

Chart 10.13 Sumitomo copper market with 2-day and 9-day WMA

You might think I choose this example because it demonstrates how a trend following program can work. Possibly, but do not think this is an unusual example, or one that is self-serving. I could have picked from literally hundreds of profitable trends this same year over a wide variety of markets. You don't have to take my word for it. Prove this to yourself by picking up a chart book. Eyeball the charts, and you tell me if the markets don't trend more than not. Paper trade the averages as presented and see for yourself this works. You may wish to play

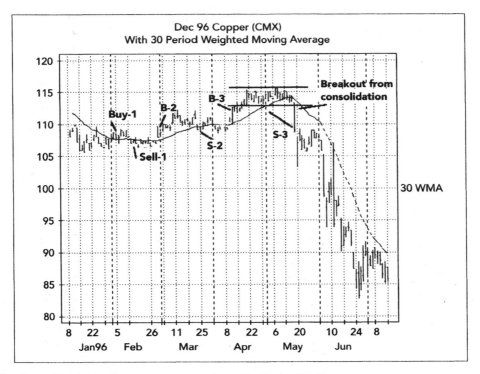

Chart 10.14 Sumitomo copper market with 30-day WMA

with different averages of your own to come up with a trend following system which works better than mine. I'm sure they're out there, and would like to hear about your successes!

Rule 7

Be consistent

Have the guts to take all the signals. Never try to fudge the system or outguess the market. Gann once said, 'The tape moves in mysterious ways the multitude to deceive.' This is true. Just when a market looks the weakest it may actually be the strongest. You must have the discipline to take all the signals, and then the patience

> ✳ *Have the guts to take all the signals. Never try to fudge the system or outguess the market.*

to wait for a bona fide signal before entering a trade. Discipline entails staying with the winning trades until you have a definite signal to liquidate. Remember, it is fun to take a profit, but taking premature profits will lead to ultimate failure. The

impulse to take profits (and try to reposition better) is very strong. There will be many time you just *know* a market is overdone and you just *know* you can re-enter better if you take your profits now. You will probably be right when this impulse hits you more times than not. If you follow your system, don't liquidate, and the market moves against you the next day, you could become frustrated and even demoralized. The temptation to fudge the system next time will be even greater.

However, this is not a recipe for success, trust me. The reason has to do with the nature of the big moves. When using this system, the best trades will be the ones you will have the good fortune to be on for the longest periods of time. There may only be a few trades each year which you will be able to stay with for months, according to the signals, before liquidating, but it will be these trades which will make your year. Also, *in an accelerating market, the best part of the move comes at the end.* This is when your biggest profits accumulate, and the temptation grows to book the profit. However, nobody I know can pick the actual top or bottom, and patience pays.

How do you acquire the required traits, discipline and patience? Write down your rules before you start to trade, then follow your game plan religiously. Know each day what needs to happen in the marketplace for you to do something. If you don't get a signal, then do nothing. The fewer number of trades you make, the odds of ultimate and maximum profitability increase!

I am not trying to say this is the holy grail, rather it is a disciplined, businesslike approach to the markets. If we were actually able to pick tops and bottoms, we could do much better than this method. However, we are not anticipating the market – here we are following it. The best we can hope to do is get into long positions near the bottom and out near the top – or vice versa. This program also has the advantage of being objective. Most technical systems do. Big losses are the result of having an opinion and not admitting or believing you can be wrong. This system tells you with certainty what the trend is and how to play it.

* Write down your rules before you start to trade, then follow your game plan religiously.

Emotions and opinions are minimized. It is impossible to be on the wrong side of a major move when you are with the trend. If the market is trending, you *will* make money here. Just be aware there will be trendless periods in all markets (even those which trend the best). The good news is markets trend more often than not. Diversification helps here, and if you are astute enough to avoid the market in a consolidation phase, or better yet catch a new move out of consolidation, you will maximize your profits!

A day trader's secrets

Why is day trading (entering and exiting positions the same trading day) so popular? In a word, it's *seductive*. There are those who believe day trading is an easy way to make a killing (but these are the people who get killed!). It looks to be liberating (but in reality day traders are slaves to their screens). The myth abounds that one can effectively day trade with a lot less money because you don't need to worry about overnight margins. In reality, those who are not adequately capitalized will ultimately drown in the financial sea. It may look exciting, but those who day trade for excitement only end up lost and dying of thirst in the financial desert.

After thousands of day trades, I can tell you this. Day trading is *much more demanding* than position trading. It takes *total* focus and *total* concentration.

It is true that advances in technology and the internet offer better opportunities for day traders. The democratic dissemination of information has levelled the playing field to a major extent, and today traders no longer need to sit by the phone waiting for their broker to call them with fills. Yet, the odds are still stacked against the day trader, so the big question is: why do it?

Well, there are positives. The big one it that you do not have *overnight exposure*, with its associated overnight stress. Day traders have a fresh start each and every trading day. They sleep like babies, not having to worry about central bank intervention or how tomorrow's USDA Crop Report might help or hurt them. Then there is the element of instant gratification which, trust me, can be very emotionally rewarding. No doubt, the shorter time frame does make for (all other factors being equal) lower risks, and without overnight margin requirements the leverage can be greatly magnified. Then again, the greater the trade activity, the greater the costs, and I am not just speaking in terms of commissions. Since slippage (price fills other than what you anticipate you will receive,

> ✳ *Those who day trade for excitement only end up lost and dying of thirst in the financial desert.*

or what you see on the screen when your order is submitted) is such an important cost of trading, it is imperative you find a brokerage firm that has excellent trade execution capabilities for the markets you trade. Slippage, in my opinion, is of even greater importance to bottom line profitability than fees, and it takes on an even greater significance when day trading.

In this chapter I plan to share with you my 'secrets' learned from twenty years of day trading. These secrets are absolutely essential to successful day trading. I will conclude by disclosing a simple strategy that has worked for me.

Your nine essential day trader's rules

1　You will not be a scalper.
2　You will be a day trader, not a daily trader.
3　You will treat day trading as a business.
4　You will feel good.
5　You will be totally disciplined!
6　You will never let a decent profit turn into a loss.
7　You will become very cautious after a 'home run'.
8　You will go only where the action is.
9　You will day trade only markets suited to you.

Now let's look at these nine rules more closely.

Rule 1
You will not be a scalper

Pit traders can successfully scalp for a few ticks because they have enormous scalper's advantages. They can buy the bid and sell the offer (you generally cannot), and they pay extremely low fees as exchange members (fees which can make trading for just a tick at a time profitable). Floor traders can react instantly to big orders as they hit the pit. They can hear the noise rising and know something is afoot, you can't. On the other hand, off the floor can be a big plus because you will not get caught up in the emotions of the pits, which often result in false messages.

Rule 2
You will be a day trader, not a daily trader

A day trader by definition is in and out the same session, but nobody can do it successfully every day. The right kinds of market conditions are not present every day, and it is psychologically too intense to day trade day in and day out. One tremendous advantage you have is freedom of choice. You do not need to take every signal or trade every market. You do not need to be in a position before an important, but risky, employment report. You have the luxury to wait and watch and witness the market's reaction before taking action. If a market is 'newsless' and quiet, or range bound, you can always relax and let your most important quality of patience work for you.

Rule 3
You will treat day trading as a business

It is not a part-time diversion. It is *very* demanding. You need *total* focus and *total* concentration. To be totally focused you must eliminate outside distractions. Lock your door, if you have to. I know from personal experience, the more outside annoyances, the harder it is for me to trade effectively.

Rule 4
You will feel good

If you do not feel well you cannot day trade effectively. If you stayed out late last night drinking, or are physically ill, or have emotional stress from outside influences, you should not do any kind of trading and this is especially important when day trading. Day trading is much more demanding and it is absolutely essential you be sharper and quicker than your competition. When the optimal 'set-up' presents itself, you must feel strong, because you will not have the luxury of hesitation!

Rule 5
You will be totally disciplined!

Period. What this means is you will follow *written* and *well-defined* rules systematically, which is the only way to avoid the emotionalism of the markets. In other words, you will construct a game plan, which *you will follow without bias*. Let me repeat this, you will have *no* biases. (I have always had my biggest losses when I have had a strong opinion about some market and overruled my technical game plan.) If you do not follow your game plan, you will miss some of the best and most profitable trades. Sound familiar?

What will your game plan look like? It will have well-defined entry and exit rules from a program or system you have tested and have confidence can win over time. Your well-tested system will have a positive outcome (not necessarily a high win to loss ratio, which is not easy to achieve for any system). If for every dollar you lose your system over time makes $2 on winning trades (after fees and slippage), then a marginally positive win to loss ratio will still result in profitability.

The best day traders are on autopilot and, just like a seasoned pilot, they operate without emotion using well-defined protocols. Your rules will be very strict in terms of capital preservation, especially during drawdown periods. (While yours may be better, let me tell you about my money management rules. I will not tolerate a drawdown of greater than 5 per cent in any single day. This is a moving target. In other words if I have paper profits this 5 per cent drawdown number is off a peak, so if I am up 1 per cent I move my stop up 1 per cent; 5 per cent is a maximum risk, most days I risk much less. To determine where my stop is placed, I use a 4 per cent number to calculate position size, with the extra 1 per cent a cushion for slippage and fees.)

Total discipline means you will always use stops (just do it), and never cancel a stop just because the market is getting close to it. Finally, never add to a losing position.

Rule 6
You will never let a decent profit turn into a loss

Here is what I do. If I have a reasonable profit on paper, I move my stop up so that if half of these profits slip away, I am gone for that day. The reason is obvious. In this way you escape with at least a portion of your profits.

Rule 7
You will become very cautious after a 'home run'

After you make a big hit, the temptation to overtrade grows geometrically. After a home run, look for singles (or better yet, take a vacation).

Rule 8
You will go only where the action is

It is essential to be aware of the current trading environment. Day trading requires volatility and liquidity. Not all markets are volatile enough to allow for ranges required for consistent profitability. You need a market that not only moves, but moves within a limited time frame. You shouldn't day trade markets like oats. Not all markets are liquid enough to minimize slippage. You shouldn't day trade markets like lumber. Even large markets should be avoided when they are quiet and/or range bound. Look for markets in the news. Of course, there will be times you think a market is going to be a mover but then it dulls up on you. Personally, if I am in a day trade which is going nowhere (after a reasonable time has passed), I will use my discretion to get out early. It does seem the best day trades work right away, and many times with little or no grief.

Rule 9
You will day trade only markets suited to you

Not every market is suited to everyone and there is no rule that says you have to trade anything and everything. While the S&P is today's day trader's favourite, I personally don't like it. It is too erratic, and in my experience the slippage and risk are too high. Better suited to my personal temperament for day trading are the currencies, crude oil, bonds and (when active) the soybeans and metals. Make a personal choice because nobody is holding a gun to your head to trade the market du jour.

One more thing, you need the right temperament to day trade. If you require numerous confirmations, or can only take action after extensive research, you are probably not suited to day trading. Additionally, I've found (maybe due to a simple mind) that simple is better. Keep it simple! Some of the most basic indicators can be incredibly profitable if you follow the rules I have outlined above.

The trend reversal day trading system

There are numerous wrong and no doubt fewer right ways to day trade profitably. The right ways come in different flavours and each trader has to discover his or her own. Here I present just one method, not the holy grail, but it works for me. It combines two simple yet effective and well-known indicators: the RSI and the simple moving average.

For the record, I am a trend follower. In other words, I do not try to pick tops or bottoms since I have personally found this just too hard to do. I would rather let the trend work for me, and find it easier to target a 'piece of the middle'. Recall what I said previously about not having a bias. This is particularly important when day trading. When using this method, we are only interested in exploiting the trend for that day; the major trend is irrelevant. A requirement is a volatile, high-volume market. We need to use our discretion and best judgement to exploit the trending days and strive to remain on the sidelines during choppy, low-volume days. How do we recognize the trending days? They tend to *follow* lower volume consolidation periods, will develop on breaks of significant chart points, generally with higher than normal volumes, and particularly on news days. You must be prepared and ready to act on days when news breaks; for example, when government reports are released. Always watch for gap opens. It is important to note that it is *not* the news, rather the *reaction* to the news, which is important. Your job is not to interpret news, but to read correctly the trend of the day. You must act without hesitation when you get a signal. Then you need patience after you take the signal. Even the best of trend days will not trend all day, as there will be intraday periods of consolidation which might only be rest periods, nothing more. You must always use stops, because no method works all the time. Finally, play it out to conclusion. At times your biggest profits will come in the final fifteen minutes of the day.

Parameters

Use a bar chart, bars no shorter than 15 minutes and no longer than 45 minutes. A shorter time frame generates too much noise and with a longer time frame the risk is too high. For the trade examples below, I use 18-minute bars. Use 23- and 30-period simple moving averages and a 9-period RSI.

Rules

1 *A signal is generated after a 'trend reversal'* A 'trend reversal' from down to up occurs when the market moves from trading under both averages, to above both averages. A 'trend reversal' from up to down occurs when the market moves from trading above both averages, to below both averages.

2 *A trend reversal can only occur after a 'set-up'* For a 'long set-up' to occur, the market must have one bar *close above* both averages (if previously below). For a 'short set-up', the market must have one bar *close below* both averages (if previously above).

3 *When the high of a long set-up bar is exceeded, a buy signal is generated. When the low of a short set-up bar is exceeded, a sell signal is generated.* Use a buy stop to enter on the long side, and a sell stop to enter on the short side.

4 *Take a buy signal only when the RSI is < 60. Take a sell signal only when the RSI is >40.* This rule will filter buy signals in potentially overbought situations, and filter sell signals in potentially oversold situation.

5 *Your initial stop is a reversal signal,* or a maximum 4 per cent of your gross equity (5 per cent including estimated fees and slippage). If by risking 4 per cent of your gross equity you cannot place your stop comfortably on the other side of the averages, do not take the trade since the risk would be too high. (For most of the markets I trade the risk is at least $400 gross per contract *not including* slippage and fees, which requires $10,000 in free equity per each single contract traded. When trading markets such as the large S&P, the risk will generally be quite a bit higher requiring a larger account size.)

6 *When the RSI moves <25 (on a short) or >75 (on a long) then lower/raise your stop to the high or low of the previous bar.* Once you have reached this step, you are tightening your stop in the exuberance phase or fear and panic phase. In many cases, you will be stopped during the next bar period, but in most cases by now you have locked in a decent profit (equal to at least your risk, and in many cases much more). This is a dynamic rule, in that you will continue to move your stop to lock in additional profits as the market continues to move your way. If your new stop is not hit during the session, then liquidate the position at the market on the close. It is important to hold the position all the way until the end of the day if you can. At times, this will result in what I call a 'mega profit' trade. You only need a few mega profits each year to really make your year!

Example 1: Long Bonds (Chart 11.1). This was a 'news day' with no less than five major government reports, including the important quarterly GDP (all released 10 minutes after the open). The numbers were somewhat conflicting, and after the releases the market continued to trend lower, but then about an hour into the session reversed and 'set up' (bar 8). The RSI on 'set up' was 52, so since it was under 60 this was a valid signal and we prepared to take the trade by placing our buy stop one tick above the high of bar 8. A long position was initiated when the buy stop was elected (bar 9) at 11320. A protective sell stop was initially placed at 11307. On this day, the RSI never traded above 75 so we were never able to tighten our stop. Since the initial stop was not touched, the position was liquidated at the close (bar 23).

It is interesting to note that the trend for this day had nothing do with the overall trend; in fact the major trend was down and the market did gap open lower on the following day (bar 24). The fact that we were day trading made this overnight risk a moot point.

Result: Long from 11320, sold on close at 11330 for a day trade profit of 10 ticks ($312.50 gross per contract).

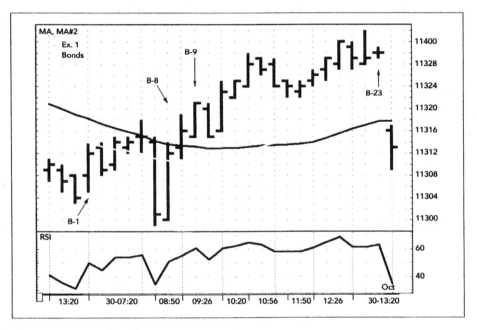

■ **Chart 11.1** Long bonds

Example 2: Short Euro (Chart 11.2). This was also a 'news day', one requiring action without hesitation. Prior to the market open, the European Central Bank raised interest rates. This was ostensibly bullish news, and the market gapped up at the open (but did so in a lukewarm sort of way). It traded modestly above the averages for the first six bars. The trend reversal came approximately two hours into the session (bar 7 with the 'set-up', and bar 8 with the sell signal). On the 'set-up' bar the RSI was above 40 (at 45), so we took the signal, and prepared to take the trade by placing a sell stop one tick under the low of bar 7. The short was filled at 10500 when the sell stop was elected at 10502. The initial protective buy stop was placed at 10542. When the RSI moved below 25 (bar 13) the stop was lowered to 10482 (just above the high of the previous bar). The stop was again lowered to 10474 or just above the high of bar 13 at the start of the bar 14 period, again to 10436, or just above the high of bar 14 at the start of 15, and again to 10406 at the start of 16.

If the market continued to trend lower into the close we would have continued to lower our stop with each subsequent bar and cover at the close. In this case, however, the stop was elected and filled at 10406 during the bar 19 period.

Result: Short from 10500, covered at 10406 for a day trade profit of 94 points ($1175 gross per contract).

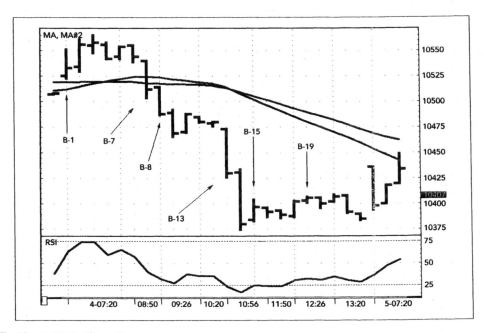

■ **Chart 11.2** Short Euro

Your state of mind

Dr Leroy, the head psychiatrist at the local mental hospital, is examining patients to see if they're cured and ready to re-enter society.

'So, Mr Clark,' the doctor says to one of his patients, 'I see by your chart that you've been recommended for dismissal. Do you have any idea what you might do once you're released?'

The patient thinks for a moment, then replies, 'Well, I went to school for mechanical engineering. That's still a good field, good money there. But on the other hand, I thought I might write a book about my experience here in the hospital, what it's like to be a patient here. People might be interested in reading a book like that. In addition, I thought I might go back to college and study art history, which I've grown interested in lately.'

Dr Leroy nods and says, 'Yes, those all sound like intriguing possibilities.'

The patient replies, 'And the best part is, in my spare time, I can go on being a teapot.'

So what does this story have to do with trading futures? Everything! All new traders believe they're 'ready to go', yet statistics on winners and losers indicate the great majority are missing an essential element. We all think we have the key to success before we trade. After all, the trading systems we develop do look like sure winners on paper, and our research makes sense both fundamentally and logically. Most traders begin confidently, so why then do so many encounter problems?

Trading is exciting, it's exhilarating, but it is also extremely difficult. While I did a decent job on the first edition of this book discussing trading tools and sharing my experiences, on later reflection, I began to believe a critical element was missing which made the first edition incomplete. This chapter, I believe, adds that missing element, and very well could be the most important chapter in this book contributing to your long-term success as a trader.

Herein, we will dwell on your inner self, we will cut to the quick regarding your personal qualities of work ethic, self-esteem and the ability to focus totally and concentrate on the task at hand. This chapter is, in one respect, a treatise on discipline, one of our essential qualities for success. This in turn relates to the all-important subject of money management, a critical subset of discipline. I could have alternatively titled this chapter, 'the psychology of trading', or 'trading consistently', yet it all really boils down to one thing, your *state of mind*. For the successful trader, the mental game is actually more important than every one of our best trading rules combined!

Motive

You want to trade futures, or you are currently trading, and the bold assumption is you would prefer to be successful at this. After all, this is why you have (hopefully) purchased this book. Have you really sat down and analyzed your true motives? Right, I know you want to make money, we all want to make money, but it should go well beyond that.

The hedgers in our markets are there for business reasons, to manage the risks inherent in the commodity and financial markets associated with their businesses. The other element, the speculators, should be in it for the same business reason, to enhance bottom line profitability. Yet, there are many, many who are trading for another reason: the thrill, the excitement, the adrenalin rush. These traders, and I think the numbers are significant, are looking for the same rush as the horse better or the crap shooter. While it is not impossible to make money as a Las Vegas gambler, some unique individuals do, most do not, and I do not think many people would treat a gambling endeavour as a means to an end.

> ✱ *The hedgers in our markets are there for business reasons, to manage the risks inherent in the commodity and financial markets associated with their businesses.*

So, my first question to you is what are your real motives? Only you can answer, but I will state very clearly that if your real motive is action, or instant gratification, you will fail. Your state of mind will prompt you to trade without regard to conditions. The conditions must favour your actions, or you will fail.

What should your motives be? Not just to make money, this is not enough. You are probably a competitive kind of person, one who enjoys playing games and the challenge of solving puzzles. You should strive to act in a disciplined, consistent, unemotional manner. Prior to each trade, you will need a well thought-out plan for that trade. The plan will expect a positive outcome, but will have a built-in contingency for an unexpected, or in other words, unprofitable outcome. You will need to act in a confident, unhesitating manner. You will need to overcome the six hurdles to successful trading.

The six hurdles to successful trading

1 Trading for the thrill of it.

2 Trading for revenge.

3 Lack of money management.

4 No well-defined trading plan.

5 Inability to pull the trigger.

6 Inability to admit you're wrong.

Let's analyze these six hurdles in more detail.

Condition yourself to be unemotional

If you are trading for the thrill of it, you will trade when the conditions favour your methods, and you will certainly trade when they don't. Since you are trading emotionally, you will overtrade, which is an inevitable outcome of thrill trading. You will also overstay your welcome on trades which are not going your way and this invites disaster. It might work for a while, but there will come a time when it will wipe you out, pure and simple. The other side of this is those people who trade for the adrenalin rush, but are subconsciously uncomfortable with risk. If you are one of these people, you will tend to undertrade, place your stops too close, and also not succeed. If you cannot condition yourself to assume the risk of a leveraged market, place your hard-earned money in Treasury Bills and go home. This is just as fatal a flaw as overtrading.

Revenge trading: another recipe for disaster

Has this ever happened to you? You have just been stopped out for a loss, a bigger loss than you had anticipated. Perhaps it was a 'gap open' beyond your stop due to some unexpected news. It is early in the trading day, and you feel you must make it back. You cannot go home today with such a large loss. How would you explain it? The market owes you your money back, it will pay you back, and it will do so today! Have you ever had this feeling? Well, I have, and let me tell you when I am out for revenge, nine times out of ten it leads to disaster. This is because the state of mind is unstable. Trading angry inevitably leads to bad decisions. When you get this feeling, force yourself to take a step back and relax. The market will be there for you tomorrow and there are always opportunities.

This is not the time to compound a problem. It is the time for your essential quality of patience to take over. Too many people let a loss affect their psychology on the next trade. I am not saying it is always easy to be unemotional, this is a very human trait. What I am saying is that you must condition yourself to remain in control, and if you feel you might be losing it, force yourself to step aside for a time.

Preservation of capital is your primary mission

When you have no money management programme in place, it is impossible to preserve your stake. Unless you tell yourself you will only risk X per cent of your account on any one trade, that one trade which looks so right will inevitably come along, and you will trade it too heavy. After all, the trade 'looked so right', 'everything is falling into place', and before you know it, you are dipping into the till once again.

Let me share a secret with you: they all look so right. I would not enter a trade unless it looked real good, but it seems there is no way to know in advance which trade is going to be the big winner. If we knew this, these are the only ones we would trade. For me, most years, it is a very small number of trades which makes my year, and usually not the trades I think will be the big winners. If I had no money management plan in place, I would no doubt be long gone before ever capturing those major moves. You must preserve your capital, and this means taking small and consistent hits on the many and inevitable losers. The goal is to still be in the game when those 'mega trades' finally materialize.

You plan must be well defined

This is crucial. Nobody enters a position expecting it will result in a loss. However, it will not come as news that even the top traders experience numerous losses over the course of any and all trading sessions. So if the best lose, why would you be any different? A well-defined plan will define failure and success both. Ask yourself why you are buying gold? If the answer is something like, 'because it just broke above the 30-day moving average', or 'because the CPI indicates inflation is heating up and we all know in the long run gold is sensitive to inflation', you have not defined your plan. You have reasons why you entered, sure, but no clear exit strategy. You are trading on hope, and this is not a recipe for success.

You must define your loss point *before* you enter the trade, and if you are not mentally prepared to lose many times, you will never win. It is essential to lose many battles in this trading war, or the war will never be won. Conversely, you should have a profit objective. Stop loss points should be written in stone, profit points can be flexible. However, you should have contingency plans when your profit objective is reached. The plan could be nothing more than something like this: 'I am risking $500 per contract on this trade, my technical profit objective is $1200. If the market moves $500 my way, I move my stop up to an approximate break-even, if it moves $900 my way, I move the stop up to approximate a $400 profit. If it reaches my technical objective I watch very closely for signs of failure. If the market shows these signs, I sell at the market. If it moves through, I tighten my stop to just under the previous low.' This plan may or may not work, but at least it is a plan, and without a plan you are doomed to failure.

You must act without hesitation (if a good reason to do so)

To paraphrase Steinbeck, 'the best laid plans of mice and men'. When you 'paper trade' you always take the loss or the profit. In the heat of the battle it is not as easy to pull the trigger. Remember, you must lose to win in this game. Too many times, even good traders will not take the loss when the planned risk point is reached. It is a human trait not to be able to admit you are wrong, and it is seductive to wait just a bit longer, or take just a bit more risk in the hope that the market will turn back your way. In the great majority of cases, this just prolongs and exacerbates the pain.

How do you overcome this shortcoming? Very simple. Place a physical stop loss order with your broker the moment you enter the trade. Then just let the 'market gods' determine your fate. Trust me when I tell you, you will not be stopped out of the best trades. The opposite, taking profits when the time presents itself, while not as critical, can be just as important. I always have a *mental* profit objective in mind (while I try to have a *physical* stop loss). It is not so bad to watch the market when it reaches the profit objective, because the best markets many times will greatly exceed your minimum profit objective. However, if the market seems to hesitate at the goal line, cash in. Just do it because many times the market will not give you a second chance. Personally, if I am unsure, I just move the stop very tight and make sure I lock in a good chunk of the profit. The majority of times I will be giving up something, but there are times I am able to squeeze out quite a bit more.

What about the 'locals' running your stops? Well, I have had stops in for significant numbers of contracts, had the market come just one tick away and never has the stop hit. Conversely, I have had the market countless times stop me out, and thank goodness it did, as it never came back to the stop price again. Unless you place your stops in very obvious places, which is never recommended, don't worry about it. Stops are valuable tools which give you an edge and are highly recommended.

Condition yourself to be humble

Another way to say this is that you cannot have an ego and be a successful trader. With apologies to Vince Lombardi, winning is *not* everything, and it certainly is *not* the only thing. I had a client with an S&P day trading system, one which made money four out of five trades. The problem was that losing trade more than offset the other four winners. Yet, he kept trading it for small profits because it felt good; that is until he ran out of money. I have seen numerous other clients try to pick tops and bottoms, yet we all know every major move has just one top and just one bottom. This is an almost impossible task. Who cares if you pick a top or bottom, and who cares if any one trade makes money or if you have more losers than winners? The name of this game is not how many winners you have, but making money at the final bell. This is the ultimate win, consistently having winning months.

> ✳ The name of this game is not how many winners you have, but making money at the final bell.

To have a winning month, my experience has been, you have probably accepted losers all throughout that month. Most people have trouble admitting they are wrong. This is why most people lose money in futures trading. In my own case, over the years, my biggest losses have come about because I have had a strong opinion on some market or another. I would end up fighting a market, taking too much risk, and voiding my money management principles. At times, I would be forced out of a market just before it would turn. In other words, I was actually right in my opinion, but my timing was off. The margin clerk, however, does not care if you are ultimately right. Other times, some new news I was unaware of would surface to demonstrate why I was wrong and the market had been right. In either case, it is better to let the market tell you what it is saying, rather than you trying to dictate, because there is no doubt who is going to win.

There is another side to this. Most people take profits too soon, because psychologically it is soothing to take profits. I always have profit objectives for my trades, but they are never written in stone. After all there is only one top in every bull, and one bottom in every bear. I am not audacious enough to assume I am the one who can pick those tops and bottoms. Can you? So, a better plan is to see how the market acts when it does reach my profit point. Many, many times it goes much further, so if the market wants to do this, just let it. Forget about being right on any particular trade and focus on making money! After all, in the long run making money is your proof.

You have probably noticed, I talk quite a bit here about conditioning. If you exercise one day, your body is not conditioned. It is the same with your state of mind. It takes constant and repetitive action or else your state of mind will go out of condition. This is because the traits which lead to success in trading are different from the traits we have learned over our lifetime, those which lead to success in everyday life. You have been taught to stick it out, persevere and you will ultimately triumph and prosper, but in trading you need to lose repeatedly to win. This takes conditioning to train your mind to act in a contrary manner to what works outside of trading. In life it is generally a recipe for disaster to act impulsively; it is better to sit back and reflect upon your situation. In trading, however, you must condition yourself to act quickly, without hesitation and unemotionally to cut a loss (or take a profit) when your pre-determined point is reached. Once you condition your state of mind, you will have control over your trading emotions. You have greater confidence when taking losses, and entering new positions, because you know your trading plan will prosper over time. You will gain discipline, one of the essential qualities for trading success.

> ✻ In trading you need to lose repeatedly to win.

There is another benefit from this reverse conditioning to your psyche. I am sorry to be the one to tell you that you are going to have a losing streak – even the best traders do. If your series of losing trades materializes because of a lack of planning, and in effect you were forced out of the market by the margin clerk, you will have an inability to bounce back quickly. You will lose focus and confidence in your ability to recoup along with your lost bank account. On the other hand, if you know you followed your disciplined programme of cutting losses according to a well-defined plan, you can never be devastated. This is because you followed your plan, and know that over time it will work for you. Your powers of focus and concentration were never lost, and in your heart you have confidence in your ability to ultimately triumph.

Money management

How can you trade relaxed, in control, unemotional and with total confidence? The simple answer is to develop a consistent money management strategy with a positive outcome. Time and time again I have heard from winning traders that a mediocre system with good money management will triumph over a superior system with poor money management. *Money management is the vital element required for success, yet so few traders concentrate on it.* Does it perhaps make sense that so few traders do well?

So, you want me to give you the best money management strategy? I think the beginning trader is looking for the holy grail here, but if there is such animal, I've not found it. I personally strive only to risk 5 per cent of available equity on any one trade going in (striving to be as close to this number as possible including fees and slippage), knowing that slippage and extraordinary events could potentially raise that number for any one losing trade. If I can keep my loss per trade to approximately 5 per cent, it would take 20 losing trades in a row to wipe me out. Even at 10 per cent it would take 10 in a row, and I have enough confidence in my system to believe the risk of total ruin under these parameters is exceedingly small. Of course, I need to stick to these parameters, and this is where your conditioning comes into play.

> ✱ *Develop a consistent money management strategy with a positive outcome.*

Now that I have defined my 'normal' risk, I should also define my 'normal' reward, and personally I am shooting for at least a three to one reward to risk ratio. Of course, many trades will result in a smaller profit, or smaller loss, and since I try never to let a decent profit turn into a loss I personally seem to have many, many 'scratch' trades (small profit, small loss, break even).

Now let's analyze the ramifications of this simple system. Suppose you had a small trading account, $10,000 (with the leverage inherent in the futures you should probably have more to start, but let's use this number to keep it simple and assume you are trading less volatile markets). You could have 7 losing trades at $500 each, and 3 winning trades at $1500 each (thus my three to one) and you would still be a nice winner.

$$7 \times (\$500) + 3 \times \$1500 = +\$1000$$

Think about this: you are wrong 70 per cent of the time, and still come out a winner. This is the beauty of a good money management programme. Now you might ask me, what about the time I placed my stop at $500 calculated loss, a bad crop report came out before the market opened (bad for me), and that loss turned into $750. I will tell you, yes I understand it happens. However, my experience is these extraordinary events seem to even out over time. At some point down the road there will be a favourable unemployment report, the market will gap open in your favour and you will reap an additional $300 per contract profit over and above your objective. I do not know why the good and the bad even out, it is one of the mysteries of nature. But believe me, my experience has been that this is the way it works!

Finally, you must continually adjust your position size based on market volatility. A small account should concentrate on only less volatile markets so the risk can be adjusted to suit the account size. A quick and simple way to evaluate volatility is to obtain a list of margin requirements by market from your broker. The clearing firm has to a major extent determined the volatility for you. Margin requirements are adjusted based on volatility. While there are always exceptions due to market inefficiencies, my general rule is the initial margin for one position should not exceed 15 per cent of your total excess equity available for trading. If you have a $50,000 cash account, and the margin for soybeans is $1250, a suggested maximum position size would be six contracts. If the perceived risk in this case is $500 per contract, you are risking $3000 with the six contracts, which is 6 per cent of total equity. Therefore you should generally pare down your position size by a contract if you want to stick with our 5 per cent rule. There is some discretion involved here. If this trade is in your best estimation a 10 on a scale of 10, you might be willing to accept that extra point risk and go for the six. If the perceived risk as determined by your system is $750 per contract, then only three to four contracts should be traded for this position. If you always adjust your position size to volatility, even in the bad times you will have capital left to stay in the game. The name of this game is to avoid the risk of ruin!

> ✳ The name of this game is to avoid the risk of ruin!

If you don't feel right, you won't trade right

Rodney Dangerfield once complained, 'It's been a rough day. I got up this morning put on a shirt and a button fell off. I picked up my briefcase and the handle came off. I'm afraid to go to the bathroom.' If this is the way your day starts out, don't trade. Your state of mind is wrong.

In conclusion, you must control your state of mind, and follow a well thought-out money management plan, but the key is your state of mind. What if you are indecisive? There is a quote I like which is attributed to Lee Iacocca when he was bringing Chrysler back from the dead: 'So what do we do?

Anything. Something. So long as we just don't sit there. If we screw it up, start over. Try something else. If we wait until we've satisfied all the uncertainties, it may be too late.'

Your advantage

This chapter has focused on your state of mind, but you have one big advantage. You've read what is presented, and if you buy into the premise (it is my belief it will be to your benefit to do so), starting today you can modify your state to your benefit. Always remember, you are in competition and the psychology on the other side is not as well informed as you now are. There are no doubt hundreds of thousands, perhaps millions of traders who have a loser's state of mind. They may not realize it today, but their actions in the marketplace will attest to this fact. The playing field has just tilted your way.

So it's time to act in a positive way. If you do this right, trading can be enjoyable, and not filled with the anxiety so many face daily. Research your trading plan, develop good money management techniques, condition your mind for success, and you will succeed!

Twenty-five trading secrets of the pros

At the times I've done well in the markets, it was usually because I did certain things in a certain way. When I've done poorly, it was usually because I didn't do these things. The 'secrets' presented below are from experience and the 'school of hard knocks', but were also originally gleaned from reading the masters. Two masters stand out, both long gone (their heyday was during the 1920s), but still living through their writings. You can still find the works of Jesse Livermore and W.D. Gann in libraries, and if you search hard enough through specialty houses. Actually, I learned more from their failures than their triumphs. The same mistakes made 50 and 100 years ago continue to be made every day. Technology may change, but human nature never does. So, I thank these two men since I know many of the 'secrets' which are discussed in this chapter while in my own words originated from them.

There have been others who have had a profound effect on my trading education throughout the years, and I have tried to thank some of them in the acknowledgments. Ultimately, the markets are the best teachers, however. There is a world of wisdom presented below. You personally may not use all of these secrets, but if you can absorb just a portion, there is no doubt in my mind you will become a success. If you disregard what's presented below, you become lost in the financial desert and die of thirst. (Perhaps that's a bit strong – but trust me this is good stuff!)

Secret 1

The trend is your friend

So, don't buck it. The way to make the big money is to determine the major trend and then follow it. If the market will not go your way, you must go its way. When you are in a bear market, and the major trend is down, the plan should be to wait for rallies and sell short; not try to pick the bottom. In a major bear market, you can miss the bottom several times on the way down and end up losing all your money. The same applies (in reverse) in a major bull market. Always go with the tide, never buck it. Let me repeat, because this is important: *the big money is made by going with the trend, not against it.*

Livermore told us, in a major bear market it is safer to sell when the market is down 50 points from the top, than when it is down just 10. The reason is, at down 50 all support is gone, and those who bought the breaks have lost all hope, are demoralized, and in a leveraged market are at the point where they must all try to exit the same small door at the same time.

> ✳ *The big money is made by going with the trend, not against it.*

The result at times can be an avalanche. I can give you many examples of markets that have trended long and far, made some people rich and wiped others out. You hear about the poor soul who lost his farm. I can almost guarantee that guy was bull-headed and fought the trend until he ran out of money.

In the 1920s New Haven was the premier blue chip railroad stock of the day and sold as high as 279. Remember, in those days you could trade stocks on 5 per cent margin, like we trade futures today. When New Haven sold 50 points from the top, it must have looked cheap at the time. How many would have had the guts to sell it short when it crossed below 179, 100 points from the top? Better yet, who would have had the guts, or the vision, to sell it short at 79, or 200 points from the top? It must have looked extremely cheap. Remember that this was the General Electric of its day. Yet the trend was down, and after the crash of 1929, it traded as low as 12.

In the year 2000 a friend of mine bought a 'new technology' stock at the offering price of 66. He added at 150, at 200 and at 300. I suggested he use stops, but he knew this company and told me it was going to 1000. It kept going up and he added at 450 and 500. It went as high as 600. As I write this book it is trading at 23 and he still owns it all.

So how do you do this, stick with the trend and not fight it? Well, it isn't easy. That's why most people don't make money in futures. You need to have a strong will. Once you can see the trend of the market, don't change your mind until the 'tape' shows the change. In any major move there will, of course, be corrective moves against the trend at times. Some news will develop which will cause a sharp correction, but it will be followed by a move right back in the direction of the major trend. If you listen to this news you will be tempted to liquidate prematurely. Avoid the temptation and listen to no one but the market. One way to do this is *never* to set a fixed price in your mind as a profit objective. The majority of people do this, and there's no good reason for it – it's a bad habit based on hope. Do not set a fixed time to liquidate either. This is the way the amateurs do it. They buy silver at $5, because their broker told them it's going to $6. Well, it gets to $5.97, turns and heads south again, and they're still holding looking for $6, watching and waiting as their unrealized profits melt. I've seen it, and this is just plain bull-headedness.

I've seen the opposite as well. The market closes at $5.95, it looks strong and is fundamentally and technically sound. The amateur has his order sitting to sell at $6, because this is his price. The market gaps up on the open the next day at $6.05 and his broker is pleased to report he sold 5¢ better at this price. However, this is a form of top picking, and who is smarter than the market? The market probably gapped up above $6 because the buying interest was able to overwhelm the sellers. I've seen many cases like this one, where the open was sharply higher, but was the low of the day; the kind of market which never looked back until it hit $8. This is all a version of bucking the trend, which is something I do not recommend. Conditions do change, and you must learn to change you mind when they do. A wise man changes his mind, a fool never. Just be sure *if* you change your position it is based on sound reasoning.

> ✳ *A wise man changes his mind, a fool never. Just be sure if you change your position it is based on sound reasoning.*

When you place a trade your objective is obviously to profit. There is no way you can possibly know in advance how much profit to expect. The market determines that. Your mission is to determine the trend, hop on for the ride, and stay on until your indicators suggest the trend has changed, and *not before*.

Secret 2
When a market is 'cheap' or 'expensive' there probably is a reason

This one goes hand in hand with 'don't buck the trend'. Livermore would tell us he always made money selling short low priced markets which are the public's favourite and in which a large long interest had developed. Alternatively, he cashed in on expensive markets when 'everyone' was bailing out because the public thought the market was high enough for a 'healthy' reaction. The public was selling soybeans short at $6/bushel in 1974, because this was an all-time high and into resistance. Who could have guessed they weren't even half-way to what would be record highs over $13? Always remember, it's not the price that's important, it's the market action.

Secret 3
The best trades are the hardest to do

You need to have guts. You will need to be aggressive on entry. You will need to quickly cut losses when the market is not acting right. *The news will always sound the most bullish at the top, and appear to be the most hopeless at the bottom.* This is why the technical tone of the market is so important. If the news is good, but the market has stopped going up, ask yourself why and then heed the call. Bottoms can be the most confusing. The accumulation phase, where the smart money is accumulating a position, can be marked by reactions, cross-currents, shakeouts and false reversals. After the bottom is in place, many traders will be looking for the next break to be a buyer. After all, the market has been so weak so long, the odds favour at least one more break, right? But it never comes. The smart money won't let it. The objective after the bottom is in place is to move the market up to the next level, and the best time to buy may actually feel quite uncomfortable. However, the train has already left the station and you need to have the courage to hop on.

Secret 4

Have a plan before you trade, and then work it

If you have a plan and follow it, you avoid the emotionalism which is the major enemy of the trader. You must try to stay calm during the heat of the session, and remain focused. To do this, you have to be totally organized prior to the opening bell. Your daily mission, should you decide to accept it, is to make money each day or, barring this, at least not lose much. In normal markets, you should take normal profits. In those unusual markets which occur rarely, you need to go for abnormal profits. This is one of the keys to success. *You must always limit losses on trades which are not going according to plan.* This takes willpower and is as essential a quality as having plenty of money. In fact, it is more important than having plenty of money. Money is not to hold on with, this is for the sheep and you don't want to be sheared. If big risks are required, don't take that trade. Wait for an opportunity where you can place a tighter stop. The way Livermore used to trade was to look for opportunities where he could enter very close to his risk point. In this way his risk per trade was small in relation to the profit potential.

> ✳ Your daily mission is to make money each day or, barring this, at least not lose much.

If you do not have the willpower to take the loss when your risk point is hit during the trading session, then you *must* use stop loss orders. Place the stop at the same time you place the trade. You have probably heard stories about the floor traders 'running the stops', but I assure you, in the good trades the majority of the time you will not be stopped out. This happens only with the bad ones.

Personally, I have a trading plan laid out the night before. I generally know what I will do if the market acts the way I anticipate it should, and just as important what I'll do if it doesn't. It is a guide, not written in stone, and somewhat flexible. However, if a market is not acting 'right' according to my plan, I know it is time to take action, either to take the profit if available, or cut the loss if not.

Generally, I've found when I try to 'fudge' the plan I get my head handed to me. Not always (and this why it's hard to follow plans many times), but enough to know the plan is smarter than I am in the heat of the battle.

When it's not going right, *when in doubt get out*. If you have a compass in the middle of the desert, and the oasis is north, don't get fooled into following the mirage to the west. There is nothing better than getting out *quickly* when you're wrong!

Secret 5

Be aggressive

Be aggressive when taking profits and/or cutting losses *if* there is a good reason to do so. A good trader will act without hesitation. When something is not right, he will liquidate early to save cash and worry. Never think too much. Just do it! And don't limit your price – go at the market! Many times a market will give you one optimal opportunity to act and that's it – go with it. As Gann said, 'The way to benefit through tuition is to act immediately.'

Secret 6

No regrets

When you liquidate a trade based on sound reasoning, never regret your decision. Go on, and if it was a mistake to get out, just learn from it. We all make them. Don't 'beat yourself up'. You will lose your perspective and become too cautious in the future. How do you do this unemotionally? Try not to think about the price you entered. This is irrelevant. If the market isn't acting right, don't try to 'get out at break-even after commissions'. This can get very expensive.

Secret 7

Money management is the key

Think about this daily. You do not necessarily need a high win to loss ratio, but your average win *must* be higher than your average loss if you want to succeed. To do this, there must be (at least some) 'big hits'. Some trades you will need to maximize. You need these big wins to offset the inevitable numerous (and hopefully small) losses which are going to happen. I've found by being able just to cut losses early, by even a small incremental amount per trade, say $100, this can make a major difference to the bottom line. This takes decisiveness, so be decisive if the trade is not acting right. Waiting a 'few more ticks' is generally not a recipe for success.

> ✳ It is bad practice to cancel or extend a stop loss order.

One more point here: it is bad practice to cancel or extend a stop loss order. You should never do this. My experience has been that 99 times out of 100 cancelling a stop is the wrong thing to do. It's OK to cancel a profit-taking order at times, but the sooner a loss is stopped the better. When you get out of a bad position quickly, and with a minimum of trauma, not only is your capital base maintained, but your judgement will improve. Without a well-defined risk point, there's no judgement, what it's called is hope.

Secret 8

Success comes easier when you specialize

Every market seems to have its own nature, its own personality. Some markets tend to make tops and bottoms with a fast run up and reverse (called an inverted V top or a V bottom). Some have rounding tops and bottoms, some double tops and bottoms, some tops and bottoms with a long consolidation. You can read a market better when you become familiar with its idiosyncrasies. Familiarity comes from concentration and experience. If a market does not fit with your nature, find another one. Just leave the markets that don't seem to work for you, and stick with the ones that favour you. There are plenty of them out there, one for each temperament.

Secret 9

Patience pays

As Gann said once, 'People are in too big a hurry to get rich and as a result they go broke.' Don't try to get rich in a few months. Don't try to catch all the fluctuations. Market movements of importance require weeks and even months to get ready. There's generally plenty of time to buy or sell one or two days, or longer, after a big move gets underway. There are times when a man or woman with nerve, knowledge and a bit of luck can turn a small amount of money into a fortune. However, this cannot be done continually. The best trades come along only rarely. You will need the patience to wait for the right trades. When they come, you will need the patience not to be overanxious and get in too soon or overtrade. When you get in and the market starts to move your way, you must have the patience to hold on tight until there's sufficient cause for closing out the trade. Remember, every act, either opening or closing a trade, must have a sound basis behind it. Never trade for the thrill of it. If you cannot see a definite trade, then use your essential quality of patience and wait!

One last point on patience: once you are out of the market with a big profit, don't be in too big a hurry to get back in. The best opportunities may be coming, but they're not there every day. You need the patience to wait. Big account balances lead to the temptation to play for less than desirable trades. If you made a good profit, look at it this way: you can now *afford* to wait a few weeks or months for the signs of the next big mover.

Secret 10

Guts are as important as patience and more important than money

Some traders are too bold and as a result overtrade. However, some have trouble pulling the trigger. This is a weakness which must be corrected. You must train yourself to trade so there is no hope and no fear. When you enter or exit a position, do it decisively and without emotion. This is particularly important after a tough losing streak. I've witnessed traders suffer a string of losses who still have some money left, and when the best opportunity of the year comes along (one they identified) they did not have the guts to act. In cases like this, guts are more valuable than money. You need the guts to press hard when you are right. You also need the fortitude to cash in when it is most pleasurable.

> ✱ *You must train yourself to trade so there is no hope and no fear.*

Secret 11

The 'tape' (quote machine) will trick you

Gann once said it's impossible for the man who day by day stands over 'the ticker' to identify a big move before it starts. The tape will fool you every day while accumulation is taking place (and it takes time to accumulate or distribute a large position). Gann actually felt the tape (today we call it the quote machine) is there to fool traders. *'The tape moves in mysterious ways, the multitude to deceive'* is the way he put it. Prices can look the weakest/strongest at the strongest/weakest times. Watching quotes all day will cause you to constantly change your mind. Trade too often and this increases your percentage of being wrong. If you get in wrong, the quote machine will tend to keep you in wrong longer than you should be because every tick your way will renew your hopes. If you get in right, and you watch the screen too closely, there will come a minor move against you which will shake you out – a move which in the long run means nothing. As a result you will lose a good position.

Secret 12

Be sceptical

Another way to put this is, it pays to be a contrarian. To be successful, a trader needs to be a student of human nature and do the opposite of the general public. Sell on your first clues of weakness, and don't wait until 'everyone' is bailing out. If you're day trading the S&P, this rule applies to moves of 15 minutes. If you're swing trading, this rule applies to moves of 3 days. It certainly applies to those moves lasting weeks or months. *And be wary of tips.*

> ✱ *To be successful, a trader needs to be a student of human nature and do the opposite of the general public.*

The tip giver may be good-intentioned, but tips will invariably influence you in the wrong direction. Remember, the market doesn't beat you, you beat yourself. Following tips and not the market is just another sign of human weakness.

Secret 13

Be time cognizant

In other words, know how much time the move has taken to get to this point. This is important, because the longer a market moves in one direction, the greater the velocity the buying or selling will have in the final stage of the move. In many cases, the most significant portion of a major moves takes place in the final 48 hours. You'll want to be there for that.

While we're on the subject of time, watch the volume after a market has made a long-term move. Volume tends to run higher than normal at the end of a move. This is the 'distribution zone', where the smart money is unloading their position to a public who is frenzied by news.

Actually, it's important to know what 'zone' the market is in. Market phases tend to act in a similar manner. Many times, at the bottom, a market can rally on small volume. This indicates there really isn't much for sale. The bottom can follow a period of panicky conditions, pessimism and apathy. Even the prior bulls will start to sound more cautious, and hint it could get worse before it gets better. It seems nobody is interested in buying. This is the time to watch your moving averages closely. If they flash a buy signal, immediately cover shorts and start to buy. Tops are the opposite of bottoms. It seems nobody notices the market is satu- rated. Yet, the market may stop going up. After the first break from the top, many times there will be a low volume 'failure test of the high'. Once the market fails at a lower high, if not out already, this could be your last best chance to liquidate.

As a general rule, the big money is made in the last stage of a bull market, when prices are feverishly active. The big profits on the short side are made in the last stage of a bear market, when everyone wants to sell and it seems no one wants to be a buyer. It is always darkest before the dawn, and brightest at noon just before the sun starts to recede.

Secret 14

Watch the reaction to the news

This is important. *It's not the news, but how the market reacts to the news that's important*. You see, it's the news that sets the public perception. Be alert for divergences between the news and market action. It all has to do with expectation versus reality. Look for the divergence between what's happening and what people think is supposed to happen. When the big turn comes, the general

> ✹ *It's not the news, but how the market reacts to the news that's important.*

public will always be looking the wrong way. There are certain ways to analyze reactions to news (or even a lack of news). Consider the following:

■ If bad news is announced, and the market starts to sell off in large volume, it's a good bet the market's going lower.

■ If the market doesn't react too much to good news, it's probably been discounted.

■ Moves of importance invariably tend to begin before there is any news to justify the initial price move. Once the move is underway, the emerging fundamentals will slowly come to light. *A big rally (decline) on no news is almost always very bullish (bearish)*.

■ It is generally not good practice to buy after a lot of very bullish news, or sell after an extremely bearish report. Both good and bad news are many times already discounted in price. Of course, you should always consider whether the trend is down or up when the news is made known. A well-established trend will generally continue regardless of the news.

I remember getting caught in the emotion of a very bullish corn report in January of 1994. Looking back, this news was the very top. An opposite (very bearish) report the following year turned out to make a significant bottom which turned out to be the springboard for the biggest corn bull market in history. The move wasn't over until corn prices doubled a year later.

■ When unexpected news occurs (news which the market hasn't had time to prepare for) and the market opens in a wide range or 'gaps' lower or higher, sell out your longs, or cover your shorts and wait. Watch the market for 30 minutes to an hour. If the market opened sharply lower, with heavy selling, and was not able to trade much lower than that, it's into support and can be bought at the market with a tight risk point. Watch the market closely at this point. Note the tone of the rally. If it is small and the market is able to fall again under the levels made when the bad news came out (or above the good), it is safe to assume the market is going lower (higher).

I remember the big bull coffee move of 1994. There was a day when the market was trading in the mid-80¢ level. I was long. Unexpected news hit the wires, something about the release of Brazilian stockpiles of coffee. These stocks were supposed to be held in reserve and off the market, but Brazil needed foreign exchange and changed their policy. The market gapped open lower and traded down 400 points, stopping me out in the process. It remained weak for a day or so, but as soon as the market was able to cross above the mid-80¢ level again, the price registered before the unexpected bad news hit. It basically went straight up. This was the time to re-enter. It was about $1.40 *before* the first freeze hit. The move wasn't over until coffee prices hit close to $2.75. And it all started when the market, on no news, crossed the level made prior to the bad news.

Secret 15
Never trade when sick or tired

Good health is essential to success. If you don't feel good, close out your positions and start over again when you do. Rest is equally essential to success. It is probably a good idea to close out all your trades periodically, get entirely out of the market and go on vacation. The market will still be there when you return, trust me on that. I've heard over and over again from some of the most successful traders that they trade their best right after a vacation. If you stick to something too long without rest, your judgement will become warped. Traders who are continually in the market day in and day out lose their perspective and will ultimately lose.

Secret 16
Overtrading is one of your greatest enemies

Gann called overtrading the 'greatest evil'. He felt it was the cause of more losses than anything else, and who am I to disagree with one of the masters? The average novice trader really doesn't have a clue as to how much money is needed to be successful, and he or she invariably buys (or shorts) more than prudence dictates. He or she may be right in his or her analysis, or determination of the major trend, but due to too big a position is forced to liquidate when the margin clerk calls. When he's liquidating so are the other novices, and that's when the smart money moves in. *The money runs out just at that critical time when it's ripest to enter.* The overtrader is exhausted and misses the profit opportunity he had once seen clearly in those more optimistic days.

Be conservative, keep your cool, and avoid the temptation to trade more contracts than your margin can reasonably support in normal markets. This is especially important at tops and bottoms where the excitement, the rumours, and the news are at fever pitch. Human nature has a tendency towards overconfidence at tops and bottoms. Study your charts, and don't let good judgement be influenced by hopes or fears.

Secret 17
Keep a cool head during 'blowoffs'

Markets nearly always seem to culminate at the top in the same way. When close to the end of a major move, markets can become wild. Volume is huge, activity is feverish and erratic, and the imagination blossoms. If you've had the vision to ride the trend to this point, your payday has come. However, in extreme markets men and women of reason lose all sense of proportion. They start to believe the propaganda that the world will literally run out of this or that. It never happens. The Hunts ran silver from $5 an ounce to over $50. They felt it would go up forever but forgot at some price grandma's silver candlesticks come out of the cupboard and into the smelter. The richest men in the world at that time lost all sense of reason and proportion and lost $2 billion in the process. The history of the world shows that there has never been a time when there was a great demand for anything that a supply in excess of demand didn't develop.

Extreme markets are *not* the time to pyramid. They are the time to become alert for the end. All good things come to an end, and your mission will be to jump before the big bump. There will be a time when the herd will all want to exit the same door at once. Make sure you've already left the room. When everyone wants to sell, and all buying support disappears, profits can run into losses fast. In the stock market crash of 1987, profits made in the first ten months of the year were wiped out in two days.

How do you turn your paper profits into cash in a runaway market? In blowoff markets the corrections are generally short and sweet. The market is feverish and everyone is bullish (the bears have already thrown in the towel). The public is buying madly. Weeks may go by without a major correction. You'll hear of fortunes being made, and if you are fortunate enough to be on the move, your paper profits will grow geometrically. The end may be near, but nobody can see the forest for the trees. In fact, only about 10 per cent of those with big paper profits will ever cash in near the top.

> **＊ There will be a time when the herd will all want to exit the same door at once. Make sure you've already left the room.**

Here's my first rule: in this type of market it does not pay to take a loss amounting to more than two consecutive days' fluctuations. If the market goes against you two days, it's likely to go more. Second, be alert for a morning when the market opens off dramatically without any news. It may rally weakly, but the rally will fail. This is the first sign of the end. The market has reached the saturation point where it's run out of buyers. Supply has finally overwhelmed demand. Third, watch for a failure test of the high. Many, many times after the first break the market will have a secondary rally which will fail *under* the high. If you failed to get out on the first break, this is your last good chance.

Secret 18

Never let a good profit turn into a loss

This is one of those trading sins which has ruined many hopes. If you have a decent profit in any position, and you are absolutely sure it is going to grow larger, at the very least place a stop where (in the worst case) you'll break even. If the market is any good, the stop won't be hit. Should the market continue to move in your favour, keep moving the stop to lock in at least some profit. The objective is always to protect your principal in every way possible, and when you are fortunate enough to start accumulating paper profits, lock 'em in.

Secret 19
When in doubt, get out!

If it's not acting right according to your plan, get out. If the market has not started to move in your favour within a reasonable amount of time, get out. Your judgement will deteriorate the longer you hang onto a losing position, and at extremes you will do the wrong thing. One of the old timers once said something to the effect that 'I am prudent enough not to stand in the middle of the railroad tracks while I try to decide if the headlight I think I see is a freight train or an illusion.'

Secret 20
Spread your risks through diversification

Distribute your risk among a variety of trades and markets. Divide your capital into tenths and never risk more than a maximum of 10 per cent on any one trade. One good profit will often totally erase four or five small losers. But if you take big losses and small profits you will have no chance of success. I also suggest concentrating on active, liquid markets, the ones which will allow you to enter and exit when you want to with a minimum of slippage.

Secret 21
Pyramid the right way

The big money can only be made by pyramiding a good position in a trending market. You have an excellent opportunity to use leverage with your unrealized profits to create a larger position than otherwise possible. Pyramiding takes both courage and self-control. The 'weak hands' seldom make the big money, primarily because they do not have the guts to pyramid and maximize the opportunities they are correct about (or they do not have the smarts to do it right). Please be advised, there is a right way and a wrong way to pyramid.

The masters suggest you never reverse pyramid (that is add a greater number of contracts than your initial position as the market moves your way). Your first risk should be your greatest risk. It is generally better to decrease the size of your position through the ride, not increase it. In this way, you have the opportunity to increase your profitability without dramatically increasing your risk.

Let's look at a hypothetical example. If you start out with a purchase of 10 cocoa contracts at, say, 1300, the way to add to this position is 5 contracts at 1350, 3 at 1400, 2 at 1450 and 1 every additional 50 points up *indefinitely* until the move is over. Of course, you would follow this position up with a moving stop loss. In this way, your last trade or two may show a loss, but all the others will show big profits. The point here is that by pyramiding with the larger position underneath (for longs) or above (for shorts), your average price is always better than the market so a correction is more likely to show bottom line profitability.

Other useful pyramiding rules:

- Never try to pyramid after a long advance or decline. The odds are against you. I did this in soybeans during the floods of 1993. I started to be a buyer at just the right time, close to the lows, but got too bullish at the top, added too many contracts, and never made any real money out of that one. The time to begin a pyramid is when the trend first turns up or down after a long move. Your technical indicators can help you here.

- It is always safer to pyramid after a market moves out of accumulation and/or distribution. In other words, a breakout from consolidation (Secret 22). Remember, the longer the time it takes prior to the breakout, the greater the move you can expect.

Secret 22

Watch for those 'breakouts from consolidation'

I've discussed this numerous times in this book, but this is powerful and cannot be overemphasized. You need to know what kind of market you are in. In a consolidating market, money can be made by scalping small moves back and forth. However, you won't make the big money with this kind of market action, and you should never attempt to pyramid. Big profits can be made in the runs between accumulation and distribution. I've found you can make more money by waiting until a commodity plainly declares its trend then by getting in before the move starts. Too many traders are fixated on picking the top or bottom and as a result miss the big picture. What difference does it make if you buy 10, 20 or 30 ticks off the lows, as long as you make money? Get the idea of prices out of your head and concentrate on market action. Forget about picking tops and bottoms.

The longer the consolidation the better. When a market has remained for a long time in a narrow range, a breakout from that range becomes more significant. The market is telling you a major shift in the supply/demand fundamentals is taking place. Because it has taken a long time to form, there is more fuel available for the coming move. This is the best type of market to play to the hilt!

One last point here: remember there is no holy grail and at times there will be false breakouts. Watch for them. You know it's most likely false if the market again trades into the consolidation range. The best ones will never retrace into the breakout range, but it is OK for a market to trade back to the upper or lower edge of the range before resuming new trend action. There is no question it was false once it breaks through to the other side. When this happens, a reversal play is the best course of action.

Secret 23
Go with the relative strength

I'm not talking here about the RSI (Relative Strength Index, a popular indicator of oversold/overbought). What is important is that you follow the trend of each market and always *buy the strong one* and *sell the weak one*. This is especially important for related markets. Silver and gold are both precious metals and will generally move in the same direction. They will move at different speeds, however. In early 1987, silver started to run, and in a very short time period ran up almost $6/ounce for profits of close to $30,000 per contract. We had clients who did not 'want to chase the market' after silver made its first $1 run-up, but they had no hesitation to buy gold. It was, after all, 'cheap' in relation to silver and would have to 'catch up' eventually – right? Gold did run up, about $60/ounce, or $6000/contract. Not too bad, but you could have made five times more by buying the strong one, instead of the weak.

Moves like this do not come along very often. If hogs are going up and bellies down, you should sell the bellies if your trend indicators tell you to do so. It doesn't matter that they're both pork products, the market's telling you no one is eating bacon, at least not now. When I first started in the business, I remember bellies (which usually trade at a 10 to 20¢ premium to the hogs) were trading at the same price as hogs. All the boys at Merrill Lynch said this was a slam-dunk. You had to make money spreading bellies and hogs. Buy the bellies and sell the hogs. It made perfect sense. The logic was, how could a 'finished product' ever sell for less than the 'raw material'. We all piled on this one, and you've probably guessed what happened. The bellies continued to head south, the hogs north, until the bellies were selling at a $5 *discount* to the hogs. This was a loss of $2000/spread at the time in a 'no risk' trade (and of course we overtraded this one because it 'couldn't lose').

The point is you need to judge a market by its own signs, and always sell the weak one and buy the strong.

Secret 24
Limit moves are important indicators of support and resistance

When a market is 'bid limit up', or 'offered limit down' (for those markets which still have limits, for example, the agricultural markets), this is a level where you could be unable to be a buyer or a seller. There is more demand at the limit-up price than available supply, and vice versa. The market 'should' continue in the direction of the limit move. On corrections, it should find support above the limit price (or below if a limit-down type move). Watch for this. If a market again trades under the limit bid price, or above the limit offered *go with the flow*. These are trades which possess reasonable risk, since it is an indication that the previous support or resistance is now absent. If anyone can now buy a market where it previously was unable to be bought (or sell where you previously couldn't) this is a major sign of weakness or strength.

One example from my memory: the day before the high price was hit in the big bull corn market of 1996, you were unable buy corn. It was not only limit bid, there were over 30 million bushels wanted with *no* sellers at the limit price. A few days later the market crossed under the limit bid price, and anyone could buy as much as he or she wanted. Once it crossed that price, the market never saw the light of day. It started on a bear rout, one which lasted for six months and didn't end until prices were $1.50/bushel lower.

Secret 25

Never average a loss

This is critical. I've talked to stock investors who have had great success averaging down. When a stock they liked got cheaper, they bought more. When the long-term trend turned back up, they make out like bandits. A leveraged market is different, however. Averaging a loss may work four times out of five, but that fifth will wipe you out. It is a bad habit to get into.

Look at it this way: if you make a trade, and it starts to go against you, then you're wrong. At least temporarily. Why buy or sell more to average the loss? When it's getting worse day by day, why do your best to potentially compound the problem? Stop the loss early before it is eternally too large, and don't make it worse.

Gann felt if you could avoid three weaknesses – overtrading, failing to place a stop loss, and what he called the 'fatal' mistake, averaging a loss – you will be a success. Good advice, plus I believe there is one final essential requirement for success. We'll discuss it in the next chapter.

'Jesse's Secret': the most important lesson

I urge you study what's presented in this chapter. Too many market axioms sound good in theory, but really don't help you very much in practice. ('Buy low and sell high', is a good example. Yeah, thanks a heap for *that* help.) This chapter is different, although on the surface what's presented may sound simplistic. Trust me, it really is quite profound.

To make the big money you need to catch and exploit the big move

Not that every trade will be a big mover, far from it. The big movers are rare. There may only be two or three major hits you'll be able to capitalize on in your lifetime. But these two or three could very well mean a lifetime of difference for you!

When I first started working on the floor of the Grain Exchange, I noticed one member, a relatively young man who would visit every so often. He would show up maybe once or twice a week. He would joke with some of the traders, check the markets, at times place a few orders, and then he would disappear for weeks, sometimes months. Over time I got to know him better. He is a very happy person, and would like his name to remain confidential. The reason we would not see him for months at times was because foreign travel was his passion, and he did a lot of it. He could well afford to pursue his passion, since he really didn't have to work for a living. It wasn't inherited money. He came from relatively modest means.

Basically his story involved the 'Russian grain steal' markets of the early 1970s. He was working for a living back then, like most of us have to today. He was trading on the side and started with a modest sum. I don't know exactly how much money he finally took out of the markets, but I have reason to believe it was substantial (judging by his lifestyle). I do know he made his big money in the soybean market. He was fortunate to be on the right side of one of the biggest soybean moves in history. He was smart enough to have a vision, brave enough to pyramid his position, and disciplined enough to stand pat until he perceived the move to be over. This was the market where soybeans ran from under $4/bushel to over $13. Bottom line, in less than two years, this man was able to change his life dramatically for the better, and forever. What he did is quite rare, almost impossible, but he is the living proof.

Think how tough it must have been to do what he did; constantly to avoid the burning temptation to cash in on what must have been huge paper profits all throughout the move. Human nature would have beckoned to 'book the profit' every time the market rallied to new highs. After all, you can always 'get back in' and re-establish a position on the next correction. Taking profits is pleasurable behaviour and by far the easiest road to follow. When the correction does come, a trader can pat himself on the back. Profitability is enhanced every time you take a profit, and are then able to buy back cheaper. After all, 'you never go broke taking a profit.' (Have you ever heard this one?)

Unfortunately, you never get rich this way either. The only major glitch in the 'taking profits programme' has to do with the corrections. While they will come, they do not always occur on schedule or from the level you decided to exit. This man, unlike most, had the discipline to forgo 'normal' profits and hold out for 'life-changing' profits. How did he do this? Well, first of all, I believe he must have had a *vision*. He had to *believe* prices could do what others could never envision.

A vision is the key, but this man must also have had the *patience* to hang in there until the trend absolutely changed direction. This isn't easy to do, and not always that easy to see. He had to have the *courage* to hang on during what looked on the charts to be viscous shakeouts. (Pull out a chart of this move; like all the major moves this one had sharp and deep shakeouts along the way and while the major trend was still pointing north.) He must have possessed the *guts to pyramid* his position for maximum profitability. This isn't all that easy either. It takes 'smart guts'. If he was too timid, he could never have achieved life-changing profitability. If too bold, he would have overtraded, become under-margined, and unable to hold his position.

Jesse Livermore

Jesse Livermore, the legendary trader of the 1920s, made and lost mega fortunes countless times over his trading career. At the height of his success, this was a man who made over $15 million in the crash of 1929: a mega fortune at the time. He must have also possessed a fatal flaw because he somehow lost these multi-fortunes. Jesse was a compulsive gambler and at the end of his life, sadly, he died penniless. He was found dead in the early 1940s in a fleabag hotel with a self-inflicted bullet wound in the head. Apparently he did not follow his own advice. For one thing, he cautioned traders always to 'lock away' half of any big hit in a safe deposit box for retirement, and to keep it locked up and unavailable for trading. He told us in his book that he did this, but I guess, sadly, he must have taken out the key and in a weak moment used it. However, to his credit, coming from an impoverished background, he developed the amazing ability to take millions out of the markets starting with relatively modest sums. It was not a fluke either – he did this numerous times throughout his career. The high point was his short position, which he covered in full at the lows on the crash day of 1929.

Jesse's secret? In *Reminiscences of A Stock Operator*, a semi-autobiographical account of his life published in 1923, the hero summed up the secret of how to make the big money. It may now be more than 75 years later, we now have computerized trading and financial futures, but the basics haven't changed because human nature hasn't changed.

Early in his career, Jesse suffered from the same malady as most of us. Unlike most of us, however, he did unlock the secret of the big money, and he shares this secret early in the book. Human nature being what it is, the lesson is easy to miss. Jesse missed it as well, but he relates the tale of old Mr Partridge, a trader who was not as frenetic as most. (Recall, in the 1920s, stocks were traded like commodities are today; highly leveraged on small margin with wild swings.) In the excerpt from the book reproduced below, feel free to substitute the word 'stock' for silver, pork bellies, S&P, or whatever you're trading now:

You find very few who can truthfully say that Wall Street doesn't owe them money. Well there was one old chap who wasn't like the others. To begin with he was a much older man. He never volunteered advice and never bragged of his winnings ... Time and again I heard him say, 'Well, this is a bull market, you know!' as though he were giving you a priceless talisman. And of course, I didn't get his meaning ... 'But I couldn't think of selling that stock,' Mr Partridge would say. 'Why not?' I would ask. 'Why this is a bull market. My dear boy, if I sold that stock now, I would *lose* my position and then where would I be? And when you are as old as I am, and you have been through as many booms and panics as I have, you'll know that to *lose* your position is something nobody can afford – not even John D. Rockefeller. I hope that stock reacts and that you will be able to repurchase your line at a substantial concession, sir. But I myself can only trade in accordance with the experience of many years. I paid a high price for it and I don't feel like throwing away another tuition fee.'

The more I learned, the more I realized how wise that old chap was. He had evidently suffered from the same defect in his young days and knew his own weakness. I think it was a long step forward in my trading education when I realized at last that when old Mr Partridge kept on telling the other customers,

'Well you know this is a bull market', he really meant to tell them that the big money is not in the individual fluctuations, but in the main movements – that is not in reading the tape, but in sizing up the entire market and its trend.

After spending many years in Wall Street and after making and losing millions of dollars, I want to tell you this; it was never my thinking that made the big money for me. It was always my sitting. Got that? My sitting tight! You always find lots of early bulls in bull markets, and early bears in bear markets. I have known many men who were right at exactly the right time, and began buying or selling when prices were at the very level which should show the greatest profit. And their experience invariably matched mine – that is they made no real money out of it. *Men who can be both right and sit tight are uncommon. I found it one of the hardest things to learn. But it is only after a speculator has firmly grasped this that he can make big money.*

It is literally true that millions come easier to a trader after he knows how to trade than hundreds did in the days of his ignorance.

(Reprinted from Jesse Livermore, Reminiscences of a Stock Operator, Traders' Library Publications 1993, by permission of John Wiley & Sons, Inc.)

I have adopted this last line as the motto for my brokerage firm.

Those who can be right and sit tight

There have been times when I have had clients who have made substantial hits in the markets we trade. I've been fortunate enough to do the same at times, but I admit not as often as I could have or should have. When I go back and look at the 'purchase and sale' confirmations statements from the clearing house I generally see the same pattern for the 'best of the best' trades. I see a position entered when it was not the popular play. I see a position held for a greater period of time than most. A position held through major shakeouts or sharp short covering rallies. These are, at times, positions which were pyramided, but not always, and not always the large positions in terms of size either. Substantial money can be made in a fairly modest position if the position is entered relatively early in a major move and held for a goodly portion of that move.

To achieve ultimate success you will need to fight human weaknesses. Human nature leads us to take short or premature profits. Why? Very simply, because it is pleasurable. The important trades, the major moves, the ones you will want to maximize, are the ones which will be the hardest and most painful to endure. Your technical tools can help here. Consider moving averages, which I believe are the best technical tool. However, any tool which can help you determine the trend and maximize profits in a systematic manner is better than emotion or too much reading or too much thinking. Technical tools can give you the discipline to stay with moves which you would otherwise cash in prematurely.

They are out there, these big moves. We see them all the time, but generally in hindsight. In fact while I first wrote this, my computer screen was showing the Swiss franc chart (Chart 14.1). It had crossed the 30-day moving average to

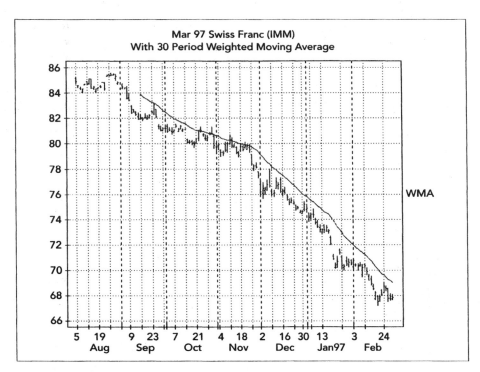

■ **Chart 14.1** Markets *do* move in downtrends

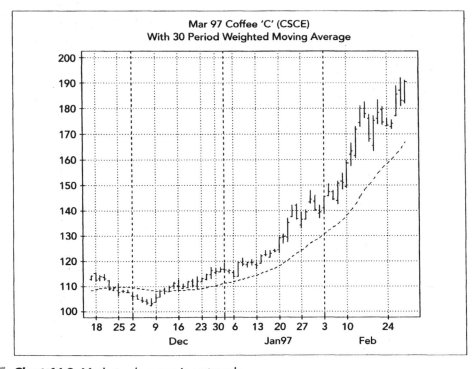

■ **Chart 14.2** Markets *do* move in uptrends

the downside about six months previous at 8350. Since that time, it had still not closed above the 30-day moving average for two consecutive days. It was trading under 6800. This was a 1550-point move (and counting), the equivalent return of about $19,400 per contract for a measly $2500 margin deposit. We're talking more than 1400 per cent *annualized* return on margin. This is *without* any pyramiding whatsoever. I believe with a relatively modest account you might have added one contract short, say every 100 points lower in a move like this, and not be undermargined, while always using reasonably positioned stops. You would have had accumulated 15 contracts with major (and I mean major) unrealized profits (and counting). This was a good market, but by no means an abnormal market. The move was quite orderly.

In the three months prior, for example, coffee had run from about $1.00/pound to over $2.00, more than $37,500 per contract (and counting), without once closing under its 30-day moving average. Check it out, take a look at Chart 14.2.

In the year this edition was written, crude oil had rallied from $12 to $32 a barrel, over $20,000 per contract, and the Euro collapsed from $1.20 to under 90¢ or over $37,000 per contract. The monster of all moves was the Nasdaq, down over 2000 points, or $200,000 profit for just one contract shorted (and counting).

Moves like this take place every year, but most of us see them only in hindsight. Look at any chart book and you will plainly see these types of moves are there for the taking, available to me and to you. In a free capitalistic society they are freely available to all, and what's really exciting is that they continue to come along each and every year. Tomorrow's markets will be as exciting as yesterday's, I can assure you of that. You can start today, and you can be successful beyond your wildest dreams. You will need discipline, guts and courage. You will need to take the road less travelled. It will not be easy, but the opportunities are out there for me and for you.

Good luck, and good trading!

World futures and options exchanges

The following information is provided without warranty of any kind.
For interactive charts, quotes, futures and commodity related news log onto
www.commodity.com

Argentina

Buenos Aires Futures Exchange
Mercado a Término de Buenos Aires
Mario Wolberg, Bouchard 454, 5° (1106) Buenos Aires, Argentina
www.matba.com.ar

Australia

Sydney Futures Exchange (SFE)
30–32 Grosvenor Street, Sydney, NSW 2000, Australia
61-2-9256-0555 Fax 61-2-9256-0666
www.sfe.com.au

Austria

Austrian Futures & Options Exchange (OTOB)
Strauchgasse 1–3, A-1014 Vienna, Austria
43-1-531-65-0 Fax 43-1-532-97-40
www.wbag.at

Belgium

Belgian Futures & Options Exchange (BELFOX)
Palais de la Bourse, Rue Henry Maus 2, 1000 Brussels, Belgium
32-2-512-80-40 Fax 32-2-513-83-42
www.belfox.be

Brazil

Bolsa de Mercadorias & Futuros (BM&F)
The Commodities & Futures Exchange, Praca Antonio Prado, 48, São Paulo,
SP, Brazil 01010-901
55-11-232-5454 Fax 55-11-232-7565
www.bmf.com.br

Canada

Montreal Exchange (ME)
The Stock Exchange Tower, 800 Victoria Square, Montreal
Quebec H4Z 1A9, Canada
(514) 871-2424 Fax (514) 871-3531
www.me.org

Toronto Futures Exchange (TFE)
Two First Canadian Place, The Exchange Tower, Toronto
Ontario M5X 1J2, Canada
(416) 947-4487 Fax (416) 947-4272
www.tfe.com

Winnipeg Commodity Exchange (WCE)
500 Commodity Exchange Tower, 360 Main Street, Winnipeg
Manitoba R3C 3Z4, Canada
(204) 925-5000 Fax (204) 943-5448
www.wce.mb.ca

Chile

Santiago Stock Exchange
La Bolsa 64, Casilla 123D, Santiago, Chile
56-2-695-8077 Fax 56-2-672-8046
www.bolsantiago.cl/ingles

China

Beijing Commodity Exchange (BCE)
306 Chonyun Building, No. 8 Beichen East Road, Chaoyang District
Beijing 100101, China
86-1-6492-8347 Fax 86-1-6499-3365

Denmark

Futop Market
Copenhagen Stock Exchange, Nikolaj Plads 6, Box 1040, DK-1007 Copenhagen
Denmark
45-33-93-3366 Fax 45-33-12-8613
www.xcse.dk

Finland

Finnish Options Exchange
Erottajankatu 11, SF-00130 Helsinki, Finland
358-9-680-3410 Fax 358-9-604-442
www.foex.fi

Finnish Securities and Derivatives Exchange
Keskuskatu 7, POB 926, FIN 00101 Helsinki, Finland
358-0-13-12-11 Fax 358-0-13-12-12-11
www.som.fi

France

Marché à Terme International de France (MATIF)
115 rue Reaumur, 75002 Paris, France
33-1-40-28-82-82 Fax 33-1-40-28-80-01
www.matif.fr

Germany

Eurex Frankfurt
Börsenplatz 7-11, D-60313 Frankfurt, Germany
49-69-2101-0 Fax 49-69-2101-2005
www.eurexchange.com

Greece

Athens Stock Exchange
10 Sophocleous Street, Athens 105 59, Greece
30-1-32-11-301 Fax 30-1-32-13-938
www.ase.gr

Hong Kong

Hong Kong Futures Exchange (HKFE)
5/F, Asia Pacific Finance Tower, Citibank Plaza, 3 Garden Road, Hong Kong
852-2531-5056 Fax 852-2824-4438
www.hkfe.com

Hungary

Budapest Commodity Exchange
H-1373, PO Box 495, 1134 Budapest, Hungary
36-1-269-8571 Fax 36-1-269-8575
www.bce-bat.com

India

National Stock Exchange
Mahindra Towers 'A' Wing, 1st Floor, Worli, Mumbai, India
022-490525, 4932555 Fax 022-4935631
www.nseindia.com

Israel

Tel Aviv Stock Exchange (TASE)
54 Ahad Haam Street, Tel Aviv 65202, Israel
972-3-567-7411   Fax 972-3-510-5379
www.tase.co.il

Italy

Italian Stock Exchange
Piazza Degli Affari 6, I-20123 Milan, Italy
39-2-724261   Fax 39-2-72004333
www.borsaitalia.it

Japan

Kansei Agricultural Commodities Exchange (KANEX)
1-10-14 Awaza, Nishi-ku, Osaka 550, Japan
81-6-531-7931   Fax 81-6-541-9343
www.kanex.or.jp

Kobe Raw Silk Exchange (KSE)
126 Higashimachi, Chuo-ku, Kobe 650, Japan
81-78-331-7141   Fax 81-78-331-7145

Osaka Securities Exchange (OSE)
8-16 Kitahama, I-chome, Chuo-ku, Osaka 541, Japan
81-6-229-8643   Fax 81-6-231-2639
www.ose.or.jp

Osaka Textile Exchange
2-5-28 Kyutaro-machi, Chuo-ku, Osaka 54l, Japan
81-6-253-0031   Fax 81-6-253-0034
www.osamex.com

Tokyo Commodity Exchange (TOCOM)
10-8 Nihonbashi Horidomecho, 1-chome, Chuo-ku, Tokyo 103, Japan
81-3-3661-9191   Fax 81-3-3661-7568
www.tocom.or.jp

Tokyo Grain Exchange (TGE)
12-5 Nihonbashi Kakigara-cho, 1-Chome, Chuo-ku, Tokyo 103, Japan
81-3-3668-9321   Fax 81-3-3661-4564
www.tge.or.jp

Tokyo International Financial Futures Exchange (TIFFE)
1-3-1 Marunouchi, Chiyoda-ku, Tokyo 100, Japan
81-3-5223-2400   Fax 81-3-5223-2450
www.tiffe.or.jp

Korea

Korea Stock Exchange (Seoul)
www.kse.or.kr/e_index.html

Malaysia

Kuala Lumpur Commodity Exchange (KLCE)
Fourth Floor, Citypoint, Komplex Dayabumi
Jalan Sultan Hishamuddin, PO Box 11260, 50740 Kuala Lumpur, Malaysia
603-293-6822 Fax 603-274-2215
www.kloffe.com.my

Netherlands

European Options Exchange (EOE)
Rokin 65, 1012 KK Amsterdam, The Netherlands
31-20-550-4550 Fax 31-20-623-0012
www.aex.nl

New Zealand

New Zealand Futures & Options Exchange (NZFOE)
PO Box 6734, Wellesley Street, 10th Level, Stock Exchange Centre
Auckland, New Zealand
64-9-309-8308 Fax 64-9-309-8817
www.nzfoe.co.nz

Norway

Oslo Stock Exchange (OSLO)
PO Box 460, Sentrum, N-0105 Oslo, Norway
47-22-34-1700 Fax 47-22-41-6590
www.ose.no

Philippines

Manila International Futures Exchange (MIFE)
7/F First Bank Centre, Paseo de Roxas
Makati 1200, The Philippines
63-2-818-5496 Fax 63-2-818-5529

Singapore

Singapore Commodity Exchange
111 North Bridge Road #23-04/05, Peninsula Plaza, Singapore 0617
65-338-5600 Fax 65-338-9116
www.sicom.com.sg

Singapore International Monetary Exchange (SIMEX)
1 Raffles Place, No. 07-00, OUB Centre, Singapore 0104
65-535-7382 Fax 65-535-7282
www.simex.com.sg

South Africa

South African Futures Exchange (SAFEX)
105 Central Street, Houghton Estate 2198, PO Box 4406
Johannesburg 2000, Republic of South Africa
27-11-728-5960 Fax 27-11-728-5970
www.safex.co.za

Spain

MEFF Renta Fija
Via Laietana 58, E-08003, Barcelona, Spain
34-3-412-1128 Fax 34-3-268-4769
www.meff.es

Sweden

OM Stockholm AB (OMS)
Brunkebergstorg 2, Box 16305, S-10326 Stockholm, Sweden
46-8-700-0600 Fax 46-8-723-10
www.omgroup.com

Switzerland

Swiss Options & Financial Futures Exchange (SOFFEX)
Selnaustrasse 32, CH-8021 Zurich, Switzerland
41-1-229-2111 Fax 41-1-229-2233
www.swx.com

United Kingdom

International Petroleum Exchange (IPE)
International House, 1 St Katharine's Way, London E1 9UN
44-171-481-0643 Fax 44-171-481-8485
www.ipe.uk.com

London International Futures & Options Exchange (LIFFE)
Cannon Bridge, London EC4R 3XX
44-171-623-0444 Fax 44-171-588-3624
www.liffe.com

London Metal Exchange (LME)
56 Leadenhall Street, London EC3A 2BJ
44-171-264-5555 Fax 44-171-680-0505
www.lme.co.uk

OMLX The London Securities and Derivatives Exchange
107 Cannon Street, London EC4N 5AD
44-171-283-0678 Fax 44-171-815-8508
www.omgroup.com

United States of America

Chicago Board Options Exchange (CBOE)
400 S. La Salle Street, Chicago, IL 60605
(312) 786-5600, (800) 678-4667 Fax (312) 786-7413
www.cboe.com

Chicago Board of Trade (CBOT)
141 W Jackson Blvd, Chicago, IL 60604-2994
(312) 435-3500 Fax (312) 341-3306
www.cbot.com/menu.htm

Chicago Mercantile Exchange (CME)
30 S. Wacker Drive, Chicago, IL 60606
(312) 930-1000 Fax (312) 930-3439
www.cme.com

New York Board of Trade (NYBOT)
Four World Trade Center, New York, NY 10048
(212) 742-6000, (800) 433-4348 Fax (212) 748-4321
www.nybot.com

Kansas City Board of Trade (KCBT)
4800 Main Street, Suite 303, Kansas City, MO 64112
(816) 753-7500, (800) 821-5228 Fax (816) 753-3944
www.kcbt.com

Mid America Commodity Exchange (MIDAM)
141 W. Jackson Blvd, Chicago, IL 60604
(312) 341-3000 Fax (312) 341-3027
www.midam.com

Minneapolis Grain Exchange (MGE)
400 S. Fourth Street, Minneapolis, MN 55415
(612) 321-6710 Fax (612) 339-1155
www.mgex.com

New York Mercantile Exchange (NYMEX)
One North End Avenue, World Financial Center, New York, NY 10282
(212) 748-3350 Fax (212) 742-5263
www.nymex.com

Index